The Work of Psychoanalysts in the Public Health Sector

This book provides a comprehensive insight into the ways in which psychoanalysts think and work. Mary Brownescombe Heller and Sheena Pollet bring together internationally known contributors trained at the Institute of Psychoanalysis to explore the broad range of clinical work, thinking, and teaching undertaken with children, families, adults and staff by psychoanalysts in the UK public health sector.

Divided into four sections, *The Work of Psychoanalysts in the Public Health Sector* covers:

- clinical work with parents and young children
- clinical work with adults and their families
- analytic thinking in health service practice
- analytic support for health service staff.

Experienced psychoanalysts discuss work with various client groups including parents with babies, children, adolescents who self harm, and adults with serious mental health conditions and psychosis. The book also explores how psycho-analytically-informed work can be used alongside other treatment methods, and how health service staff can best be trained and supported.

The Work of Psychoanalysts in the Public Health Sector offers the reader a broad perspective and a clear understanding of the various analytical concepts used in clinical practice. It will be invaluable reading for anyone interested in, or already using psychoanalytic ideas and techniques in the health sector, as well as students in training.

Mary Brownescombe Heller is a Consultant Clinical Psychologist and Psychoanalyst who worked full-time in the NHS in Teesside for nearly 25 years, where she managed an NHS psychoanalytic psychotherapy service. She now works largely in private practice. She is a Lecturer, Psychotherapist and Supervisor for the BPC accredited training of the North of England Association of Psychoanalytic Psychotherapists (NEAPP).

Sheena Pollet is a Consultant Psychiatrist in Psychotherapy in the 5 Boroughs Partnership NHS Trust in Cheshire. She also works as a Psychoanalyst in private practice.

The Work of Psychoanalysts in the Public Health Sector

Edited by
Mary Brownescombe Heller
and Sheena Pollet

Routledge
Taylor & Francis Group

LONDON AND NEW YORK

First published 2010
by Routledge
27 Church Road, Hove, East Sussex BN3 2FA

Simultaneously published in the USA and Canada
by Routledge
270 Madison Avenue, New York, NY 10016

Routledge is an imprint of the Taylor & Francis Group, an Informa business

Typeset in Times by Garfield Morgan, Swansea, West Glamorgan
Printed and bound in Great Britain by TJ International Ltd, Padstow,
Cornwall
Paperback cover design by Aubergine Creative Design

This publication has been produced with paper manufactured to strict
environmental standards and with pulp derived from sustainable forests.

British Library Cataloguing in Publication Data
A catalogue record for this book is available from the British Library

Library of Congress Cataloging-in-Publication Data
The work of psychoanalysts in the public health sector / edited By Mary
Brownescombe Heller and Sheena Pollet.
     p. cm.
  Includes bibliographical references and index.
  ISBN 978-0-415-48428-2 (hardback) – ISBN 978-0-415-48429-9 (pbk.)
1. Mental health services—Great Britain. 2. Psychoanalysis—Great Britain.
3. National health services—Great Britain. I. Heller, Mary Brownescombe.
II. Pollet, Sheena.
  RA790.7.G7W67 2009
  362.196'891700941–dc22
                                                         2009018204

ISBN: 978-0-415-48428-2 (hbk)
ISBN: 978-0-415-48429-9 (pbk)

This book is dedicated to the memory of two of our colleagues, both of whom died before the book was completed.

William 'Bill' Brough, who began his working life in the 'Friends Ambulance Service' in Burma during the Second World War, later trained as a doctor and is remembered with great affection by patients and staff from the many years that he worked as a Consultant Psychiatrist and Psychoanalyst in the National Health Service.

Richard Lucas contributed enormously to the analytic understanding of psychosis and the 'psychotic wavelength'. Using his deep understanding both as a psychiatrist and as a psychoanalyst, he wrote many papers and taught several generations of young doctors and health professionals working in mental hospitals in the NHS. His was a unique contribution and his untimely death leaves a considerable hole in psychiatry as well as psychoanalysis.

Contents

Acknowledgements

We would like to thank the following for allowing us to reprint these papers:

A version of Robin Anderson's paper, Chapter 3: Assessing the risk of self-harm in adolescents, was originally published in: *Psychoanalytic Psychotherapy* (2000), Vol. 14, No. 1, 9–21, reprinted here by kind permission of Karnac Books Ltd. A slightly different version was also published in *Assessment in Child Psychotherapy* (2000), Margaret Rustin and Emanuela Quagliata (Eds.), London: Duckworth (Tavistock Clinic Series, Nicholas Temple and Margot Waddell, Eds.).

Rob Hale and Liam Hudson's paper, Chapter 16, was originally published in *Stress in Health Professionals* (1999), Jenny Firth-Cozens and Roy L. Payne (Eds.), Chichester, UK: Wiley.

We would also like to thank Professor Joan Raphael-Leff, who published brief versions of the papers by William Brough and Sheena Pollet (Chapters 5 and 1) in *Between Sessions and the Couch* (2002), Colchester, UK: CPS Psychoanalytic Publications, University of Essex.

Introduction

Mary Brownescombe Heller and Sheena Pollet

It was a source of some surprise to us when, as editors, we undertook the task of compiling a book of collected papers by psychoanalysts about their work in the UK public health sector, that no such compilation had ever been published. We believe that these papers will provide a lively and informative cross-section of the important contributions that psychoanalytic thinking and clinical input can provide within health service settings. The main authors of these papers are all psychoanalysts trained by the Institute of Psychoanalysis in London and members of the British Psychoanalytic Society (BP-AS). While London has been seen as the traditional home base of psychoanalysis in Britain, the number of psychoanalysts living and practising across the UK continues to increase. We have considered it important that our book represents the work of psychoanalysts across the UK. The papers are intended to be of interest to the general reader who wants to know more about psychoanalysis, to psychotherapists of many persuasions, to health service professionals, health care managers and lecturers, and supervisors involved in psychoanalytic teaching and supervision.

Our aim in bringing together these papers has been to portray just some of the ways in which psychoanalytic thinking and practice continue to flourish and to contribute to the day-to-day work of the National Health Service in the UK, as well as to some of the most challenging environments within the mental health sector. We have included contributions from those psychoanalysts who, while not directly employed within the NHS, provide supervision and teaching services to medical, nursing, psychology and other professions working in health service settings.

The authors in this collection of papers take somewhat different analytic approaches, convey their thinking in a range of different styles and are all fascinating in their own right. We begin the book with papers on parenting and childhood development, followed by clinical work with adults and families. Next, we sample some of the ways that psychoanalysts think in health sector settings, and we end with a selection of papers describing the kinds of support that psychoanalysts provide to health service staff.

It is sometimes claimed that psychoanalysts work primarily in the private sector, seeing people who are sufficiently wealthy to afford their services. This is very far from the truth; indeed, there has been a long and distinguished tradition of psychoanalytic involvement in health sector services within the UK health services from the 1920s and 1930s onwards. Melanie Klein, Wilfred Bion, John Bowlby, Herbert Rosenfeld, Hanna Segal, Henri Rey and Murray Jackson are just some of these early pioneers. Their seminal contributions include understandings of psychosis and of how important it is for an infant's development that he or she has secure and loving parenting. Our authors are some of the many psychoanalysts who continue to contribute in various ways to health service provision, not only in child and adult health services, in organizational management and professional groups, but also in learning disability, forensic provision, neurophysiology, and physical disability. Many of these analysts work at the very limits of therapeutic treatability. (For an example, see Cockett's Chapter 6.)

Psychoanalysis, both as a clinical treatment and as a body of theory about the mind and its vicissitudes, has much of value to offer in a variety of different settings and is a fascinating and worthwhile subject of study – as attested by the current number of university degree courses in psychoanalysis across the country. Moreover, psychoanalytic understanding has recently provided valuable insights into the role of emotion and unconscious phantasy in contributing to the current global financial instability (Tuckett and Taffler, 2008).

The BP-AS was founded in 1919. It has nearly 500 registered members, including those from overseas and candidates in training, and its rigorous standard of training is widely regarded as an inspirational model for other psychoanalytic and psychodynamic training. As well as being a member of the British Psychoanalytic Council, the BP-AS is a component society of the International Psychoanalytical Association. This is a body with members across five continents whose major function is to safeguard professional psychoanalytic standards.

Regrettably, at the current time in the UK health sector, there is an overreliance on so-called 'evidence-based' (randomized control trials, RCTs) research as a means of making decisions regarding which forms of manualized psychological therapy should best be offered to those with mental health difficulties (e.g. National Institute for Clinical Excellence Guidelines, 2004). Such an attitude is inherently discriminatory, in that a manualized approach cannot be so easily employed in the dynamic forms of psychotherapy. Analytic psychotherapy views the unique relationship and unconscious processes taking place between therapist and patient as central to the treatment process. RCT methodologies, we would argue, cannot but be limited as a means of understanding the complexities of human behaviour; nor can the non-replicable relationship between analyst and patient be reduced to the kind of quantitative statistics required by 'evidence-based practice' research (Perron, 2006). Therapies that target behavioural and thought-related *symptoms* may risk missing out on those deeper areas of distress and conflict that have brought so many patients to seek help. From this perspective, a narrow-focus approach to mental health research, *treatment* and practice in the NHS not only is unhelpful, but does a serious disservice to the consumers of mental health services and their families by limiting the availability of choice for those with complex needs. Importantly, the limitations of RCT evidence have now been accepted by Professor Sir Michael Rawlins, Chairman of NICE, as he made clear in his 2008 Harveian Oration to the Royal College of Physicians (Rawlins, 2008, p. 2).

> The notion that evidence can be reliably placed in hierarchies is illusory. Hierarchies place RCTs on an undeserved pedestal for . . . although the technique has advantages it also has significant disadvantages.

The NICE recommendation of cognitive-behaviour therapy as a treatment modality of choice (2004) has its relevant and helpful place, particularly among the shorter-term talking therapies, but it is by no means a cure-all, nor does it provide the kind of in-depth, long-term therapeutic help that is so essential for those large numbers of individuals who experience complex and deep-rooted mental health difficulties. Equally important, such restrictions do not give health professionals access to an understanding of the complex dynamic processes that they need to know about, in order to make sense of the impact of unconscious forces on their patients, themselves and health service institutions.

We would argue that *practice-based evidence* is always important and needs to be seen as an essential part of the work. Research, both as a discipline and as a means of developing theory and practice, does need to be undertaken within the analytically based psychotherapies, but it needs to be 'fit for purpose'. In a recent article Smith (2007) pointed out that an increasing number of methodologically impressive research studies highlight the benefits of analytic psychotherapy. These studies demonstrate the efficacy, relevance, cost-effectiveness and long-term therapeutic potency of psychodynamic and psychoanalytic approaches to mental health difficulties. Such evidence is not currently seen as conforming to the statistical requirements of the RCT paradigm.

Nevertheless, in some London NHS Trusts and treatment centres, psychoanalysts *are* undertaking research using RCT and manualized psychoanalytic psychotherapies. These include David Taylor and colleagues at the Tavistock Clinic studying treatment-resistant depression, Marco Chiesa and colleagues at the Cassel Hospital studying borderline personality disorder, Peter Fonagy, Mary Target, Amanda Joyce and others at the Anna Freud Centre studying parent–infant psychotherapy and child psychotherapy. As an exemplar of the work of these analysts, our book includes Fonagy and

Bateman's brief summary of their ground-breaking work on 'mentalization-based treatment' with borderline personality disorder (Chapter 14).

To conclude, Freud himself always argued that analytic work carried all the hallmarks of good research, in that it involved a careful and systematic observation of the data arising from the relationship between patient and analyst. Such data would include both verbal and non-verbal components, fleeting perceptions, physical sensations and sensory impressions, 'acting-out' behaviours, as well as dreams and day-dreams. One of the major tasks of psychoanalytic work is for these disparate elements to be thought about and linked together, so that a deeper level of therapeutic understanding can be gained by both analyst and patient.

The contributors and their papers

The book is divided into parts. The first part explores ways of working analytically with parents and babies, children and adolescents (Sheena Pollet; Judith Trowell; Robin Anderson). This is followed by descriptions of clinical work with adult patients and families (Mary B. Heller; William Brough; Susan Cockett; Brian Martindale). The longest part of the book takes a more general look at how analytic thinking can be employed to illuminate health service practice; how it can contribute to, or indeed conflict with, the role of the psychoanalyst who is also a health service practitioner; how it can inform research and provide new ways of working with personality disordered patients (Veronica Gore; Colin Thomas; Anne Ward; Christopher Phillips; Siobhan O'Connor; Mary B. Heller; Peter Fonagy and Anthony Bateman). The last part describes ways in which psychoanalysts provide support, training, teaching and supervision to health service and other public sector staff (Richard Lucas; Rob Hale and Liam Hudson; Graham Ingham and Vic Sedlak).

Chapter 1: Making a little go a long way: Early intervention (Sheena Pollet)

Sheena works in Cheshire as a consultant psychiatrist in psychotherapy in the 5 Boroughs Partnership NHS Trust and as a psychoanalyst in private practice. She gives a description of a service provided to families in difficulties who have children under five years of age. Psychoanalytic, systemic and cognitive behavioural treatments are available to families; the approach depends on what kind of help the family can best use at the time. Whichever approach is employed is underpinned by the staff keeping an analytic framework for thinking, so that underlying painful feelings can be understood and given words. In this way the family is enabled to understand and bear such feelings.

Chapter 2: Child protection and 'looked-after children': What can psychoanalytic ideas contribute? (Judith Trowell)

In this chapter, Judith reviews her psychoanalytically informed work over many years of working with children, parents and families, with the NSPCC and social workers, with psychiatrists and the Royal College of Psychiatry. Over the course of her work she reached the conclusion that being able to think analytically for herself, and to provide analytic thinking to staff on individual and group situations, not only was of benefit for those she worked with, but also enabled her to maintain a creative space inside herself that has acted as a secure bedrock in dealing with the often traumatic situations she and care staff encountered through the years.

Chapter 3: Assessing the risk of self-harm in adolescents: A psychoanalytic perspective (Robin Anderson)

Robin is a training analyst and consultant adolescent psychiatrist. He was head of the adolescent department at the Tavistock Clinic for many years. He lives in London and now works mainly in private practice. His chapter explores the way psychoanalytic thinking can be used to extend and improve the quality of the assessment of adolescents at risk of self-harm. While conventional risk factors are clearly of value in identifying those young people who require admission or other interventions, a consideration of the interaction of internal and external factors, as manifest in the transference and in a consideration of the history and present circumstances, allows shape and depth to be added to the assessment. In this way an assessment can be a therapeutic intervention in its own right, and can play a part in reducing the risk. This approach is described and illustrated with clinical examples.

Chapter 4: A chance to dream: Asperger's syndrome and symbolic activity (Mary Brownescombe Heller)

Mary is a consultant clinical psychologist and psychoanalyst who worked full-time in the NHS in Teesside for nearly 25 years, where she managed an NHS psychoanalytic psychotherapy service. She now works largely in private practice. She is a lecturer, psychotherapist and supervisor for the BPC-accredited training of the North of England Association of Psychoanalytic Psychotherapists (NEAPP). Her paper describes the progress in psychotherapy of a seriously mentally ill young man who was said to be a 'stalker'. It soon became clear that his obsessional behaviour and thinking could best be understood within the designation of Asperger's syndrome. Although at first claiming never to engage in dreaming, it was not long before he was able to bring in a number of dreams. These are described in the chapter and the author discusses how such dreams enabled meaning and symbolism to play an important role in David's psychotherapeutic progress.

Chapter 5: Mrs ABC and the three uncles (William Brough)

'Bill' Brough (1919–2007) was highly influential in the development of psychoanalysis and psychoanalytic thinking, both in Scotland and in the north-east of England. Bill worked for many years in the NHS as a consultant psychiatrist and psychoanalyst, and this book is dedicated to his memory. His paper provides an account of the psychotherapy that he undertook with a chronically suicidal psychiatric in-patient. Over the course of the treatment, Mrs ABC was able to take charge of her life, move out of hospital and set up home with her sister. Bill, who was then aged nearly 80, presented this paper in 1999 at a conference describing the work of an NHS psychoanalytic psychotherapy service, based in Teesside.

Chapter 6: Murder in the dark: Surviving a murderous pathological organization (Susan Cockett)

Susan is a recently qualified psychoanalyst and is a consultant clinical psychologist in Central and North West London NHS Foundation Trust, working in Hillingdon. The chapter's focus is on the difficulties of working with a severely disturbed patient, and uses perspectives from both psychoanalysis and clinical psychology. The patient was seen in the context of a Community Mental Health Team, for five years on a twice-weekly basis. During this time, she spent several periods on the acute ward as well as attending the hospital's day programme. The account follows the patient's progress from suicidal attempts, violent behaviour and frequent self-harming to a more thoughtful and contained capacity to get on with her life and relationships – a capacity that ultimately broke down in the face of yet another significant loss.

Chapter 7: Psychoanalysis, psychosis and the NHS: Just a pipe dream or a new beginning (Brian Martindale)

Brian works as a consultant psychiatrist to the Early Intervention in Psychosis Service for the Northumberland, Tyne and Wear NHS Trust. He is a psychotherapist and supervisor for the BPC-accredited training for NEAPP. He has a particular interest in psychosis and is book series editor of the ISPS (The International Society for the Psychological Treatments of the Schizophrenias and Other Psychoses). He was the founder and is now Honorary President of the European Federation of Psychoanalytic Psychotherapy in the Public Sector. His paper explores the approach and past history of psychoanalysts working with families and psychosis in the public services. Brian provides clinical illustrations of engagement with families where there is a psychosis, illustrating the potential as well as the difficulties of such an approach. All the case illustrations are based on work in an NHS context.

Chapter 8: A4C and the dissemination of anxiety (Veronica Gore)

Veronica is a clinical psychologist and psychoanalyst who worked in the NHS for many years in Newcastle-upon-Tyne. She currently works mainly in private analytic practice near Oxford. In her chapter, Veronica points out that in today's health service we are surrounded by abbreviations such as A4C, PFI, EIP, KSF, BPD and IWL. She argues that these abbreviations are fragments of words, denuded of real meaning. She discusses how the abbreviations mirror attempts in mental health services to minimize the degree of disturbance that NHS staff experience – which then leaves them bereft of proper words that could convey meaning and contain anxiety. Instead this anxiety is managed via dissemination and projection.

Chapter 9: The impact of the archaic on mental health work (Colin Thomas)

Colin is a consultant clinical psychologist and joint lead in psychological therapies in Wolverhampton Primary Care Trust. He is also a psychoanalyst in private practice and is involved in the training of psychotherapists in the West Midlands. His paper considers the conflicts that arise in today's NHS where there is increasing pressure related to the need to protect the overall quality and effectiveness of both an internal thinking space and the external clinical work, within the context of an atmosphere of increasing confusion about objectives and financial restraints. In such situations, reality-based, thoughtful work becomes increasingly difficult to preserve. Colin describes, with examples, how these difficulties can become played out in the external world via group 'enactments'.

Chapter 10: Confidentiality matters (Anne Ward)

Anne is a consultant psychiatrist in psychotherapy in South London and Maudsley NHS Foundation Trust and a recently qualified member of the British Psychoanalytic Society. She lives in London. Her paper discusses the stresses and strains imposed on analytic confidentiality, and the difficulties in holding an analytic framework, when working with very disturbed patients who come under the Care Programme Approach held within the Multi-Disciplinary Team. She illustrates how difficult it can be for teams to keep the psychotherapeutic aspects of confidentiality in mind and how, in the current electronic age, fears can arise that patient records may be circulated more widely than is appropriate.

Chapter 11: Why do a psychoanalytic training? (Christopher Phillips)

Chris is a consultant psychiatrist and psychoanalyst who works in a Child and Adolescent Service. He explores how his analytic training and thinking have contributed to his work in the service and provides an illustration of such thinking in relation to an anorexic patient.

Chapter 12: Psychiatrist or psychoanalyst? Do these disciplines combine or conflict? (Siobhan O'Connor)

Siobhan is a consultant psychiatrist who has always worked in acute NHS psychiatry, while at the same time continuing to work as a psychoanalyst in private practice. She previously worked in Northern Ireland and now works in London. The focus of her chapter is on how she applies the discipline of psychoanalysis to issues arising in the area of major mental illness and its acute presentation. Her clinical examples demonstrate how psychoanalytic interventions can enable patients and their relatives, as well as the staff working with them, to return to 'good' or 'evidence-based' practice, when the intensity of the emotional issues has misled them. In the world of acute psychiatry, however, there may be little time for psychoanalytic reflection and decisions may have to be taken quickly when one is faced with acute crises. Siobhan highlights the value of shifting perspectives between the psychiatric and psychoanalytic models.

Chapter 13: It was an accident waiting to happen! (Mary Brownescombe Heller)

Mary's paper is a description of research using the 'Adult Attachment Interview' (AAI). The interviews were undertaken with 22 individuals who had been referred to an NHS psychotherapy clinic and who were all diagnosed with post-traumatic stress disorder. Using audiotaped excerpts from the AAI transcripts of four cases, she explores the usefulness of this form of assessment in revealing aspects of early history that have contributed to the individual's vulnerability to PTSD, when a traumatic event in adulthood resembles, either literally or metaphorically, childhood traumatic events that have not been sufficiently contained, thought about and worked through.

Chapter 14: A brief history of mentalization-based treatment and its roots in psychoanalytic theory and practice (Peter Fonagy and Anthony Bateman)

Peter is a clinical psychologist by background. He is the Freud Memorial Professor of Psychoanalysis and Head of the Research Department of Clinical, Educational and Health Psychology at University College, London. He is also chief executive at the Anna Freud Centre, London.

Anthony is a visiting professor in the Psychoanalysis Unit at University College, London. He is a consultant psychiatrist and psychotherapist and honorary senior lecturer at University College and Royal Free Medical Schools, Barnet, Enfield and Haringey Mental Health NHS Trust, and St Ann's Hospital, London. He is also a visiting consultant at the Menninger Clinic, Baylor College of Medicine, Houston, Texas.

Peter and Anthony have written many books and papers. In this chapter they describe how they developed and manualized an innovative, psycho-analytically informed treatment for personality disorder: 'mentalization-based treatment' (MBT). MBT has undergone successful clinical trials and can be implemented by trained mental health professionals.

Chapter 15: Relating psychoanalysis to general psychiatry: The role of a psychosis workshop (Richard Lucas)

Before his untimely death, Richard worked for many years as a full-time consultant psychiatrist and psychoanalyst in NHS psychiatric hospitals. He describes the role of a weekly psychosis workshop offered to junior doctors to help them make sense of their bewildering experiences with patients presenting in psychotic states of mind. As a psychoanalyst working in general psychiatry, Richard always argued that it was necessary to develop a framework of approach, where the theory meaningfully related to the presenting problems. This is described in the first part of the chapter. Clinical examples taken from the psychosis workshops follow. These illustrate the kinds of problems presented by the junior doctors and how their fellow members of the workshop respond. The challenge for psychoanalysts working in psychiatry is how to raise confidence in the junior doctors, in order to convert the patient's psychotic monologue into a meaningful dialogue. The psychosis workshop offers one forum for such endeavours.

Chapter 16: Doctors in trouble (Rob Hale and Liam Hudson)

Rob was Director of the Portman Clinic and worked at the Tavistock Clinic for many years as a consultant psychiatrist and psychoanalyst; he now works mainly in private practice. Liam was, among many other roles and prestigious appointments, a visiting professor of psychology at the Tavistock

Clinic and the author of several books and papers. He died in 2005, aged 71. The chapter describes a service run by Rob for GPs who were experiencing psychological difficulties. Two cases are described: The first is that of a suicidal doctor who needed immediate support and then long-term psychoanalytic psychotherapy; the second gives extracts from a session with a young woman who was struggling with the stresses and demands she experienced, both in dealing with adulthood and with her medical career.

Chapter 17: Teaching a psychoanalytic approach to public sector mental health workers (Graham Ingham and Vic Sedlak)

Graham and Vic are training analysts, with backgrounds in social work and clinical psychology respectively. Both work in private practice in Leeds. In this chapter, they argue, on the basis of their experience, that it is possible to convey some of the important elements of the psychoanalytic model to a wide range of mental health professionals, using a simple reading/clinical seminar structure over a relatively short period of time. They describe how they found it helpful to stress some relatively simple factors such as the importance of a reliable physical setting. Since many of the course members regularly bring very disturbed patients, it was felt to be important to give them a basic knowledge of the more destructive elements of human functioning and experience. The use of such clinical material not only was helpful in supplementing the reading of selected texts, but made possible a more thorough and convincing discussion about such concepts as transference and countertransference. In this way, the course members were helped to understand that feelings they had hitherto dismissed in themselves were clinically informative and could be dealt with in a professional and therapeutically enabling manner.

References

National Institute for Clinical Excellence (2004) Depression: The Management of Depression in Primary and Secondary Care. London: NICE.

Perron, R. (2006) 'How to do research? Reply to Otto Kernberg', International Journal of Psychoanalysis, 87: 927–932.

Rawlins, M. (2008) De Testimonio. On the evidence for decisions about the use of therapeutic interventions. The Harveian Oration. Delivered before the Fellows of The Royal College of Physicians of London on Thursday, 16 October 2008. Available at www.rcplondon.ac.uk/pubs/brochure.aspx?e=262 (accessed 25 January 2009).

Smith, J. (2007) 'From base evidence through to evidence base: a consideration of the NICE guidelines', Psychoanalytic Psychotherapy, 21: 1, 40–60.

Tuckett, D. and Taffler, R. (2008) 'Phantastic objects and the financial market's sense of reality: A psychoanalytic contribution to the understanding of stock market instability', International Journal of Psychoanalysis, 89: 389–412.

Part 1

Clinical work with parents and children

Chapter 1

Making a little go a long way
Early intervention[1]

Sheena Pollet

This chapter describes how one consultant psychiatrist with a psycho-analytic training – myself – working in the NHS in the borough of Halton, Cheshire (an area of high socio-economic deprivation in the North West of England near Liverpool) has attempted to ensure that her psychoanalytic resource benefits as many patients as possible.

In 1986, when I was first appointed to a consultant post in general adult psychiatry there, I had 14 hours of my week designated for psychotherapy. To spend these hours to most effect, I followed two guiding principles. Firstly, much of my clinical work would be psychoanalytically informed, rather than full-blown formal psychotherapy. This meant that alongside direct work with patients, I needed to develop indirect working relationships with colleagues in other disciplines and other areas, such as Primary Care. Such indirect work included supervision, consultation and work discussion. I also aimed to use time-limited therapies wherever possible. Where a patient's needs were for long-term work, I used 'slow-open' group analytic psychotherapy, unless a group was contra-indicated. Some patients needed time-limited analytic therapy (usually 18 to 24 months) or cognitive analytic therapy (16 to 24 sessions) before they could enter such a group.

My second guiding principle was to pick a target population where change could be achieved rapidly, thus enabling the potential for enormous secondary preventive effect. Halton's first consultant child and adolescent psychiatrist, Dr Margaret Bamforth, was appointed shortly after me and we soon shared patients who made us forcibly aware of the transmission of mental health difficulties across the generations. In general psychiatry I treated young mothers, with severe borderline personality difficulties, presenting with serious deliberate self-harm in the early lives of their first children. In childhood, these women had suffered neglect and abuse such that their attachments to their children were impaired and they frequently experienced severe depression. Research was already beginning to show the effect of maternal depression on child development (Cox *et al.*, 1987). Sometimes, the growing child developed some of his mother's symptoms and/or conduct disorder, leading to his referral to child psychiatrist, Margaret. The child might also be on the Child Protection Register.

We soon saw that it would be much more effective if we could intervene at the stage of the parent–infant relationship. Working with that relationship capitalizes on the invaluable resources of the plasticity of the developing infant brain and parents' usually high motivation to do their best for their baby. The rapid change that such brief therapy can achieve is highly rewarding for parents and therapists alike. Work in this area is also intellectually exciting, situated at the intersections of research and development in neuroscience, child development and psychoanalysis. In the past 20 years, an explosion of research has provided abundant evidence about the early development of the human mind, how crucial the parent–infant relationship is for that development and the value of such early intervention. (Mayes *et al.*, 2007).

In 1988, Margaret and I obtained funding to develop a small shared team – mainly nurses – to target psychotherapeutic help on families in difficulties when their children were under five years of age. We began by studying Selma Fraiberg's ground-breaking long-term psychoanalytic work with very disadvantaged families (Fraiberg *et al.*, 1975). Her team worked to dispel 'the ghosts in the nursery': the projections on to the child from the parents' internal worlds. Traumatic events in the parents' past had been managed by such psychic means as *identification with the aggressor*, so that, whether or not they were remembered as facts, affective memory was unavailable, dooming the traumas to be re-enacted between parent and child. They discovered that the parent could not 'hear her child's cries until her own were heard'. For that to occur, therapists had to be attentive to the splitting of the transference and prompt in addressing the negative transference. If they failed to do so, the mother was likely to drop out of therapy. The psychotherapy took place once weekly in the home – 'psychotherapy in the kitchen' – with the father present as much as possible. They combined adherence to psychoanalytic principles with practical help and tactful 'developmental guidance' – by which they meant using naturally occurring opportunities to help parents notice their baby's developing abilities and needs and the evidence of their vital importance to their infant. The latter could be shown by 'speaking for the baby', for example: 'Oops! That bump stopped hurting once you saw Mum notice!'

Halton's resources would not stretch to a long-term approach, so we sought a brief model to combine with Fraiberg's insights. I was fortunate to obtain supervision from Dilys Daws, then Principal Child Psychotherapist at London's Tavistock Clinic, to learn the approach of their Under 5s Service – rapid access to a five-session parent–infant psychoanalytic therapy, defined as *a containing space* with free-floating analytic attention in which to think with the family about their situation.

Containment is a concept described by Bion (1962). A baby depends on his mother to help him manage his unbearable experience, which he can convey to her without words. Mother takes in his experience, reflects on it and returns a modified, more bearable, experience to her child. Bion called the piece of unmanageable experience disposed of by projection into mother a *beta element*. The mother's capacity to reflect on that he called *reverie*, and performing her *alpha function*. The modified experience she returned to the infant was an *alpha element*. Alpha elements can be used for thinking, so the baby can then think a rudimentary thought. The whole process is *containment*. Bion considered it a crucial factor in the infant's developing the capacity to manage his own experience and to think. (Fonagy and Bateman's Chapter 14 in this book refers to the scientific investigation of this analytic concept and its being operationalized as *reflective function* and *mentalisation*.) Bion described a range of relationships between *container* (mother's mind) and *contained* (baby's projected experience) from benign to malignant: the success of the process depends on features of both baby and mother.

Our families' presenting complaints are seen as indicative that something in the parent–infant relationship is interfering with this essential containment process. The therapist brings her alpha function and containing capacity to bear on the family's plight to help them regain their thinking capacity and so metabolize their experience. Reasons for referral have included complaints about a baby's 'maddening' inconsolable crying, feeding difficulties, a toddler's oppositional behaviour, mother's post-natal depression, overt attachment problems, a parent putting a pillow on their baby's face. Families are referred by health visitors, general practitioners, Child and Adolescent Psychiatry, the Crisis Resolution Team and adult psychiatric wards. Usually other attempts to help have failed.

We call Halton's model *Brief Parent–Infant Psychotherapy – BPI* for short. We offer a family six sessions to think with them about their situation. I aim to offer a first appointment within three weeks of receiving the referral. Wherever possible, I make my first contact by telephone. This allows me to enquire about the family composition and learn when it is likely that the family can attend in order to accommodate their hours of work, nursery and school and the problems of public transport. The whole family is invited but I work with whoever comes, keeping absent members alive in our conversations. My focus is on the parent–infant relationship and the freeing-up of space in the mind(s) of the parent(s) for the child(ren).

I seek the meaning of the presenting difficulties through my free-floating analytic attention both to the family's verbal and non-verbal communications and to my countertransference. Over six sessions I hope to learn about current difficulties, the story of this and previous children (born and unborn), the stories of the parental relationship and previous important partnerships, the family stories of each parent and the current partner, who may not be the baby's father. The stories we hear are full of meaning and pain. It is clinical death to take them tidily as case histories. We act more as midwives to each story, which must tumble out as it comes, in a jumbled, fragmented chaos, or tight and constricted and full of gaps.

I aim for emotional contact with the family's difficulties, acknowledging the feelings that are expressed, looking for those that are missing, wondering aloud how something may have felt for my patient (say, in the postnatal ward surrounded by babies with mothers while hers are very ill in the special nursery). Often the missing feelings are negative ones towards the baby and parenthood, and terror for the survival of baby and parents – feelings of which the parent is very frightened and ashamed. Keeping analytic attention on the parent–child relationship, and the contact I am allowed with it, takes discipline but pays dividends. Parental preoccupation with self, partner, marriage or child is often defensive, as I will illustrate shortly.

Non-verbal behaviour affords understanding that I can then share with the family. For example, three-year-old Andy, unable to reunite a doll's torso and head, places them imploringly in my lap, showing his anxiety about Mummy's mind and his wish that I would mend her. After worriedly watching Betty repeatedly ignore her twins' dangerous antics, I could give voice to her fear that her life was over unless they died.

We often find *unmetabolized trauma*. Frequently there is *loss* – of necessary time as a couple before parenthood, of old identities, normal conception, a foetus, the imagined pregnancy and delivery or the perfect imagined child. A partner or parent may be far away, be estranged or have died. Full up with loss, a parent has no room in their mind for the baby. Preoccupied with concerns for the infant's survival and growth, a mother has little room for her own struggles. In her unconscious, it can often seem that it is the loved baby who has injured her and is stealing her life. Occasionally violent retaliatory feelings against the infant are painfully evident. Usually, however, parents are left desperately warding them off by splitting and projection onto whatever suitable and safer target is available.

The following clinical example is a fictionalized composite of several families. After recovering from prolonged post-natal depression during which she had been suicidal, 'Mary' had returned to work and been horrified to find it too much for her. She had come to us because she was concerned and very angry that she still did not feel as if nine-month-old Jason was her child.

In her first session, speaking angrily about the birth, she told me of suddenly finding herself rushed to theatre by brusque nurses. Moments later, her husband had been hustled away. Mary's severe pre-eclampsia had put her baby's life at risk. Her tale was an angry, jumbled catalogue of complaints about rough, impatient doctors and nurses but, through the muddle and fog, I began to suspect Mary had some fragmentary awareness that there had been enormous anxiety about losing both lives. I eventually said that she had been preoccupied with the danger to her baby, but it had been too terrifying to contemplate the equal risk to herself. Nodding and suddenly in tears, she told me frantically how she had felt desperately alone, wanting to pass through the doors to join her husband. I said I had the feeling that she meant letting herself die rather than staying alive for Jason. Sobbing, Mary agreed.

I found myself wondering why no-one else had got to this before. Feeling pleased with myself led me to become suspicious that I was colluding in viewing all rough, thoughtless helpers as elsewhere. This helped me interpret that our clinic was a place Mary had come for help, but that part of her was terrified that this would be yet another place where everything would go terribly wrong and she would be expected to cope with far too much. She seemed very relieved to have this 'negative transference' acknowledged. Soon after, she spoke of a kind doctor who had visited her on the ward the day after the delivery, to make sure she could understand what had happened.

Next session, when Mary complained of her painful feeling that Jason wasn't hers, I said I thought it might be hard for her to love and feel safe with him when she felt they had so nearly killed each other; easier to leave him with her attentive parents, whose help she now found so intrusive. Immediately, she blurted out that, when she had eventually found enough courage to lift Jason, her Caesarean wound had burst open, terrifying her: '*Only my clothes held me together.*'

This comment enabled me to understand that she had been holding herself together with an idealized view of a fragile mother, along with a view of herself as able to manage everything for herself and everybody else. Her mother had never recovered after having a stillborn child some years before Mary's birth. Mary had always prided herself on being no trouble to anyone. To be having a terrible pregnancy and labour, be exhausted by her beloved job and find motherhood so difficult felt utterly shameful. As she acknowledged her terror of contact with her son, her bitter resentment towards him for disappointing all her expectations and for shattering her idealized view of herself, Mary gradually began to enjoy him more and take over his care.

In our fifth session, I learned that the couple had conceived immediately they were married and had had to take in a lodger to make ends meet. I commented that they hadn't had time for themselves to form a couple before encountering parenthood, and I said that important work still needed to be done. I never managed to persuade Mary to bring her husband, but I frequently asked her what she had told him about our talks and what he thought about it all.

The main mental defences Mary had used to 'hold herself together' were *splitting* and *projection*. She used them unconsciously to manage a terrible conflict between her intense love and her intense fear and hatred for her baby, as well as to deal with the severe threat that this conflict posed to her identity and her capacity to manage her life. Her use of these defences had left her depleted and depressed and her relationship with Jason deadened. The defences directing her anger, hate and terror outwards had succeeded in their job of keeping everyone in the dark about their real source and target.

In BPI, we find we work best within a fixed contract of six sessions, which we sometimes extend by an agreed number of sessions. For us, a definite ending enhances the treatment's chance of allowing the expression of intense feelings and evoking issues of separation. (The latter often underlie difficulties with a baby's sleep or feeding.) Many of our referred parents have considerable personality difficulties. The definite boundary around the therapy helps us keep it firmly focused on the parent–child relationship, separating it from a later follow-up meeting where the adults can consider help in their own right.

Writers on parent–infant psychotherapy emphasize that much infant mental health work relies on a positive transference, sometimes advising that one should eschew direct work in the transference. Perhaps because so many parents we see have backgrounds of childhood neglect and abuse, we find like Fraiberg that families are more likely to engage and stay in therapy if we are very active in addressing the parents' negative transference, as well as the difficult projections and the unacknowledged warmth that exists between parents and child.

Our parent–infant relationship work has opened our eyes to the number of patients in adult mental health services whose presentations have not been recognized as resulting from becoming or being a parent. Once this is realized, appropriately focused work can be offered as the most helpful first step. Usually that is to offer a prompt extended psychoanalytic consultation aimed at answering the questions, 'Why this presentation and why now?' Once it becomes clear that the answers are to do with becoming and being a parent to this particular child, we would aim to involve any partner in the exploration.

The manifest problem may be in the parental couple's relationship. If the underlying problems in the parent–infant relationship cannot be reached, such partnership difficulties and the mother's underlying depression can become intractable. This is especially likely if the mother–infant relationship is idealized.

Commonly, the intense feelings are directed against a past trauma, typically memories of childhood sexual abuse that may have been evoked by a traumatic birth or the mother's (sometimes unconscious) anxiety that, like her mother, she will be unable to protect her baby from such abuse, maybe even from her baby's father. This often presents at least a year later as a request for individual work focusing on that abuse, but by then the couple's relationship and the relationship of the abused parent with their infant can be seriously impaired. A factor in a mother's depression may be that the baby's father is unsupportive, even behaving like an out-of-control adolescent. It is important to realize that the man may well have had his own past sexual or parent–child traumas reawakened by fatherhood and be doing his best to avoid contact with his baby, terrified that he may harm his child.

When their childhoods leave a legacy of cruelty and neglect, parents usually strive to give their children the opposite experience. Some may become depressed without realizing how intolerably envious they feel of their loved children or because they feel drained by loving them when they feel so empty inside. Such parents may be referred to adult psychotherapy services for long-term individual work. Again an extended intake consultation is the most useful first step.

We have also found that the repeated admissions of women with severe borderline personality disorder are often inappropriate responses to a decompensation or breakdown that has been precipitated by being or becoming a parent, or phases in her daughters' sexual development – puberty, becoming sexually active, pregnancy and motherhood.

The analytic concept that is most helpful in detecting all these situations is Freud's finding that in the unconscious there is no time, place or person. For the unconscious, such situations are the same (Freud, 1900).

We have found it essential to have a range of ways of working with the families referred to us. While I imported the psychoanalytic model from the Tavistock, Margaret received training in the *Parent/Child Game*, a brief, enabling therapy based on behavioural principles, in which the parent plays alone in the room with her child while the therapist watches by video-link and communicates with the parent through an ear-piece (Jenner, 2000). In the early sessions – the Child Game – the parent is helped to attend encouragingly to the child's play. In the final sessions – the Parent Game – the parent is helped to give clear commands and to see that they are followed. In each session, after the period of observed interaction, the parent has time alone with the therapist to reflect on the feelings, thoughts and memories aroused by the interaction. This often leads to exploration of the parent's childhood relationship with their own parents; work in which the therapist can use her analytic skills.

Parents usually see the Parent/Child Game as being taught parenting skills. Our child and adolescent mental health (CAMH) colleagues also offer the well-studied *Webster-Stratton Parent Management Training Programme* for parents of children over four years old. In it, a group of parental couples and single parents meet weekly for several weeks to view and discuss video-clips of parent–child interactions.

More recently, we have introduced *Watch, Wait, Wonder Infant–Parent Psychotherapy* (Cohen *et al.*, 1999). In it, in a room with appropriate toys, the parent is instructed that s/he must only follow the child's lead, other than to ensure safety. The therapist sits quietly by and does not intervene until the play period is over. Then, while the child plays alongside, the therapist slowly follows a set procedure to develop the parent's reflective capacity and her awareness of the child as having its own mind full of feelings, thoughts and intentions. First, he asks the parent what she noticed about her child. Next, he asks what she thinks was going on inside the child and only then does he enquire what was going on for the mother during the playtime. That last element can lead to analytic exploration and insight.

Parents do not fall tidily into those who need parent training and those who need space to think. On the whole, if we feel a parent is full up with unresolved trauma and loss, we will offer BPI alone or before one of the other three therapies. However, some parents find BPI unbearably intrusive and persecutory, construing enquiry into their childhood and inner world as blaming them for the presenting problems. Some parents who seek parent training find that the brief exploration periods make them aware that exploration is needed, so move on to BPI. Other parents are horrified to find that the Parent/Child Game involves intolerable contact with their child, and need to be changed at once to BPI. Some parents in the Webster Stratton Groups find the video-clips too disturbing and drop out. BPI can help some of them.

Inevitably, the adult's attachment pattern determines their relationship with services. Each week, I spend a little time with Halton's Crisis Resolution Team and learn of young parents, usually women, who have presented in crisis, because of deliberate self-harming acts or their contemplation in pregnancy or the first postnatal months. These adults have invariably experienced childhood abuse and are terrified that their relationship with their babies will emulate theirs with their parents. Their backgrounds make it hard for them to trust and engage with services. It is essential to pace parent–infant mental health work to suit them. They often feel much more able to use practical support from family support workers and Children's Centres, alongside their health visitor's support. By liaising with the health visitor, I can help inform her work and she can involve me more directly when the family is ready for more intensive involvement.

Health visitors' comprehensive knowledge of the most difficult families who reach us, some of whom may never engage with our Tier 2 and 3 services, has taught us that it is a service planner's fantasy that we deal with the difficult cases and leave the easy ones to our Tier 1 colleagues. The hardest cases to help probably never reach us or, if they do, slip back to their health visitor and GP, or return to them after we discharge them. This makes it essential for NHS infant mental health services and services for 'children-under-five' to work indirectly.

The indirect work of our service with health visitors was inspired by Dilys' paper 'Standing next to the Weighing Scales' (Daws, 1985), describing how important it is to find an ordinary, non-intrusive way to be available in the working space of primary care colleagues – to absorb the strengths, strains and stresses of their work and to let them find their own way to use one's psychoanalytic knowledge and skills.

From the start, we offered our health visitor colleagues consultation by phone or face-to-face, but were always concerned that this implied that the gradient of expertise was just one way. Eventually our opportunity came when the health visitors asked the nurse therapists to become co-therapists with them in the eight-week semi-structured support groups they provide in local Health Centres for mothers who have post-natal depression. The therapist and health visitor together do assessment and follow-up visits to the women in their homes. Some mothers may need parent–infant work at our clinic instead or subsequently. Whether or not the assessed women attend the group, we find that contact at home often makes it easier for them to seek our help later. The joint car journeys provide opportunities for discussing other cases and getting to know and respect each other. Our 'Watch-Wait-Wonder' Clinic is a joint venture between the Mental Health Trust (with myself from Adult Psychiatry and a consultant psychiatrist from CAMH) and the Primary Care Trust (with their Maternal Mental Health Specialist Health Visitor).

This chapter can give only a flavour of psychoanalytic parent–infant work. An excellent collection of key papers underpinning this area of work is edited by Raphael-Leff (2003). The reader is also encouraged to consult three recent edited books providing an overview of the many creative ways in which such work is employed and can be adapted to public sector health services. From the Anna Freud Centre comes Baradon (2005)'s contribution *Claiming the Baby*, and from the Tavistock Clinic Emanuel and Bradley's (2008), *What Can the Matter Be?* A third is an international kaleidoscope of papers edited by Pozzi-Monzo and Tydeman (2007), *Innovations in Parent–Infant Psychotherapy*.

The minimum requirement for beginning such work is to find a suitable supervisor, for example, an adult psychoanalytic psychotherapist or a child psychotherapist. In the UK, courses in infant mental health (IMH) work at diploma and master's level have been developed by the Anna Freud Centre and the Tavistock Clinic. Shorter courses are also available at the Scottish Institute of Human Relations.

Note

1 This chapter began life as a contribution to a celebratory conference at the Tavistock Clinic, of the work of Dilys Daws at her retirement in 2000. It is also an extended version of a brief paper: Pollet, S. (2002) 'Brief psychotherapeutic work with parents and children' in J. Raphael-Leff (Ed.), *Between Sessions and Beyond the Couch*, Colchester: CPS Publications.

References

Baradon, T. (2005) *The Practice of Psychoanalytic Parent–Infant Psychotherapy: Claiming the Baby*, London: Free Association Books.

Bion, W.R. (1962) 'A theory of thinking'. In *Learning from Experience*, London: Heinemann. Reprinted 1984, London: Karnac.

Cohen, N., Muir, E., Parker, C.J., Brown, M., Lojkasek, M., Muir, R., *et al.* (1999) 'Watch, wait, and wonder: Testing the effectiveness of a new approach to mother–infant psychotherapy', *Infant Mental Health Journal*, 20, 4: 429–451.

Cox, A.D., Puckering, C., Pound, A. and Mills, M. (1987) 'The impact of maternal depression in young children', *Journal of Child Psychology and Psychiatry*, 28: 917–928.

Daws, D. (1985) 'Standing next to the weighing scales', *Journal of Child Psychotherapy*, 11: 77–85.

Emanuel, L. and Bradley, E. (Eds.) (2008) *What Can the Matter Be? Therapeutic Interventions with Parents, Infants, and Young Children*, London: Karnac.

Fraiberg, S., Adelson, E. and Shapiro, V. (1975) 'Ghosts in the nursery: A psychoanalytic approach to the problems of impaired infant–mother relationships'. In S. Fraiberg (Ed.), *Clinical Studies in Infant Mental Health* (pp. 164–196). London: Tavistock, 1980.

Freud, S. (1900). 'The Interpretation of Dreams', *Standard Edition*, Vols 4 and 5. London: Hogarth Press.

Jenner, S. (2000) *Parent/Child Game*, London: Bloomsbury.

Mayes, L., Fonagy, P. and Target, M. (Eds.) (2007) *Developmental Science and Psychoanalysis: Integration and Innovation*, London: Karnac.

Pollet, S., Bamforth, M. and Collins, G. (2000) 'Adult psychotherapy and child and family psychiatry: Ten years of working together for parents and infants', *Psychiatric Bulletin*, 24: 139–141.

Pollet, S. (2002) *Brief Psychotherapeutic Work with Parents and Children*. In J. Raphael-Leff (Ed.), *Between Sessions and Beyond the Couch*, Colchester, UK: CPS Psychoanalytic Publications.

Pozzi-Monzo, M.E. and Tydeman, B. (Eds.) (2007) *Innovations in Parent–Infant Psychotherapy*, London: Karnac.

Raphael-Leff, J. (Ed.) (2003) *Parent–Infant Psychodynamics: Wild Things, Mirrors and Ghosts*, London: Whurr.

Chapter 2

Child protection and 'looked-after children'

What can psychoanalytic ideas contribute?

Judith Trowell

When Freud was in training he spent time in Paris and witnessed many autopsies. He recognized the extent of the abuse of women and children, and this led him to listen very carefully to what women said. In his early psychoanalytic practice, he always accepted and took seriously women's accounts of their seduction (or sexual abuse) by their fathers or other males in their childhood or adolescence. Later, while not by any means denying the occurrence of sexual abuse and the reality of its harmful effects on children, he also recognized that fantasies (or unconscious phantasies) of seduction could be equally important in their effects. He developed the Oedipus complex to explain and understand the very powerful feelings he was witnessing which had led to such distressing symptoms.

Clinical work

Working as a trainee child and adolescent psychiatrist and undertaking the psychoanalytic training, I found myself working as part of my training rotation at the National Society for the Prevention of Cruelty to Children (NSPCC). I came from general practice after paediatrics and in my adult mental health training had spent time in a mother and baby unit, which meant that I had an interest in family dynamics and what happens between parents and children. By then, I had also seen a number of children physically injured by their parents. The NSPCC that I joined had evolved a way of working that led to a marked reduction in re-abuse, but they were aware that the children were still not doing too well. This was in the days of physical abuse and neglect; there was really no awareness of sexual abuse at that time.

My task was to assess the children and share this, verbally and in writing, with the child protection team meetings. What I found were many damaged children who were unable to learn and whose emotional and psychological development was impaired or distorted. Psychoanalytic thinking informed my ideas – psychoanalytic child development and previous infant observations in particular. Undertaking an infant observation had developed my skills; I could observe myself and the child and the family during the assessment interviews. Some of the assessments involved home visits; all the cases had a home visit and I was included in some of these. During the home visits, the splitting and projection and projective identification were powerful and often these dynamics were repeated in the team meetings. Understanding the transference and my developing recognition of the countertransference and an ability to use it thoughtfully began to be valued by myself and the team during case discussion. An ability to understand and think about violence and sexuality, fantasy and reality as well as being able to consider risk was very helpful. However, I soon found that the most useful concept was containment and I began to recognize that many parents had never experienced a containing relationship and had no idea about child development and play. The suggestion that two boxes of toys went for the assessment, one for the child and one for the mother, substantially helped the assessment process, as did the suggestion that the focus of the assessment was not only the child, but the mother needed to have the opportunity to reflect on her own childhood and relationships, rather than simply offering her practical parenting skills. The major innovation, however, was to press for resources for the children: a child psychologist to assess the children and to work with the nurseries and schools, and a child psychotherapist to provide psychotherapy for the children and to consult to the social work team.

Slowly my role became supervisory of the child team but also with the senior staff and management. A team meeting was followed by a team group where not only issues from the work but also team dynamics and institutional issues could be discussed. Understanding group process was crucial, and my own supervision essential. Over time other NSPCC teams and senior managers began to seek consultations and supervision.

Child and Adolescent Mental Health Services began to do more work with families involved in child protection, assessments and interventions, and 'looked-after children' services. This was largely driven by the recognition of child sexual abuse during and after the 1989 Cleveland Inquiry and then the 1989 Children Act, which came into operation in 1991. It was recognized that agencies needed to work together, share information and have policies and procedures to protect children. Area Child Protection Committees were set up to take a lead on developing local policies and procedures, to review cases when they went wrong (for example, if a child was seriously abused or killed) and to develop inter-agency training.

It was rewarding as well as interesting, as the local child and family mental health representative, to try to find ways of sharing an understanding of children and family dynamics in a way that could be heard and thought about. It seemed important to constantly hold the child in mind, as the needs and concerns about the parents were often overwhelming. Without an understanding of group process and individual psychopathology, it would have been almost impossible. The internal world of the family cases with their processes of splitting, projection, denial and projective identification dominated the interpersonal and inter-agency relationships. Gradually, the agencies felt safe enough to share and build working relationships, to manage conflict and begin to find a shared language. Slowly, the agencies felt less embattled and believed themselves to be part of a network working together to protect and safeguard children.

Most of my caseload was child protection cases or long-term looked-after-children cases. Sexual abuse for a while seemed to swamp the service and Court attendance became a regular event. Court introduced a whole other language and organization, as well as a very different way of thinking. The Court and the lawyers had a 'snapshot' mentality and seemed unable to think about their interventions as part of a feedback loop. The judge heard all the evidence from the past and decided in the light of this what was in the child's best interests but also what was thought to be just in the circumstances. Yet as health professionals, we constantly review and reassess – and then adjust our interventions in the light of the response to the first step.

The difference in approach was challenging. Giving evidence in Court was often helpful as a discipline, because I needed to be clear myself as to what I thought and I could not hide behind jargon or waffle. Cross-examination was rigorous and searching, so I needed to be able to explain both what I thought and why I thought it. I also needed to be aware that there were dynamics in the courtroom that I ignored only if I was foolish. The lawyer for mother, the lawyer for father, the lawyer for the local authority and the child's lawyer were often caught in the family dynamics and it was easily enacted in the Court. Speaking on behalf of the children was frequently painful and difficult. Mother could be sitting there weeping while father was angry and verbally threatening, or abusive. The judge might or might not appreciate quite what was going on; at times the judge also became caught up in the dynamics. How one responded to questions was often important; this included not only my verbal, but also my non-verbal communications. Managing all the projections, both during the hearing and afterwards, at times could feel very painful and difficult.

Physical abuse cases were very distressing, but the task of 'child and family mental health' was usually to look at the emotional and psychological sequelae and see if such interventions as individual or family therapy would be helpful. Paediatricians were in the front line and had to make the diagnosis and treat the damage. It was usually the health visitors or Accident and Emergency staff that raised suspicions and initiated child protection procedures.

Neglect and emotional abuse were rarely recognized, although 'child and mental health services' were often where emotional abuse cases were referred for a range of problems.

The recognition of sexual abuse changed the role of 'child and family mental health'. Initially, there was great reluctance to consider it and anyone suggesting that such a thing might be part of the underlying problem in a case was treated with suspicion. The analytic community struggled with the idea of the reality of children being sexually abused by adults, and it felt like an uncomfortable place to be. The clinical work involved trying to understand what was reality and what was unconscious phantasy or conscious fantasy. As more knowledge accumulated and there was recognition of the emotional and psychological impact of trauma, which included post-traumatic abuse, this area of work became more acceptable. Adult analytic patients talked more of their abusive experiences as children, and more children and families were able to seek help. Sadly, the main area currently is the growth of abuse allegations in the context of the breakdown of the relationship between adults in matrimonial cases.

Psychoanalytic ideas have been invaluable in considering treatment post-abuse and the links with neuropsychoanalysis, physiology and psychology have been exciting. As we understand brain mechanisms to cope with trauma, psychoanalytic concepts can make greater sense. Experiences that are stored in islands or bubbles, or as sensations and emotions that are not yet symbolized and therefore not able to be communicated in language, connect with the emerging understanding of the developing brain. But perhaps one of the more important contributions of psychoanalysis is that it provides a robust way of understanding the impact of abuse on the patient, the family, professionals and the self which, despite the horror, enables thought and reflection to continue.

Often I wondered why I did this work, but it seemed to me that as a psychoanalyst and child analyst as well as a child and adolescent psychiatrist, if I did not feel I had important and useful things to say about these troubled children, then I was avoiding a setting where I could make a real difference.

Training

The ACPC Area Child Protection Committee was now developing local child protection inter-agency trainings. The Tavistock too developed a training in observation for Social Workers (Trowell and Miles 1991) and then the MA in Child Protection and Family Support which had a particular emphasis on sexual abuse. The President of the Family Division Interdisciplinary Committee set up by Lord Justice Thorpe undertook continuous Professional Development Conferences involving lawyers, child and adolescent mental health services, social workers, paediatrics services and court services. All these trainings struggled to provide knowledge as it emerged, but more importantly to look at the emotional impact of this work on the professionals involved. Psychoanalytic, or the perhaps more acceptable psychodynamic, ideas were always fundamental to this, as long as the language used was not full of jargon. The emotional issues that the cases presented stirred up everyone, but some professionals could manage the emotions more easily within their working practices. Social workers were usually left carrying the projections for everyone else and were blamed and attacked by the parents and society. Recognition of this led to work with social work trainers to promote and develop social work pre- and post-qualification training. None of this would have been sustainable for me without my awareness and understanding of psychoanalytic processes and without ongoing supervision to understand what I encountered.

Alongside these training developments, there were two further developments. One was the move into management within the Tavistock Clinic Child and Family Department and the other was the development of research and an academic presence.

Management

My management role in the Tavistock was exciting but also taxing. Conflicts with the external world over funding and staffing were a constant battle at that time. Internal conflicts were more complex and the outcomes were mixed. There were conflicting visions of the role and task of the institution: was it to promote 'pure' psychoanalysis, or was it to promote the application of psychoanalytic ideas in the community? Perhaps this was irresolvable and a clash of visions inevitable. At times, psychoanalytic ideas and internal conflicts, such as those between groups, were used to attack and denigrate, but this was mainly in the service of personality clashes that manifest in an unpleasant manner. Promoting services for children and families and the training of outside professionals grew rapidly; these generally had to include an observation and an understanding of individual and organizational dynamics, as well as the concepts of transference and countertransference. The work and ideas of Bion underpinned such training and at its centre were his concepts of the container/contained, beta-elements and alpha function.

It has always been important to promote the next generation of psychiatrists, psychologists, social workers, psychotherapists and nurses in child and adolescent mental health. Maintaining a psychoanalytic stance is not always easy and may not be directly appropriate in every case. It is however, always helpful when trying to understand the dynamics of the child and family and the professional network. Some cases may need other types of intervention, or medication, but encouraging the trainees to seek personal therapy as an essential component of training was a constant. Time given to supervising trainees, particularly psychiatrists, was particularly important.

In addition, in order to promote an analytic way of thinking for psychiatrists who could not undertake the formal analytic training, an additional training skills course was developed. Many of the psychiatrists did part or all of this and, at the current time, psychiatrists come from across the country and from overseas, so this continues to grow. The psychiatrists value specific skills of dynamic understanding in their work with children and young people, in addition to having their own individual psychotherapy, alongside their formal specialist training for Royal College recognition.

For a number of years, these management and training developments led me to be involved with the Royal College of Psychiatrists on a number of sub-committees. I found that this experience of contributing, but not belonging, could be more or less stressful. The voice of psychoanalysis in the child and adolescent psychiatry section or faculty has always been limited and can be felt to be of doubtful value, with the result that joining with child and adolescent psychiatrists tends to involve keeping psycho-analysis underground and using it primarily to sustain oneself.

Research

The other and continuing development has been the undertaking and promoting of research. It seemed important to try to explore the use and outcome of working psychoanalytically. A start was made with evaluations. The Monroe Young Family Centre had been set up to offer assessment and treatment to families with children under five years where there were serious abuse concerns, or where children in care needed consideration of their long-term placement. The families came for the day and were offered, alongside practical parenting work, family therapy, individual therapy for the children and parents, parental couple work and a group. The evaluation demonstrated that those parents who kept their children, or had their children returned, improved in their parenting skills, but did not progress emotionally – despite all the therapy. This led us to realize that it was only by the time of discharge that these very worrying families (if they had their children) were just beginning to be ready to engage in psychoanalytic therapy work. Early on, they did not, or could not, grasp what was being offered (Trowell and Huffington, 1992).

Observation training was a cornerstone of all the training, and so to look at its outcome seemed the next step. Again, the intuitive outcome was not found. It was not the observation training that helped trainees so much as their own personal therapy. Where trainees were in (or had received in the past) personal psychotherapy or psychodynamic counselling, we found that they could more easily grow and develop (Trowell, Paton, Davids and Miles, 1998). These and other small projects led on to bigger, funded projects.

Using an outcome study with sexually abused girls and a childhood depression study, individual psychoanalytic psychotherapy was compared (with random allocation) to other psychological therapies – a group for the sexually abused girls and family therapy for the depressed children. Both these projects were very demanding and needed determination as well as analytic understanding. In both studies, the young people had up to 30 sessions once weekly and the therapists had fortnightly supervision. Both studies showed that the children made considerable improvement and both showed how the work with the parents was crucial in promoting or holding back the child's improvement.

The problems were immense and created many tensions and conflicts. Can 30 once-weekly sessions be considered psychoanalytic therapy, or would it have been better to call it a brief psychodynamic intervention? It did, however, demonstrate that working in this way had helped the young people. The research methods and research instruments available were not really designed to look at psychoanalytic work, and perhaps the studies were done before their time. Certainly, clinicians found the demands of the research very difficult, but now quote them in these days of evidence-based practice, so it does feel it was an important project to tackle, even though the research methods did not meet the 'gold standard' criterion of the 'randomized control study' and thus the outcome could be said to be of limited use.

Reflections

Reviewing all this, it seems clear to me that a psychoanalytic understanding made it possible for me to undertake this work. Throughout, I have had a private practice of cases across the age range and this has been the bedrock of my professional life. The supervision that has gone with it not only has enabled me to think about the cases, but also has held me connected to the importance of all the ideas and experiences of the analytic community.

The 'Leicester' and 'Mini-Leicester' group relations conferences were also essential; my capacity to think about group dynamics, whether this is in Court, in management committees, in Department of Health policy meetings or research committees, has been based on this experiential learning. The label of psychoanalyst has, I feel, both helped and hindered my professional life. In the psychiatric and research world, there was sometimes so much suspicion and scepticism that some situations had to be recognized as hopeless. Now, as a senior professional, the psychoanalytic world feels like coming home. The language, the ideas, the settings all feel comfortable and the conflicts and rivalries have become less important. It is clear to me that these ideas have enormous value in themselves and are of interest and help to many patients, many academics and many in all walks of life. I could not have done the work I have without being able to draw on the whole body of psychoanalytic work at different times and in different places.

References

Trowell, J. and Huffington, C. (1992) 'Daring to take the risk: setting up a Young Family Centre', *Bulletin of the Association for Child Psychology and Psychiatry*, 214, 3 (May): 114–118.

Trowell, J. and Miles, G. (1990) 'The possible contribution of observation training to professional development in social work', *Journal of Social Work Practice*, 5, 1: 51–60.

Trowell, J., Paton, A., Davids, Z. and Miles, G. (1998) 'The importance of observational training: an evaluative study', *International Journal of Infant Observation*, 2, 1: 101–112.

Chapter 3

Assessing the risk of self-harm in adolescents

A psychoanalytic perspective[1]

Robin Anderson

Suicide, attempted suicide, and other forms of self-harm are rare in younger children, but once adolescence is reached the rate of deliberate self-harm rises steeply. In 1990, the suicide rates per million for 15-19-year-olds in England and Wales for males and females were 57 and 14 respectively. This is almost certainly an underestimate, because of the reluctance of Coroner's courts in this country to bring a verdict of suicide for all but the most certain cases. Even so, mortality rates were higher only for accidents. Of course, many fatal teenage accidents may have a suicidal aspect to them as well. Of great concern at the present time is the increase in the male suicides in this age-group. Between 1980 and 1990, the increase was 78 per cent. This is particularly disturbing because the rate for adolescent girls and for all other age-groups is falling (Flisher, 1999).

Seventy-one per million is of course a very small proportion, though even one wasted life would be too many. The effect on others, however, of an adolescent suicide cannot be overestimated. It is a trauma that is devastating for other family members, who frequently suffer for years afterwards. Siblings can have their own development grossly interfered with, and are at risk of suicide themselves. It is also deeply upsetting for the surrounding community, especially in schools and university campuses, where it can trigger waves of suicide attempts or even actual suicides. When the young person has been receiving help from professionals it is very upsetting for them too, giving rise to strong feelings of guilt and distress and loss of a sense of competence, often not helped by the ensuing inquiries, which can become dominated by hostile and blaming attitudes, which are at the heart of suicidal behaviour and the response it can evoke.

It has been argued that those who attempt suicide are a different population from those who actually kill themselves, but this seems unlikely. A study in Oxford by Hawton and colleagues (1997) showed that there was a parallel increase in the rate of attempted suicide during a similar period. Empirical studies in the psychiatric literature in relation to the risk of suicide conclude that young people who are depressed are far more at risk of suicide than those who are not, and that those who attempt suicide immediately identify themselves as part of a group at particular risk. Studies vary, but the risk of suicide in the next twelve months increases by a factor of more than a thousand for those who have attempted suicide (Hawton and Fagg, 1988).

Other risk factors that appear to be important are a history of being bullied, of being sexually abused, and, for young men, of being imprisoned. Suicidal thoughts and wishes are also common in adolescents. Sometimes they are transient, and not signs of serious risk. Those with persistent ruminations about suicide are likely to be depressed and are at risk of suicide.

As I will attempt to show in this paper, an assessment of risk consists of paying attention to known risk factors, and then putting these into an overall context of the young person's situation at the time of the assessment, their history, and their personality characteristics. Insofar as circumstances permit, the more information that is available, the more chance there is of finding an explanation of the young person's behaviour. Often we get only a partial picture of what is going on, either in the mind of the patient or in their external life history; but the more coherent and convincing the explanation based on an appraisal of internal and external facts, the more we are able to take appropriate action. It is also true that a sound understanding of the patient's state of mind has a calming effect, both on the patient and on those carrying the anxiety and responsibility. In other words, a good assessment can reduce the risk.

Putting the risk into context: The adolescent process

The reason why adolescents are more at risk than younger children becomes somewhat clearer with a consideration of the biological, psychological and social changes of adolescence. Adolescents are thrust into a state of rapid change. Hormones induce physical changes to sexual organs, and changes in physical size and strength. These changes are accompanied by powerful feelings, not only as a direct result of circulating hormones, but also as a consequence of the alterations in psychic balance that come from changes in how young people feel about themselves – for example, from the knowledge of being stronger and being able to conceive or father a baby.

These biologically induced developments interact strongly with infantile feelings, so that the young person's fantasies about themselves and their bodies are given a powerful new context. Sometimes these are a great relief: for example, a girl's breast-development and menstruation may confirm that she will be able to be a mother after all, and help to overcome depressive fantasies of being damaged and infertile. At other times, extreme anxiety is produced as a result of a merging of frightening infantile fantasies and sexual maturity. Those whose defences against helplessness are based on powerful omnipotent fantasies may be quite terrified when their physical capacities allow them to act out a murderous fantasy. Or they find that the new circumstances of adolescence come with a sense of the past repeating itself.

> A 15-year-old girl cut herself badly after her first boyfriend dropped her. Later she revealed that her parents' marriage had begun to deteriorate during her infancy, culminating in her father leaving when she was four. In fact her parents were reconciled, and by this time had a happy marriage. However, it became clearer that her own fears about her parents' past unstable marriage, and her belief in her part in it, resulted in a catastrophic identification with her mother when an upsetting but entirely normal event in her social development took place.

The other context of adolescence is that the developmental thrust is towards moving from a state of dependence on parents to an interdependence with others – ultimately towards sexual partnerships and the acquisition of a capacity to be a parent. There are of course many fluctuations, but all these developments create powerful surges of contradictory feelings between dependence and independence that, for those who are vulnerable, can manifest themselves as unbearable anxieties that can lead to drastic defences.

In adolescence, unbearable feelings are frequently followed by action. The whole process of experiencing feelings, processing them and working through them is frequently replaced by an enactment. The girl who cut herself did not at that time remember her father leaving home or her mother's unhappiness, but when her boyfriend left her she enacted both the father who wounded and the mother who was wounded. It was only later, in the context of an assessment interview, that it was possible for her to bring her capacity to think about her emotional experiences and to connect past and present. This type of enactment, based on rapid projective identification of unprocessed experience, is common to most adolescents. But in those at risk it is usually more extreme, and is associated with issues of death, destructiveness and damage in which guilt is a strong feature.

Thus, suicide in adolescence is not an act of self-euthanasia. It is an irrational act based on the very primitive idea that a psychological problem will be solved by the physical act of ending one's life. This may be for a variety of motives: killing off an unbearable part of the self; destroying a destructive internal object; finding peace to escape from persecutors. It is most unlikely that a clear consideration that death really seems to be the best way out is the explanation.

> A young man whom I worked with for several years, who had made many serious suicide attempts, told me once that he imagined jumping out of a window and flying away, leaving his battered and scarred body to fall to the ground. This was not an ordinary religious belief, but a

delusion that he could solve his terrible internal state by creating a split between two parts of himself.

When we are faced with assessing a young person who may be at risk, one of the first tasks is to try to establish what is their story. Where are they developmentally? What are their main preoccupations? And how are they dealing with them? Sometimes one can get a sense of this by a thoughtful discussion, often by a consideration of their behaviour; but central to any assessment, and indeed treatment, is an exploration of the relationship that develops between the assessing therapist and the patient. The way in which a professional is regarded – whether as potentially helpful, or with suspicion, or perhaps with indifference – gives some indication of the young person's internal capacity to use help: the quality of the internal parents. This may bear a close relationship to actual parents, past and present, though it may not.

Containment in adolescence

Part of adolescent development is the revival of the importance of containing parental figures. The other side of all the acting-out that goes on – which, as I mentioned, was closely related to the increased use of projective identification in adolescence – is that the target of many of these projections is the parents themselves. This is like a revival of the infantile situation in the very different circumstances of adolescence. What is similar in babies and adolescents is the intensity of feeling, which those close to both babies and adolescents are asked to bear. It is the subjection to painful projections that can make aspects of parenting adolescents so difficult at times. Sometimes it feels as though all the unwanted feelings, hopelessness, incompetence and fear on one hand, and responsibility and worry without the power to go with it on the other, are left with the parents. Yet just as it is impossible to be unscathed by parenting a baby – babies require this of us – so it is that a part of normal adolescent development is that parents are often worried and uncomfortable. This is one of the reasons why the circumstances for children in care are so difficult. Not only do they have a past history of disturbance, making them more vulnerable, but they are often deprived of parental figures who feel a special obligation to help them in these ways.

When adolescents are assessed, professionals often find themselves in a parental type of role, in receipt of these projections. This is uncomfortable, and at times unnerving, but it is also very informative, and enables them to get a feel of what is going on.

In normal adolescence, there is a fluctuation between the need to use parents as temporary recipients of projections and the ability to take on these functions and to be more independent. Maturation involves the gradual taking over of the function by the young person. It is a regulatory process that allows the more disturbed parts of the personality to be managed, without causing too much danger to the person themselves and those around them. Bion often used the analogy of detoxification. In adolescents it is the more destructive and disturbed parts of the personality that can lead to states of mind in which there is a risk of self-harm when they take control. If there is an internalized capacity to manage these parts of the self – something that will either take control and overrule the destructiveness, or know when external help is needed, such as a parent or friend – then even quite dangerous states can be managed.

Thus, a crucial question in assessing suicidal risk after an act of self-harm is to assess the presence in the patient of a capacity to care for and help themselves. Do they have evidence of a good internal object and a wish to turn to it? If a young person has taken an overdose, what did they do next? Did they simply go to bed, indicating that they abandoned themselves to a murderous situation? Or did they go and tell someone, who could take them to hospital, indicating that there is some presence in them of an internal parent, temporarily silenced, who can care about them and make sure that they are helped?

As in any assessment, an examination of the quality of internal containment is crucial, and can be arrived at by exploring the quality of the young person's relationship, both to themselves and to others. To what extent do they show concern or even interest in their actions? Do they see themselves as a cause for concern? Do they have a capacity to have an overview of themselves – to see their own plight? It may be that such ideas are around, but more in a projected form – for example, they might complain: 'My mother [or my boyfriend] keeps asking me if I am all right.' In this situation, where the responsibility is projected, the risk is greater, because more is expected of another person; but often there is a very careful unconscious selection of a helpful object or a deep knowledge that a parent will carry the anxiety. An assessment of this capacity to select an object who will care for them, or alternatively to choose an unhelpful or unresponsive object (sometimes repeating infantile situations) is crucial.

A young woman in therapy, prone to wild acting-out and suicidal behaviour, reported to her therapist before a holiday break that she had been driving her car with her boyfriend and had deliberately driven it into the path of an oncoming lorry. The boyfriend had grabbed the wheel and steered the car to safety. The therapist was naturally very concerned, and in discussing this in a supervision had tried to weigh up the risks. On the face of it, this suggested a young woman in an extremely dangerous state of mind, who seemed to be at risk of killing both herself and her boyfriend. Her past history had included many self-destructive acts – sometimes literally suicidal, like taking overdoses, and sometimes acts of a more symbolic kind, like getting herself repeatedly thrown out of school and wrecking her education (she was very bright). She seemed to be caught up internally, and to a lesser extent in her current external life, with a seductive and destructive father, with whom she formed a collusive alliance against a denigrated and weak mother. This recent episode had come in the context of some good work in the therapy and the presence of a long-suffering and essentially good boyfriend who was not at all like the father. The countertransference of the therapist had been very intense, and she was familiar with the emotional pressure that this patient put her under.

In weighing up the risk, the crucial questions seemed to be: Was this a communication of a dangerous state of mind, but also of a presence of a part of her, represented internally by the boyfriend, who would take her out of the path of danger? Could this be seen as a communication to the therapist, as well as an attack on her? An important consideration was how she had imparted this material to her therapist in the session. Had it been in a cut-off or triumphant manner? If so, this would have supported the view that she was more in the control of something cruel and destructive that wished to terrify her therapist, just as her boyfriend had been terrified. On the other hand, was there more desperation and anxiety in her tone? This would suggest a more internalized insight that recognized her dangerous state and a wish to be helped.

The decision the therapist took was that, although it was difficult to be sure, there was enough of the patient who had brought this dangerous state to her for help: The patient herself had indeed been shaken by what she had done. This allowed the therapist to feel that she could afford to wait, and to go on assessing whether the patient was coming out of a crisis before the break in her therapy. The weighing-up of whether waiting is helpful, or simply avoiding the necessity to act and therefore dangerous, is always a crucial and difficult decision. Fortunately, in this case it did prove to be the right decision, and the patient, having communicated the danger and felt that she had been heard, survived the break without further suicidal behaviour.

Writing in a *British Medical Journal* publication on clinical risk management, Lipsedge (1995) notes the danger of relying too much on a cross-sectional rather than a longitudinal approach to the assessment of risk-management. He emphasizes the importance of developing a sense of history about patients' behaviour, as well as being prepared to repeat assessments.

One of the features of this example is that the countertransference of the therapist was very active. She was full of anxiety, and one could see this as the patient mobilizing her objects and filling them with projections that were therefore finding their target. This does not mean that there was no risk of suicide, but it does imply an active relationship going on, both externally between the patient and her objects (including her therapist) and internally between different parts of herself – for example, the boyfriend representing a more responsible parenting side of her.

One capacity that was clearly demonstrated was ability to enter into a relationship in which intense interaction could take place: a relationship in which the seeking of an object to project into and achieve a response was possible.

Some of the most worrying and dangerous young people are those in whom this capacity is markedly impaired. Many such young people do not reach professionals. Some of those who commit suicide without ever having sought help probably come into this category. Not surprisingly, when such people do reach us they are very difficult to assess, and may not know themselves that they are at risk. We get some clue of their impairment from their history of unpredictable, dangerous behaviour. Often this is not accompanied by distress – or at least we cannot get access to, or contact with, a distressed part of themselves. Such young people often have histories of deprivation and disturbed early relationships, which may include sexual abuse. What we meet at assessment is someone who may feel very untrusting, and who is therefore very difficult to engage in a cooperative dialogue. This quality of relationship produces a very difficult counter-transference because we cannot use our usual sensitivity as a guide to where the young person is. It may emerge that their means of coping does not involve an idea of being cared for, but instead are based on being in the grip of a more ruthless and omnipotent type of relationship, which often appears to promise to care for them but in fact is quite murderous, especially if there is any question of disloyalty in it.

> A girl of 14 was referred by her doctor with a history of a serious suicide attempt a year previously, followed some months later by her drinking a whole bottle of vodka, for which she was also hospitalized. She had broken off treatment at another unit and was refusing to be seen with her parents. Indeed, she did not want her parents to know about her referral to us.

A request for the parent not to know of the referral is not uncommon, and, apart from the legal issue of consent to treatment, raises diagnostic questions. Why has the young person requested that her parents be excluded? It is a sign of an impaired relationship with the parents, but what does it mean? Is there a wish to deny the need for parents? Or is it a sign that the parents are mistrusted, perhaps for good reasons? The problem, of course, is that often one just does not know at this stage; and an even more important consideration must be how to engage with the young person in a way that will allow an assessment and treatment to take place. We understood from the doctor that the parents were very concerned about Paula, but felt helpless; and we decided to see her on her own, as she wanted, but we insisted that her parents should know of the referral to us; and we planned to see them once we had engaged with Paula. We knew that Paula's sister had died three years previously, from an 'accidental' drug-overdose, and that Paula herself was behaving in a wild, out-of-control way, which was terrifying but paralysing her parents.

During her first assessment session her therapist reported as follows:

'Paula is a small, pretty girl with streaked hair who looks both younger and older than her age at the same time. During most of the session she was willing to answer questions, but offered very little information about herself. She quickly withdrew almost as if in a fog and she frequently yawned. When she went to the A and E department she was surprised when they said she could have died if she had come half-an-hour later. She had taken close to 70 paracetamol tablets. It was chilling to hear her talk about her suicide attempt with no emotion or meaning to it.'

Paula's disturbing detachment both from the therapist and from her own dangerous behaviour was very striking. The therapist found that she had to work hard on herself during the sessions to remain concerned and appropriately anxious rather than be caught up in what seemed to be a defence against despair, which took the form of a cut-off and disinterested state. When the therapist could hold on to her sense of tragedy with this girl (and of course with her sister's death, which had no space to be spoken of at this stage), there would be moments when Paula would come more to life. However, during the therapist's four-session assessment, she took a planned one-week holiday. During that week Paula took another large overdose and was hospitalized.

It seemed most likely that her sense of being dropped by the therapist was behind the overdose, but, not surprisingly, there was nothing else that Paula conveyed that gave any indication of her attachment to the therapist or any idea of what had been in her mind when she took the overdose. When these things were pieced together, it was possible gradually to build up a picture of a process at work that could give some sense of Paula's actions. Paula seemed to 'think' and communicate almost entirely through her actions – she could communicate depression and despair, but only by taking an overdose which might then give others, if not herself, some knowledge of what had been in her mind at the time. We suspected that the loss of her sister had had a profound effect on her as well as on her parents; but instead of being able to mourn her she seemed to be in a manic identification with her. The desperation was apparent to her helpless parents and those around her. She seemed to be pushing into them feelings of helplessly watching something wildly and dangerously destroying their life. In this way, the pain of the loss of the sister could be inferred, but at the same time with a sense that this was not just a communication, but a very dangerous identification that might well end with her losing her life and her parents losing another child.

This provisional hypothesis was used to provide the basis for thinking about how to complete her assessment and form a treatment plan. With such a dangerous disturbance, including the risk of dangerous acting-out, inpatient treatment was obviously indicated. But Paula was adamantly against this. Compulsory admission certainly does have a place in an acute situation, but in the circumstances of Paula's suicidal behaviour, which was ongoing and intermittent, this did not seem to be the solution. In addition she liked her school, and seemed to be well supported there. It was decided to set up a plan of weekly sessions with a psychotherapist, together with at least three-weekly appointments with a psychiatrist to evaluate her mental state and supervise her antidepressant medication. Her mother was given charge of these drugs. Her parents were also seen regularly.

With this structure, despite one more slightly weaker suicide attempt, Paula was gradually able to use her sessions to become more open and to talk about her sad feelings behind all the partying, including how she had not been able to protect herself properly, and had been sexually assaulted as a result. Her dangerous behaviour diminished, and although she broke off treatment after nine months, she was in a less dangerous state and was willing to continue her appointments with the psychiatrist. It was not until right at the end of her treatment that she was herself able to speak with feeling about the loss of her sister.

Other types of impaired container-contained relationships may emerge in assessment. Young people with a history of more perverse or abusive experiences often have had prolonged experience of being used as recipients of unwanted projection by others, such as their parents. This seems to be especially pathogenic when it is in the context of violence. Such relationships impair the development of a capacity for self-care, and emerge in adolescence as the presence of impaired relationships with others, abusive peer relationships, and inability to use professional help. Often the experience of being understood does not bring relief for them, as it produces great conflict, and so it is very difficult both to assess them and to set up appropriate treatment programmes. But the more these circumstances can be properly understood, the more it is possible to find ways of making a contact with the young person, or to help those who are struggling to help them.

An integrated assessment

An assessment that is conducted in a way that will allow psychodynamic features to emerge is one that needs to be conducted in a relatively unstructured way. Many structured interviews used for empirical research programmes or checklists could be seen to clash with a psychodynamic approach. If too much of the assessment is spent asking the patient rather than listening to them, it will not be possible to 'hear' the subtleties of what lies behind Paula's silence about herself, or the young woman who tried to kill herself and her boyfriend. A checklist of questions can be used as a means of acting out countertransference anxiety. Instead of holding on to feelings of helplessness or worry, asking a series of questions can be a way of not holding on to the anxiety, or of properly processing it in order to arrive at a fuller understanding of the patient, and allowing them to feel heard in a deeper way.

On the other hand, to avoid taking a more active part in an assessment that is full of avoidant behaviour can also be a collusion with the patient not to name the risk, something that they may have persuaded those close to them to do. Careful use of standardized questionnaires, such as the Youth Self Report Form (Achenbach, 1991) or for older adolescents the Beck Hopelessness Scale (Beck and Steer, 1988) can also have a place, as well as being of value for audit and research.

Provided the therapist is aware of the dynamic significance of asking or not-asking, the use of questions in an assessment becomes a sensible and reality-based piece of equipment that can enormously improve the quality – the degree of accuracy – of risk-assessment. It is therefore helpful to have at the back of one's mind a list of risk factors to draw on which can be converted into questions or lines of enquiry when appropriate. No assessment of any young patient should be regarded as complete without the therapist feeling satisfied about the presence or absence of a significant suicidal risk.

The following is a list of risk factors that can be borne in mind.

- Preoccupation with themes of death expressed in talking or writing
- Expressing suicidal thoughts or threats
- Actual suicidal threats or gestures, even in the distant past
- Prolonged periods of depression, such as change in sleeping patterns, too much or too little sleep or sudden extreme changes in weight and eating habits
- Withdrawal and isolation from family and friends
- A history of prolonged family conflict and instability
- Deteriorating academic performance reflected in lower grades, dropping lectures and tutorials, and dropping out of school or college activities
- Pending disciplinary issues in school or college
- A history of severe or prolonged bullying
- A history of family suicides
- Persistent abuse of drugs or alcohol

- Major personality and behavioural changes indicated by excessive anxiety, or nervousness, angry outbursts, apathy, or lack of interest in personal appearance or the opposite sex
- Recent loss of close relationship through death or suicide, or a suicide within school or college
- Making final arrangements, leaving a 'goodbye' note, drawing up a will, or giving away prized possessions
- Telling someone of one's state and intentions
- Previous suicide attempts
- Sudden unexplained euphoria or heightened activity after a long period of depression. The decision to commit suicide is felt as an abandonment of a painful conflict that can actually lift depression
- The development of a psychotic illness – schizophrenia is associated with a markedly increased risk of suicide.

Whom to assess?

Similar principles can guide the therapist in trying to decide who should be seen and in what combination. It is essential to establish a setting in which the young person can feel listened to and in which the dynamics can be visible, and that other relevant people in the young person's life (such as parents or social workers) can be heard and involved too, as they can make a vital contribution.

However, it is important that the trust of the young person is not lost, nor the possibility of examining the transference and countertransference situation. Where professionals are working single-handedly, there is no alternative to making the best compromise between being there for the young person and giving space to other involved adults. When it is possible to have a team, even of two, then these tasks can be divided. Whichever way it is used, there will also be important questions of confidentiality. The young person must feel that confidentiality will be respected, but not to the point of allowing a collusion in which suicidal plans are kept from parents or others *in loco parentis*.

Conclusion

An assessment of risk is at best imprecise. It should get as close as it can in establishing what the risks are. However, it is essential to understand that it is also a therapeutic intervention which, when well conducted, will allow both the young person and those concerned for them to feel more understood and therefore to feel less at risk. It is a relationship with the young person and their system that contains anxiety. In these days of increased litigation, and a greater tendency to practise defensively, there is a risk that this valuable intervention can become more obsessional and defensive itself, and thus be less containing. Professionals at the centre of an assessment of risk do carry responsibilities, and can be at risk themselves if they have not conducted their work to adequate standards. But this pressure not to carry and live with some risk needs to be firmly resisted. In this way, an essential dynamic can operate which can both reduce the risk and allow important information about the patient's state of mind to be included in the assessment of risk.

Acknowledgements

The author would like to thank Professor Phil Richardson and Dr Helen Keeley for their help with the epidemiological and questionnaire references.

Note

1 A version of this chapter was originally published in: *Psychoanalytic Psychotherapy* (2000), Vol. 14, No. 1, 9–21. A slightly different version was also published in *Assessment in Child Psychotherapy* (2000), M. Rustin and E. Quagliata (Eds.), London: Duckworth (Tavistock Clinic Series, N. Temple and M. Waddell, Eds.).

References

Achenbach, T.M. (1991) *Manual for the Youth Self Report Form and 1991 Profile*, Burlington, VT: University of Vermont Department of Psychiatry.

Beck, T. and Steer, R.A. (1988) *Beck Hopelessness Scale Manual*, San Antonio, TX: Psychological Corporation.

Flisher, A. (1999) 'Annotation: Mood disorder in suicidal children and adolescents: Recent developments', *Journal of Child Psychology and Psychiatry*, 40: 315–324.

Hawton, K. and Fagg, J. (1988) 'Suicide and other causes of death following attempted suicide', *British Journal of Psychiatry*, 152: 349–366.

Hawton, K., Fagg, J., Simkin, S., Bale, E. and Bond, A. (1997) 'Trends in deliberate self-harm in Oxford 1985–1995. Implications for clinical services and the prevention of suicide', *British Journal of Psychiatry*, 171: 556–560.

Lipsedge, M. (1995) 'Clinical risk management in psychiatry'. In C. Vincent (Ed.), *Clinical Risk Management*, London: BMJ Publishing Group.

Part 2

Clinical work with adults and their families

Chapter 4

A chance to dream

Asperger's syndrome and symbolic activity

Mary Brownescombe Heller

> The study of dreams may be considered the most trustworthy method of investigating deep mental processes.
>
> (Freud, *Beyond the Pleasure Principle*, 1920, Ch. 2)

The capacity to dream, or its absence, in those individuals diagnosed as functioning within the Asperger's spectrum is not something that has received much attention in the growing literature concerning this condition. Yet in psychoanalytic thinking dreaming has a major part to play in the understanding of psychic structure, the nature of unconscious phantasy and the capacity to engage in symbolic activity. As Freud (1900) so memorably put it, the interpretation of dreams is the 'royal road' to an understanding of what goes on in the unconscious levels of the mind. The ability to own one's dreams, to think about them and make insightful use of them is, as Flanders (1993) has pointed out, a sign of developing psychic health and reduces the potential for 'acting out' unconscious conflicts.

In this chapter, I shall be describing how dreams and their interpretations formed an important part of the work undertaken with a seriously depressed young man diagnosed with Asperger's syndrome, whom I shall call David.[1] I think that having the experience of bringing dreams that were not only welcomed but also sympathetically understood, played some part in his recovery.

Uncertain beginnings

I might never have seen David. When his psychiatrist telephoned the NHS psychoanalytic psychotherapy service that I then managed, asking if we would accept his referral, my reaction was an uncompromising refusal. This was not my usual response to referrers; I felt uncomfortable about having been so abrupt and I began to wonder what had produced such a rejection.

The psychiatrist had described a young man, only 20 years old, who was clearly quite seriously ill and currently an in-patient in the local mental hospital. He was said to be highly obsessional, depressed and suicidal. There was mention of borderline psychopathology, schizoid personality disorder and possible schizophrenia – not that these features would necessarily have deterred me from accepting David into the psychotherapy service, assuming that he had wanted to explore the possibility of psychotherapy and that he was well enough to attend the clinic where the service was based. What had led to my unusually negative response was the psychiatrist telling me that David had been stalking the nurses, finding out where they lived and noting their telephone and car numbers. The ward staff had become so angry and so frightened by this that he was about to be discharged from the hospital – so would we please see him? It felt like a most unwelcome projection and, without allowing myself time for reflection, I had said that we would *not* see him. I did not want my staff being exposed to this kind of anxiety; they already had enough to deal with. I could have added that I too felt that I had enough to deal with, what with managing a scarce psychotherapy resource, which was insufficiently funded, overloaded with referrals and harassed by a long waiting list.

Six weeks later the psychiatrist telephoned again. She was at her wits' end, she said, as to what to do about David; he still needed to be in hospital, but she was going to have to move him elsewhere because of the fear his stalking had generated in several of the ward staff. Couldn't we at least see him for an assessment? By that time I think I had sufficiently processed the projection to feel less alarmed by the prospect of seeing this young man. I had begun to wonder whether we might have something to offer David that could be helpful to him. I was also intrigued by the powerful nature of what seemed to have got into both the hospital staff and myself that was leading us to want to rid ourselves of it, without allowing any space for thinking. I'd had no experience of working with stalkers, but I assumed that such behaviour must relate to some kind of early trauma, possibly of an attachment kind. Given the enormous anxiety that so many of the ward staff were feeling in relation to David, might this be some kind of enactment of early experiences that David himself had undergone? Were the ward staff reacting to a projective identification to do with feelings of primitive terror being unconsciously communicated to them by David? I didn't know, but I was becoming interested in finding out.

To the psychiatrist's evident relief, I said that we would see David, with a view to assessing whether there was anything we could offer him in the way of psychoanalytic understanding that he might find helpful. I decided that I would interview him in the company of a colleague. I had in mind a very experienced member of our staff: a psychoanalyst and retired psychiatrist (WB) who was then working one day a week at the clinic. Not only would this mean that there would be two of us to think about what might be going on in David's internal world, but if psychotherapy was what he chose to undertake, we would also function as a parental couple who could support each other, as well as David, in what was likely to be complex work. That was more than eight years ago. My co-psychotherapist retired from the clinic after we had seen David together, on a once-weekly basis, for 18 months. I continued to see David once a week, moving to a fortnightly basis after he had been attending the clinic for about three years; by this time he was no longer requiring hospital appointments.

The assessment

> From the earliest days onwards frustration and discomfort arouse in the infant the feeling that he is being attacked by hostile forces.
> (Klein, 1952, 'The Origins of Transference', Ch. 4 in *Envy and Gratitude*)

What we saw was a very tall, markedly overweight young man, who had great difficulty in looking at us, let alone meeting our eyes. His talking style was polite in a rather old-fashioned, formal and stilted sort of way. He was very hesitant and at times what he said scarcely seemed to make sense. He frequently broke off from what he was saying and engaged in an agitated, repetitious, sub-vocal counting that was accompanied by stereotyped hand flapping. He told us that he had been undertaking a university degree, but had become increasingly unwell after an upsetting rejection by a young woman student whom he had thought was his girlfriend. She had behaved, he believed, as if she reciprocated his feelings, but had then made fun of him in front of his fellow students. He later found out that she was seeing someone else and he had felt devastated. We put it to David that he must have felt quite angry with the young woman and her unkind behaviour. This idea was categorically dismissed. David said that he was never angry – being angry was bad, he added. When we wondered aloud whether this young woman had taken the relationship as seriously as David clearly had done, he became even more noticeably agitated, saying repeatedly, in the manner of a religious mantra, 'She betrayed me three times!' It gave us the impression that David had felt quite crucified by this experience.

There had followed what sounded like a major psychological breakdown with psychotic features. He had taken numerous overdoses, cut his arms almost to ribbons and had been unable to return to university – feeling terrified at undergoing further humiliations and frightened of everyone. Eventually he was taken into hospital where, if anything, he had become even more ill. He was currently on a massive drug regime. When we raised the question of the stalking behaviour, David again became agitated, with increases in hand-flapping and repeated sub-vocal counting. He told us that he had been appalled at having been called a stalker. He'd had no idea that this was how his behaviour would be seen. Stalking was bad and he was not a bad person. It was true, he said, that he had written down the registration numbers of some of the nurses' cars; he had also looked up their telephone numbers and addresses. With some difficulty he told us that this was because he had felt so frightened of them. Finding out where they lived and what cars they drove helped him to feel safer. He liked numbers; numbers were safe. When we commented that this behaviour had helped him feel more in control of a world that had become chaotic and terrifying, he looked at us briefly for the first time and nodded agreement. At the end of this first meeting, when we put it to David that he might like to come again and talk some more with us, he told us that he didn't like women; he didn't understand them and he didn't trust them. What his girlfriend had done had confirmed that he was right not to trust women. He didn't think he would want to come for psychotherapy, not if it was going to be with a woman. Even so, he added, not quite managing to look at me, he wouldn't mind coming one more time.

In discussing this after David had left, we felt that what he'd told us had been an accurate, albeit partial, representation of his psychic reality. The so-called stalking behaviour was undoubtedly David's way of trying to keep control over a world that was becoming increasingly fragmented. In his current state of mind there seemed to be nothing to separate external reality from terrifying internal phantasies in which a cruel, ridiculing and persecuting regime held sway. The ward staff – or at least some of them – had become just such figures in David's mind. It seemed to us that what he was unconsciously communicating to them, through the processes of projective identification, was the contents of his own internal terrors. Ridding himself of these unbearable anxieties by evacuating them into other people was partly in the hope that these feelings might be contained, processed and understood; and partly, we thought, out of an unconscious motive of angry revenge for the way he felt the world (the world of women, in particular) had treated him – it was a case of 'Let *them* know what it's like. Let *them* feel as threatened and terrified of me as I do of them!' It seemed to us that David not only was evacuating this aspect of his inner world as a way of dealing with it, but also was in identification with a cruel and powerful internal regime. We wondered whether our difficulties in understanding David might contain a reflection of his own difficulties in understanding people and whether maybe this paralleled something of his parents' difficulty in understanding him.

Later, when David was able to reflect on the state he had been in when he first came to the clinic, he said that he had been convinced that the psychiatrist and all the nurses on the ward were mad – he had felt terrified of them and what they might do to him in the way of horrific tortures. He was able to acknowledge, somewhat shamefacedly, that he had indeed wanted to stalk some of these people and he still occasionally had fantasies of doing just that. Never anyone in the clinic, he hastened to add; he liked us here and would never do such a thing to people he liked. At this time, David's world was still split into the good people that he liked and the bad people that he did not like; and these two sorts of people were to be kept determinedly apart. As Klein (1958) has noted, splitting is a fundamental defence against intolerable anxiety and it had been very important for David to keep us, his two psychotherapists, as good figures in his mind. He was able to say however, that when he had first met us he had thought that we too were mad. It had felt to him, in the early stages of meeting us, that these two psychotherapists who were purporting to offer him something helpful were talking to him in a way that sounded duplicitous; he thought that we must have some sort of hidden agenda. The only reality that made sense to him at the time was that we were part of the insane world of the psychiatric ward. He had come to believe, he told us, that all NHS staff were mad and he was the one sane person left. It was a truly mad and frightening world in which he was then living.

The Asperger's syndrome diagnosis

> Even today, when more is known about the condition, some young adults with Asperger's Syndrome are referred for a psychiatric assessment for schizophrenia . . . and there is research evidence that individuals with Asperger's Syndrome tend to score higher on measures of paranoia than do normal controls.
>
> (Attwood, 2006, p. 341)

Asperger's syndrome was originally documented by Asperger in 1944, although the term 'Asperger's syndrome' was not widely used until the 1980s (Hodges, 2004).

From our first meetings with David, it seemed to us that his whole demeanour was 'odd' in a way that could not be fully explained by his depression, psychotic episodes and obsessive-compulsive behaviours. His difficulty in making eye-contact, his formal way of communicating, his excessive concern for accuracy, his inability to hold a flexible belief system, his love of numbers, his need for safe routines and dislike of change, his inability to 'read' other people's intentions or to observe himself from the point of view of others, the concrete, 'tram-line' quality of his thinking despite his high intelligence, his rigid body posture, his hand-flapping and other stereotyped gestures were all, in combination, suggestive of the autistic spectrum. He was also very sensitive to sounds and smells, particularly liking, for example, to sniff the insides of books. As a child and now as an adult, he had a particular fascination with refuse lorries. What he found intensely exciting was the way the metal teeth chewed up the rubbish as the content of each dustbin was thrown into the back of the lorry. It became increasingly clear to us that his presentation was best understood in diagnostic terms through the perspective of Asperger's syndrome, as described in such texts as Attwood (1998, 2006), DSM IV (American Psychiatric

Association, 1994) and Ehlers and Gillberg (1994). In addition, his child-hood history supported such a diagnosis. He'd had a difficult, protracted breech birth. He was somewhat late in talking and had a significant delay in his fine motor skills; for example, he had not been able to catch a ball or tie his shoelaces, which had led to teasing from the other children. He was very intolerant of frustration and of any kind of change in the environment. He was hyperactive as a young child and had frequently been verbally dis-inhibited in school, where he was often in trouble with his teachers and sometimes bullied by the other children. His parents were caring people who had done their best to deal with his childhood difficulties, despite feeling bewildered by their young son's unusual behaviour. There were no external traumatic incidents or close relationship losses during his child-hood that might have rendered him vulnerable to a late adolescent break-down, and he had never taken drugs.

Individuals who come within the Asperger's syndrome spectrum appear to have a particular difficulty in developing what Peter Fonagy and Mary Target (1995) have referred to as 'reflective functioning'. This is the capacity to form an imaginative understanding of other people's states of mind. Being able to attribute reasonably accurate mental states to other people enables their behaviour to become more meaningful and predictable. It was this ability that David so clearly lacked. Fonagy and Target argue that if the child cannot construct a coherent representation of their own and other people's mental states, then not only do internal and external realities become confused, but the capacity for symbolization becomes limited to concrete representations.

Thus David's vulnerability to psychic breakdown was, we felt, best understood in the context of an Asperger's developmental history in which the world would have seemed a confusing, bewildering and frustrating place to a little boy to whom other people were a mystery, who found it so difficult to understand socially what was expected of him, who had always experienced himself as different from other people and who, despite his efforts to fit in, was frequently told he was stupid or daft, or a 'bad boy'. This must have built up inside him, we thought, an enormous reservoir of rage that was always threatening to overwhelm him, unless kept rigidly under control, by means of splitting and projective identification. His pre-occupation with refuse lorries represented, we felt, something of the pleas-ure and relief at having, at least temporarily, a concrete sense that strong and powerful father figures could empty out and dispose of the bad 'rubbish' contents of his mind.

We thought that his universal dislike and distrust of women was likely to be based on very deep-seated, primitive feelings of grievance towards mother who, as his primary attachment object, would have been held responsible, at an unconscious level, for his Asperger's developmental difficulties. In failing to produce a perfectly normal baby, all women, of whom the prototype was mother, would have been experienced as betraying him and not worthy of his trust. The betrayal by the girlfriend he had thought loved him, and her humiliation of him in front of his friends, was the final straw. Rather than attack her, in his fury and shame he attacked both his own body and his mind through the laceration of his arms, his overdoses and his retreat into psychotic episodes. Viewed from this perspective, his breakdown could be said to have had a protective aspect, in that it defended himself, his girlfriend, his mother and other women from a potential violent acting-out of feelings that could have culminated in tragic consequences.

As Hanna Segal (1957) has pointed out, when projective identification is in the ascendant there are problems with symbolization. The symbol and the object are experienced as one and the same, since the ego is identified and confused with the thing to be symbolized, leading to the kind of concrete thinking so apparent in David. She terms this the 'symbolic equation'. It soon became apparent to us that David had great difficulty in distinguishing facts and beliefs; as Britton points out, *'To believe something is not the same as to know it'* (Britton, 1998, p. 12). In a ward case conference, for example, an opinion had been expressed that David had a schizoid personality disorder. This was heard by him as something bad, not as a diagnostic possibility but an indisputable fact that condemned him for all time and meant, in his mind, that he was irredeemably bad. For David, there were no such things as beliefs or hypotheses that might or might not be true, or that could be partially true, or be the opinion of one person but not that of another, or indeed, be something with which he could agree or disagree. He had no ability to play with ideas. If someone expressed an opinion, this was a fact and a fact had to be incontrovertibly true – otherwise all was chaos. This inability to tolerate uncertainty and 'not knowing' appears to be typical of the 'tramline' or 'black-and-white' thinking in Asperger's syndrome. It is a state in which splitting and symbolic equations predominate. When 'bad facts' were applied to him, David became almost driven mad by having to contend with two entirely split and highly conflicting perceptions. He was good, therefore a bad fact could not apply, or if what he perceived as a bad fact had been stated about him, then he must be bad – and this was intolerable, because it was imperative to him that he should be a good person. Hearing a perceived bad fact applied to himself created an internal situation that was akin to stalking, in that he felt relentlessly and obsessively pursued by an impossible conflict from which there was no escape. All he could do was empty his mind of the terror such bad facts created inside him by way of the sub-vocal counting and rituals, or evacuate the fear and rage into other people – *they* would then know what it was like to be so relentlessly pursued.

We discussed the likely diagnosis of Asperger's syndrome with David, to whom it made a great deal of sense: so much so that over the years he has read most of the books that are available on the subject and is probably more knowledgeable now about Asperger's syndrome than are most of us. I think that this diagnosis has provided him with an identity that he can feel more comfortable with, that helps him to understand himself, to feel less alone and, existentially, to find a way of being in the world. His current psychiatrist, whom he sees every few months, writes his diagnosis in her letters as 'Asperger's syndrome with obsessive compulsive disorder'. Asperger's syndrome is not like some illness that can be 'cured'; it is a life-long condition but, as Ehlers and Gillberg (1994) point out, long-term psychotherapy can help increase the capacity for self-reflection and concern for others, and make social contexts more comprehensible. This point is also taken up by Tony Attwood (2006, p. 326) who states 'Long-term psychotherapy can help the person with Asperger's Syndrome understand key events in his or her life, and cope in a world that does not always understand the perspective and intentions of someone with Asperger's Syndrome'.

Given his fear and distrust of women, David continued to be quite suspicious of me and not at all sure that he wanted to attend the clinic for psychotherapy sessions. He reluctantly agreed to attend once a month; it seemed that this really was all that he could manage at the time. As he got used to both of us, however, he was able to come on a more frequent basis; once weekly for about two years, then fortnightly. For the next year or so David continued to be quite ill, with periods in hospital. There was no repetition of the 'stalking' behaviour, or of his overdoses. His arm-cutting stopped within a year. It took him some time to grasp that what we were particularly interested in exploring with him was what went on in his mind – his thoughts, his feelings, his wishes, fantasies and dreams. For example, we wanted to know what he was thinking or feeling just before he went into his sub-vocal counting, and how we might understand the anxieties that underlay this behaviour.

A chance to dream

> Interpreting a dream implies assigning a 'meaning' to it – that is, replacing it by something which fits into the chain of our mental acts as a link having a validity and importance equal to the rest.
>
> (Freud, *The Interpretation of Dreams*, 1900, Ch. 2)

Bion (1962) stressed that projective identification is not simply an omni-potent phantasy, but is also a primitive means of communication and the forerunner of thinking. What is projected needs a container, not only for the purposes of evacuation but in order that what is experienced as unbear-able can be taken in by the container where it may be processed, understood and modified. Eventually, based on the experience that such feelings *can* be contained and thought about, the communications can be reintrojected in a more bearable form. Bion also makes the point that dreaming is a way of converting what he refers to as 'beta elements' (undigested and unmetabolized sensory fragments) into a form that can be symbolized and thus converted into 'alpha elements'; that is, conceptions that can be consciously thought about and communicated in a verbal form.

An early dream

> Dreams are perhaps residues of a primitive infantile process of self-reflection that developmentally antedates full self-awareness.
>
> (Fonagy, 2000, p. 76)

David brought his first dream nearly a year into the psychotherapy, in a tentative and rather embarrassed way. He appeared worried that we might dismiss this offering from him, or treat it as nonsense. After that, there were a great many dreams, most of which gave a vivid and rich reflection of those states of mind that David found difficult to access from a conscious position. As we continued to explore with him the content and possible meanings of these, David became increasingly interested in thinking about them for himself and in suggesting possible meanings. I shall give a brief selection of these dreams, taken from different periods in the psychotherapy.

> He was at university with his friends. A Tyrannosaurus Rex had escaped and was threatening to attack everyone at the university. David called out to his friends that if they stood completely still the dinosaur would not be able to see them because its eye could only detect moving objects. However, David sneezed, which caused him to move slightly. The dinosaur could now see him and began moving towards him in a very menacing way. It was about to attack him when he woke up feeling terrified. He went back to sleep and the dream continued. This same Tyrannosaurus Rex was now attacking a city. It was tearing up all the houses and pulling them to pieces. David was running from one house to another, trying to hide from this terrible creature. He woke again and was too frightened to get back to sleep.

The dream gives us a vivid portrait of the state of David's internal world in which a classic monster roams the earth, stalking its prey. This terrifying creature from the distant past – perhaps representing the frustrated rages of his infant self – now threatens to destroy the whole world.

Freud (1900) described dreams as 'the guardians of sleep', implying that one of the functions of dreams is to deal with psychic anxieties by working them through in such a way that the anxieties become less disturbing to the individual. Freud (1920) has referred to this as 'mastery'. The dream represents a compromise between the instinctual urges, desires and passions of the id and the disapproving, guilt-inducing strictures of the super-ego. In effect this means that through the production of a dream, the anxieties (which are based on a combination of unconscious phantasy and traumatic experiences) are moderated. Thus they become less likely to produce symptoms of physical or mental ill-health, to be 'acted out' in inappropriate behaviours, or to be evacuated in the form of projective identifications. This is one of the reasons why psychoanalytic therapists welcome dreams as an indication that psychic 'working through' is taking place. In the above dream, the task of construction fails on two occasions when it meets up with terrifying, nightmare anxieties that cannot be contained within the dreaming process. After a second dream attempt, David wakes up altogether and cannot get back to sleep. Even so, the very fact that he has remembered this nightmare dream and brought it to his psychotherapy indicates that he wishes to communicate something of the tyrannizing quality of his internal world.

I think that David's dream acts as a container for his intolerable feelings of not only being stalked by internal persecutors, but also of being identified with them. Instead of being evacuated in the form of a projective identification in which the hospital staff had to experience what it was like to be stalked, the hearers of the dream were now being asked to act as containers of these terrifying anxieties, to process them and to make some sense of them. In this way, David's tyrannical internal stalking scenarios were able, over time, to become less powerful and thus less likely to be acted out in the external world.

David's association to this dream was a memory of attending the reception class when he was four years old. He remembered that his mother always had to drag him to school kicking and screaming, because he was so terrified of his teacher. We commented to David that this was how he had experienced us when he had first come to see us – it had felt to him that we were terrifying dinosaurs who had been forcing him to come to this psychotherapy school and, once he was here, were going to tear him to pieces if he so much as sneezed. This interpretation caused him to laugh (an unusual event) and he said 'I don't think I did think that, not consciously'. Clearly he had experienced us as terrifying, as he was able to acknowledge at a later date, but at that stage he was not able to bring such thoughts into his conscious mind.

I think the dream also cast an interesting light on David's rigidity, lack of spontaneity and fear of change – as if he had a menacing and tyrannical internal eye, or 'ego-destructive super-ego', as described by Bion (1962), O'Shaughnessy (1999) and Britton (2003), forever stalking him and threatening to attack him if he engaged in anything that was outside the eye's omnipotent control, even if it was as human and ordinary as a sneeze.

The girlfriend dreams

David had several of these. This is a typical example.

> He was climbing up the outside of his girlfriend's house to her bedroom. He climbed through her bedroom window and began to look through her drawers. He was very anxious that someone might come in and catch him, because he knew that he should not be doing this. Eventually he heard her parents shouting at him and calling him names. He ran off and got lost in a wood.

This dream has a classical 'wish-fulfilment' function, in that it clearly represents an enactment of David's sexual fantasies. Yet again there is the disapproving, repressive 'eye' of the super-ego which cannot allow him to entertain such a relatively ordinary sexual desire. In discussing this dream with us David said, with some embarrassment, that in the dream he had been looking through his girlfriend's underwear drawer. We said that he was very interested in what women had inside their panties, or drawers, but was afraid that if he told us about his sexual curiosity then we would shout at him and call him names like his girlfriend's parents. We wondered whether the running off and getting lost in a wood was a bit like the sub-vocal counting behaviour he got lost in whenever he was feeling anxious – it protected him from all this shouting and name-calling that went on inside him.

The nightmare dreams

These generally appeared when David was feeling particularly low, or tormented by obsessional repetitions of what he referred to as his 'dirty thoughts'. The following is a long, episodic dream he had at a time when he was at a low ebb, hearing voices again and feeling quite suicidal.

> He was at a hotel staffed by beautiful young ladies, but he was sitting alone in his hotel bedroom watching a 'dirty' TV channel. He was afraid that the young ladies would come in and see what he was watching and be disapproving of him. The channel changed to the film *Hellraiser*. A monster called 'Pinhead' was chasing David, who was trying to escape from him by jumping from the tower block of one high-rise building to the tower block of another. David began to realize that the only way he could escape from this menacing character, who was catching up with him, was to jump off one of the tower blocks and kill himself. He jumped off, crashed to the ground and killed himself. Pinhead came up and began to examine David as he lay dead on the ground – while he himself looked on from a safe distance. Then he was

back in the psychiatric unit. He had been put in a black pit with a deranged monster who had massively long arms. David was desperately trying to escape from this monster, but he couldn't escape these terrible long arms. David woke, just as the monster had finally got him in its grip. When he went back to sleep, he was again in the Unit, with several other patients. The patients were all put in black holes which were being used as rooms. There was no sunlight or daylight of any kind, no beds and no toilet facilities. David managed to escape, but a nurse found him and took him back to the black hole.

This dream scenario graphically represents the persecutory nature of David's internal world – an anal world – of stalking monsters, from which he feels there is no escape, other than death or madness (the black hole). There are, of course, many ways of thinking about this dream and who and what it represents, including the apparent reference to my name in the film *Hellraiser*. We wondered whether we were being seen as the 'Pinhead' in the dream; after all, psychiatrists and psychoanalysts are sometimes referred to as 'Shrinks' and I think that in the early years of our seeing David, he may well have felt at times that it was us who were stalking him, with our sustained interest in his mind and in his dreams.

We can see again the tyrannical nature of his 'ego-destructive super-ego' as it stalks him with a ferocious, relentless intensity. It acts as an internal persecutor; the 'long arm' of a very harsh lawgiver, examining him and finding him guilty for his interest in the 'young ladies' and his 'dirty thoughts' about them. The tower blocks have a phallic, omnipotent quality and vividly depict the dreadful crashing down into a black hole of depression that David experiences when he moves from a state of identification with these morally disapproving, high-and-mighty, punitive and omnipotent figures into a state that is more dependent, deprived and needy.

Suicide can be understood as an act of enraged revenge, but it can also take place in the context of a despair of ever being able to escape from the clutches of cruel internal persecutors, other than by death (e.g. Asch, 1980). In this view, the suicide represents an acting-out of the conflict between two parts of the self that have been entirely split off from each other. In David's dream the 'monstrous Pinhead' self is stalking the 'good David' self and threatening to overwhelm the good self – so that death becomes the only means of escaping this terrifying fate. Fortunately David was able to enact this impossible conflict in his internal dreaming state, rather than in external reality.

A psychotherapy dream

After about five years, David's dream productions reduced considerably in number and he rarely brought any to his psychotherapy. By this time he was off most of his medication, attended a gym regularly and was of normal weight. He had begun another degree course at university and was keen to continue coming for his psychotherapy. He was also receiving support from his psychiatrist, a woman, along with his care-worker, a male psychiatric nurse, both of whom he liked and trusted. His obsessional preoccupations and unwanted intrusive thoughts continued but were, on the whole, less persecuting. He had managed to cope with the retirement and loss of my co-psychotherapist (WB) and would frequently ask after him, remembering him with affection. In this way, he was able to keep WB alive and present as a good paternal object, both for himself and for me, his remaining psychotherapist. The following is a dream that took place on the night before a psychotherapy session.

> His left arm was covered with white scaly scabs, which he was trying to rub off. The more he rubbed, the more irritating they became. He woke up with the thought that the irritating scabs would feel better once he had been for his psychotherapy.

In his associations to this dream, David remembered that as a young child he had suffered from eczema on his hands and forehead. His mother had used an emollient cream to smooth on him. It had felt very soothing and had taken away the irritation. This had been one of the good memories of his childhood. I commented that one of the reasons he came for his psychotherapy was to talk about all the things that got under his skin and irritated him; in this way his feelings became soothed and didn't trouble him so much. He agreed, adding that he thought I had a very soothing voice.

This is a different, less persecuted dream than the earlier ones. The painful, angry scabs are on the surface of his psychic skin, rather than remaining deeply unconscious. Scabs indicate that there has been a traumatic lesion, but that a healing process is now taking place. David is aware in the dream that his own punitive, self-lacerating methods of dealing with the irritations only make matters worse, but he now has the idea, albeit manifesting as a waking thought rather than a dream, that there is help at hand. There is the hope that the persecutory objects that continue to irritate him can be helpfully dealt with, if the good maternal object can be re-found and thus recovered internally. Melanie Klein notes that the infant's ability to deal with internal bad objects is strengthened by his mother's capacity to soothe as 'the primal good object' (Klein, 1958). Bion (1962) points out that the maternal capacity to contain her infant's bad object feelings enables him to develop an increased capacity to internalize this idiom of care – self-soothing – and use it for himself in the absence of mother.

In my reflections on this dream, after the session, it occurred to me that while the soothing hands and voice of mother had clearly been helpful to David, and the waking thought and associations attached to the dream represented a re-finding of a good object, I should also keep in mind that there was something seductive about a 'very soothing voice'. These white scaly scabs were difficult to eradicate – they had a concrete rather than a symbolic form and easily became worse when touched or scratched – so I should not be lulled into a false sense of security about David's progress. I needed to keep in mind that it did not take very much in the way of change to exacerbate the scaly scabs of his obsessional ruminations and to promote in his internal world a return of the persecutory stalkers.

Such concerns became evident when he obtained his first-class honours degree and had been accepted to do a Master's course. David was delighted, as I was. It was not long however, before he became persecuted by guilt-ridden ruminations that he did not deserve such a degree, he was not a first-class person, he had obtained the first-class qualification by false means and he should explain to the examiners that the additional time he had been given by the university to sit his examinations, as a consequence of his OCD, was unwarranted and amounted to cheating. Although we explored this for several weeks, I did not feel that much progress had been made in enabling David to moderate these entrenched and self-torturing preoccupations which, as I had pointed out to him, themselves confirmed the continuing presence of an OCD severe enough to merit the additional help given him by the university. It seemed to me that not only were we back in the area of the symbolic equation, but we were in the presence of an 'ego-destructive super-ego' that was bent on enviously spoiling all the hard and good work that had been done.

Having eventually become somewhat more settled in his mind about his 'first-class' depiction, David brought in a further self-accusation. This time it was to do with the lap-top computer that he had been given by the university to assist him in undertaking the Master's degree course. He told me that his previous lap-top, which he had bought himself, was 'riddled with viruses' and could not be used to access Internet information. He was now torturing himself with the idea that he should not have been given the new lap-top by the university, because he had obtained it by deception. He had not told the whole truth about his need of it, because sometimes he liked to play computer games on it. He had telephoned the university and told them this – adding that he would give the lap-top back to them once his Master's course was completed. The university had said that it was not their policy to take back computers once they had been allocated, so he must feel free to keep it. This information, far from allaying his preoccupying guilt, had exacerbated it.

I pointed out that we could think that it was David himself who was 'riddled with viruses' – these viruses were like the torturing thoughts of his OCD that were now stalking his mind, in just the same way that the computer hackers stalked the Internet looking for outlets in which to plant their viruses. David looked puzzled, but then his face lit up. 'Yes,' he said, 'it is just like that. My OCD acts on my mind like a computer hacker, it stops me being able to think. It interferes with everything that I do and messes it up.' After a pause, he said that he hadn't put any virus protection on his old lap-top, but he was making sure that he had proper protection for this new one.

David moved to a different university within the next year, where he continued his studies for his Master's degree. The location was some distance away and we agreed that this was a good time for his psychotherapy to come to an end. He found out that should he need further therapeutic help, it could be made available to him at the new university. This knowledge enabled both of us to feel less anxious about saying goodbye to each other. It remains my hope that the psychotherapeutic work that we have done together will continue to provide a 'proper protection' for his mind, so that the internal computer hackers may continue to be kept at bay, if not entirely eradicated.

Note

1 The author would like to thank David for permission to write this chapter and remains grateful to Dr William Brough for his many helpful thoughts in the early years of this work.

References

American Psychiatric Association (1994) *Diagnostic and Statistical Manual of Mental Disorders, 4th Edition*, Washington, DC: American Psychiatric Association.

Asch, S.S. (1980) 'Suicide, and the hidden executioner', *International Review of Psycho-Analysis*, 7: 51–60.

Attwood, T. (1998) *Asperger's Syndrome: A Guide for Parents and Professionals*, London: Jessica Kingsley Publishers.

Attwood, T. (2006) *The Complete Guide to Asperger's Syndrome*, London: Jessica Kingsley Publishers.

Bion, W.R. (1962) *Learning from Experience*, London: Karnac Books (1984).

Britton, R. (1998) *Belief and Imagination*, London: Routledge.

Britton, R. (2003) *Sex, Death, and the Superego: Experiences in Psychoanalysis*, London: Karnac.

Ehlers, S. and Gillberg, C. (1994) *Asperger Syndrome: An Overview*, trans. C. Olsen (2006), London: The National Autistic Society.

Flanders, S. (Ed.) (1993) *The Dream Discourse Today*, London: Routledge.

Fonagy, P. (2000) 'Dreams of borderline patients'. In R.J. Perelberg (Ed.), *Dreaming and Thinking*, London: The Institute of Psychoanalysis.

Fonagy, P. and Target, M. (1995) 'Understanding the violent patient: the use of the body and the role of the father', *International Journal of Psycho-Analysis*, 76: 487–501.

Freud, S. (1900) *The Interpretation of Dreams*, Standard Edition, Vol. 4. London: Hogarth Press.

Freud, S. (1920) *Beyond the Pleasure Principle*, Standard Edition, Vol. 18. London: Hogarth Press.

Hodges, S. (2004) 'A psychological perspective on theories of Asperger's Syndrome'. In M. Rhode and T. Klauber (Eds.), *The Many Faces of Asperger's Syndrome*, London and New York: Karnac.

Klein, M. (1958) 'On the development of mental functioning', *International Journal of Psycho-Analysis*, 3: 84–90.

Klein, M. (1975) *Envy and Gratitude and Other Works 1946–1963* (The Melanie Klein Trust, Hogarth Press). London: Virago (1988).

O'Shaughnessy, E. (1999) 'Relating to the superego', *International Journal of Psycho-Analysis*, 80: 861–870.

Segal, H. (1957) 'Notes on symbol formation', *International Journal of Psycho-Analysis*, 38: 391–397.

Chapter 5

Mrs ABC and the three uncles

William Brough

Mrs ABC was 48, but looked more like 84, when I first met her. She was the picture of misery – grim, gaunt and worn. She had been in and out of psychiatric hospital many times over the past 15 years, with 'severe depression'. This included cutting herself and overdosing with whatever came to hand, reinforced with excessive amounts of alcohol. She'd had most treatments known to modern psychiatry – except psychotherapy. And so she came to us at the psychotherapy clinic.[1]

Mrs ABC declared that her experience of this world was that the sooner she departed from it, the better. It had now reached the stage of not being worth the effort to stay alive. Her recent attempt to end her life had almost succeeded, and she regretted to find, on recovering consciousness, that she was still alive. Yet she had once had a good job – owned a house, and at one stage in her life had been, so the referral letter informed me, a presentable and attractive woman.

Mrs ABC had been married in her thirties to a Mr ABC. After six weeks, he left her for a woman whom he had not even met at the time of the marriage. It was shortly after this event that she became severely depressed and suicidal. The essentials of her history are that from the age of 5 to 13 she had been sexually abused by three uncles, whom I have called X, Y and Z. Uncle Z was her mother's brother; the other two were 'honorary' uncles, who were married with children, while Uncle Z was single and childless. They were all friends and neighbours of her parents, and had a babysitting function for them. I do not know whether, at this early stage, when she was very young, she had ever wondered if this curious sexual activity was associated with babysitting, or whether it was something that happened to everybody. Nor do I know whether she was ever involved with more than one of these men at the same time, or if it had ever been a group or a gang activity – or even if the involvement of any of them had been known to the others. It was presented to me as if it were three separate arrangements. I had no reason to suppose that it was not penetrative, genital intercourse at some time.

At her menarche, when there was now a possibility of pregnancy, one of these uncles dropped out, but the other two continued. I do not know how long it continued into adult life, but one thing was sure – her parents did not know what was going on. She felt adamant that they must never know about it. The knowledge would kill her mother, if she knew that her own brother was treating her daughter, his niece, in this way. Furthermore, she was sure that her father would kill the uncles, all of them, and so end up in prison. I suspected that the two wives of uncles X and Y not only knew but colluded. The two uncles, X and Y, were now dead, while Uncle Z was still alive. These three uncles were of my vintage, which meant that there was a clear route for the transference that might gather around a therapist of my advanced years.

In recent years she had lived with her frail mother, who needed her care. When Uncle Z also became frail, her mother and he decided to join households – without the consultation and agreement of Mrs ABC. This, unsurprisingly, led to an increase of her hospital admissions. Furthermore, she was so committed to the protection of her mother that she allowed her mother to extract a 'death bed promise' from her to the effect that after the mother died, my patient would stay on as housekeeper for Uncle Z and continue to care for him. This amounted to a returning of Mrs ABC to the earlier setting of childhood. Thus she was 'caught' in the same way as she had been long ago.

Uncle Z seems to have seen this as an opportunity to 'try it on again', as he had done when she was a child, this time in the middle of the night in an otherwise empty house. Following further overdoses, she was admitted yet again to hospital: this time only for a brief period, because the ward was to be closed for repairs. She knew this in advance, but when the time came for her to be discharged she was distressed and protested vigorously. This made it possible for her to remain in hospital, while attending her psychotherapy.

What I was able to offer to Mrs ABC was fortnightly visits of an hour. There was a lot of talking to do and some painful reliving of her past. She was certain there was *Nothing* and *Nobody* that could help her. The enormity and the extent of her problems and the utter impossibility of changing anything, in this '---- world', was beyond human capacity. The message I received was that the countdown had already begun. This time she really was going to succeed in killing herself. She bombarded me with her anger from the word go. She did not want to live in such a world. In the telling of it, she was pouring her pain and misery into me. This was the grief that had lain embedded in her since early childhood. This is what we call 'containing'. The cutting and the overdosing and drunken bouts eventually began to abate somewhat, because there was now a different or additional vehicle for the evacuation of the misery, the pain and the despair that she had carried inside her for so long.

However, the major issue remained. The attacks on herself, although fewer, were continuing. In any of them, she could end up dead. It became clear to me that she had taken over the abusing role from these uncles and was continuing to do this to herself. Formerly she had been the victim and others were the attackers, but now, although she remained the victim, as she saw it, she had taken over the role of being the punisher of herself. This she did not see, and it led me to wonder aloud to her whether she felt there was something that she had done for which she felt she ought to be punished.

Central to it all, was the fact that I was of the same vintage as the uncle trio, and proposing to spend an hour a fortnight alone with her in my room. She needed to feel secure with me yet, as before, this situation held the potential of exploitation. As well as all this, it was likely that she had some anxiety that I might press her to discover whether she had had any gratification, or satisfaction, or pleasure, or even curiosity, about the sexual activities in which she had participated. Whatever she had felt about this at the time, not only did she now regard the whole thing as wrong, but she felt she ought to have stopped these activities at the time.

I chose to deal with this in two ways. If there was something she ever wanted to tell me about, I told her she could do so when she was good and ready – and I was prepared to wait. The other way was to point out that during much of the time of the activity, she had been young, if not very young. At that time, she'd had the resources, the strength, the appearance, the courage of a child, but she had been confronted with the task of an adult. The others involved, while they had the appearance and age of adults, were in fact immature and fell short of being grown-up. So if there was something that she and they did not get right at the time, we need not be too puzzled about it. While there was nothing to applaud about the uncle trio, or anybody else on the scene, I also let her know that I did feel a twinge of pity and sorrow for them. But to whitewash them, or to let them off, was the last thing I wanted to do. They could have done with help themselves, because I could see that they must have missed out on some of their own growth and development in childhood.

At first, Mrs ABC was not clear what bearing or relevance her past experiences had on her present predicament, or what she wanted to do about it, or what she wanted me to do about it. There had been, and still was, a mixture of anger, hate, shame and disgust inside her. She still held on to an intense wish for punishment and revenge, and to lash out and disgrace those involved, including herself – although most of the participants were now dead.

I am going to take an aside to tell you something about my early days in China, during the Second World War. Every possession left unguarded was stolen. The rationale was that if the owner did not value and regard as precious what they had, then others, who wanted these things more, were justified in taking over possession. Something similar seems to have happened for my uncared-for little girl who had grown up to be my Mrs ABC. My guess was that the adults in her life had not been cherished or properly cared for themselves. So not having learned to value themselves, had found it difficult to value her. Her task now, with me, was to find the ability to value and care for herself.

There came a particularly bleak point in the treatment, when a profoundly depressed woman friend of my patient killed herself. This was a great loss to Mrs ABC, who had shown considerable kindness and compassion for this similarly afflicted friend. She herself now became very suicidal and I began to think that I had taken on more than I could manage and would lose her, despite the support I was having from my colleagues. I eventually pointed out to Mrs ABC that while she could show considerable kindness and caring to others, all she was showing to herself, so far, was anger, hate and defeat. I told her that she knew something about *giving* kindness, but not about how to *receive* it.

Once, when her Uncle Z was 'trying it on' after her mother had died, I was able to point out another piece of the problem to her. That is, that she was continuing to act as if she was still the little girl that she had been, and not the grown woman that she now was. This led to the understanding that 'the uncle nonsense that took place in the night' would go on for just as long as she allowed, unless she told him plainly and clearly to stop it. Eventually, this was just what she did; she stopped her uncle by the use of an expression that I had frequently heard among my soldier colleagues during the war. She told him to 'piss off' – and so he did.

One of the things that now became clear to her within the discovery of her new-found power was that she might now stop punishing herself. She had suffered more than enough for whatever she had done intentionally or unintentionally. I let her know that in my opinion, any time now would be right for her to stop attacking herself – and to replace this with a little cherishing. She began to have something to smile about. Her weight increased from six to seven and a half stone, and the pleasure about this showed on her face and on that of her junior nurse escort.

Mrs ABC now had a new problem to cope with; she had to make a financial decision. If she stayed where she was as her uncle's housekeeper, she would almost certainly inherit his house – to which in a sense she was entitled for her cooking and cleaning care of him in recent years. But to benefit financially, or in any other way, from Uncle Z's estate was difficult. The idea of taking money from someone who had sexually abused her was not straightforward. There was something about it that was akin to being a prostitute – though we were both at pains not to use that word.

Then I discovered something that she and I already knew, but had lost from the front of our minds. It was that she herself had a house: a derelict, almost abandoned house. This was not far away and was in much need of redecoration. Until now, it had just been left there and was rotting away. Now we could see that this unoccupied house represented something of Mrs ABC herself. That is, her own unused, abandoned self. This derelict house needed repair work done to it, just as she herself had needed repairing. So she contacted a younger sister, whom she found had also been molested by the same Uncle Z, but who, unlike my patient, had dealt with the uncle very promptly in the appropriate manner at the time – and had lived to tell the tale. This sister was very good at wallpapering and painting. She was delighted to make contact at last through the blanket of despair that had separated the two sisters during those lost and precious years. So not only was the house being recovered and renovated, but also the two sisters and their relationship. The sister was delighted with my patient and her achievement and these two now got their acts together. Thus the physical act of restoring and mending the house was part of the equation of her repairing and restoring her own life and her existence.

We decided to delay the ending of our sessions until her own house was ready and she was well into it. Then she could let me go with the knowledge that she had been able to face something that she had hitherto felt was unfaceable.

Note

1 This paper was first presented at a Specialist Psychotherapy Service Conference, held in Middlesbrough on 20 March 1999. A brief form of the paper 'Mrs ABC' was published in *Between Sessions and the Couch*, edited by Joan Raphael-Leff (2002), Colchester, UK: CPS Psychoanalytic Publications, University of Essex.

Chapter 6

Murder in the dark

Surviving a murderous pathological organisation

Susan Cockett

In NHS mental health services, we see many patients with narcissistic types of object relationships, who present for help when the balance in their lives is disturbed. In extreme cases, patients present with deliberate self-harm, sometimes with psychotic symptoms and potential violence to others. They come desperately wanting relief, but can become quickly caught up with services in unhelpful ways, and present professionals with a real challenge. The psychoanalytic literature addressing the psychodynamics of individuals who occupy this borderline between sanity and madness can help us understand, work with and contain them.

This chapter summarises the usefulness of theory when working with such very disturbed and disturbing patients as Ms B, who was diagnosed with borderline personality disorder, and whom I saw in my role as clinical psychologist in a Community Mental Health Team.

Ms B's initial presentation followed a violent sexual assault in which she had feared she would be murdered.

It was soon apparent that any actual or potential experience of loss posed an extreme challenge to Ms B's resources, causing her intense persecutory anxiety and driving her into the hands of an internal 'them'. I became very familiar with these figures, who resided in a complex and powerfully destructive pathological organisation. Frequently, I felt helpless in the face of 'their' power over Ms B and caught up in the grip of this gang myself. I too could feel trapped within the same kind of threatening tyranny that had entrapped the more dependent part of her personality.

'Murder in the Dark' was the 'game' Ms B had had to play as a child, while staying with friends of her family. She described nighttimes when she was separated from the other children, in a darkened room where adults would try to catch her. She would hide, be caught and then used in a sexual way.

In my work with Ms B what emerged was murder, excitement, confusion, and the sense of being caught up blindly in a drama where players were both victims and perpetrators.

During our work, I learned much about unbearable psychotic anxiety and how Ms B coped with this; evacuating it from her mind not only by violent projective identification but also by violent acts that became increasingly difficult to contain.

Theoretical discussion

Herbert Rosenfeld (1964, 1971a, 1971b) was one of the early psychoanalytic writers to describe and develop thinking about severe narcissistic conditions and to describe an organisation of the personality into a gang. He used the ideas of Melanie Klein, who took forward Freud's (1920) dualistic theory of life and death instincts.

In her work with children (1957), Klein observed and described a constant struggle between an urge to destroy objects and the desire to protect them. She believed that much anxiety arose from this struggle, with the operation of the 'death instinct' experienced as a fear of annihilation. Good and bad were split to keep them apart and then projected into objects. The subsequent introjection of these objects into the ego led, if all went well, to the healthy development of personality. These processes coloured the baby's experience of the outside world. Mrs Klein viewed splitting and projection as normal processes that predominated in the early paranoid-schizoid position. The destructiveness of envy was seen as a direct derivative of the death instinct. This envy was directed at the good feeding mother who was hated *because* she owned the source of food the infant depended on and that he wanted to possess for himself.

Rosenfeld (1971a) saw envy as being stimulated by dependence and experiences of separation. Any therapeutic work aimed at enabling the patient to give up the narcissistic position (of being entirely self-sufficient and omnipotent) inevitably provoked aggression towards those on whom the patient depended. He considered that the strength of the envious destructive impulses was closely connected with the strength of omnipotent narcissistic object relations. Rosenfeld (1964) stressed that *excessive* projective and introjective identifications of self and object caused a fusion of self and object in these narcissistic states. This functioned to deny separation, and thus avoid feelings of dependence, and envy.

Rosenfeld (1964) distinguished between the libidinal and destructive aspects of narcissism. Where libidinal aspects predominated, an awareness of a separate good object led to experiences of humiliation and defeat in the patient. Although there is considerable psychic pain associated with these experiences, sensitive therapeutic work can help to make them more bearable. However, where destructive aspects predominate, envy results in violent attacks on the good object, both internal and external. This is the negative therapeutic reaction, which can be seen when deterioration follows progress. The aim is to destroy the object that provides what the patient/infant needs, in order to maintain an unconscious fantasy that the patient/infant provides everything for himself. These self-destructive attacks are directed towards the needy, dependent part of the self, which has turned towards the object for help.

Thus destructive narcissism is manifest in attacks on both the self and its objects. Rosenfeld described this as being a kind of gang-like 'Mafia' organisation, which ensures that the dependent part of the personality does not step out of line, in exchange for the gang's protection. The aim of the organisation is to maintain the *status quo* and therefore prevent the development of reality-based object relations. In less disturbed cases this may be hidden behind a sense of superiority or cut-offness, and might emerge more clearly in dreams. In more disturbed cases the organisation can be quite explicit and very dangerous. Violent, dangerous attacks can emerge and threaten both the patient's and the therapist's mind and body.

I found this theory very helpful in my work with Ms B, where violent attacks of this kind were common.

Good as well as bad parts of the self can be projectively identified with the therapist. Henry Rey (1979) considered that such patients often come for help to *protect* good aspects of the self from the predominant destructiveness within their ego. Excessive projective identification can lead to intense dependency on the presence of the object, in order for the subject to continue functioning. When the object goes away the patient is left feeling frantic and without the essentials for living. This explains the extreme sensitivity to loss and abandonment that one sees in patients with borderline personality disorder.

Bion's (1957, 1962) concepts of the 'container/contained' and the development of an apparatus for thinking, in normal as well as pathological development, are central to the way psychoanalytic thinking about pathological organisations of the personality has developed. Following his experience of offering analysis to schizophrenic patients, Bion made a distinction between normal and pathological projective identification, and in particular was interested in the qualities of the object/container into which the patient or infant projects. In his model, when things go well, the mother is able to 'take in', or contain, those parts that are projected by the infant into her mind, and to think about them, without the balance of her mind being unduly affected. Again, if things go well the infant can take back these projected aspects and re-introject them, now in a moderated form, so that they are not so frightening or persecuting, and in this way the infant's ego is strengthened.

If the container/mother cannot do this, then the projected material comes back in exaggerated form, perhaps with some additional characteristics added by the mother herself – for example, if the mother has felt persecuted by her baby's projections. This leads to the infant needing to expel such material more forcefully from his ego. Thus Bion understood how excessive projective identification could lead to the patient/infant, in unconscious phantasy, emptying out the contents of his mind, including those aspects of his mind responsible for the perception of reality. Such evacuation was seen by Bion to fundamentally damage the basic capacities necessary for thinking and the perception of reality. This is his contribution to our understanding of psychosis. What happens between an infant and his primary caregiver, and the qualities of this containing object, are crucial to the way the baby's mind develops and the extent to which he can face and bear reality.

Rosenfeld (1971b) discriminated between several different forms of projective identification.

1   A *communicative* form where an aspect of the ego is projected into the object in order that the object knows something of the subject's experience, which cannot be readily conveyed in words. This would be the basic form of non-verbal communication between mother and baby.
2   An *evacuative* form where the aim of the projective identification is to get rid of something unbearable from the self and place it in an object.
3   An *avoidance of separation* form where the self and object become fused.
4   An *omnipotent control* of the mind and the body of the other – in the therapeutic situation, the therapist.
5   A *parasitic* form occurring in psychotic patients, which involves a phantasy of living *inside* the body and/or mind of the object.

John Steiner (1993) has written comprehensively about different aspects of pathological organisations in his work with borderline patients, particularly those patients with whom it is difficult to make emotional contact. He underlines their difficulty in being able to make and maintain contact with reality, and describes how the organisation of their defences is structured to avoid any contact that might leave them open to the experience of psychic pain. The pathological organisation offers a 'retreat', which protects the patient from psychic pain and promotes a withdrawal from object relationships to shelter behind a kind of armour. In psychotic and borderline patients Steiner (following Freud, 1911) argues that this organisation functions as a patch to repair an ego that has suffered a catastrophic breakdown. In less ill people, psychic retreats are utilised during periods of particular stress where the subject's resources are overly stretched. This retreat is more temporary and reversible. However, in severely disturbed patients pathological splitting and projection results in a fragmented ego. The qualities and capacities of this ego are split, projected and then re-introjected to form a defensive organisation, which holds extreme dependence and extreme destructiveness in a complex relationship. This structure *simulates* a containing object, which seductively offers supposed support to an ego in chaos, but Mafia-like threatens and coerces to force the dependent part of the personality into line.

O'Shaughnessy (1981) describes how such patients present for help in order to urgently re-establish a defensive structure that had previously enabled some, albeit limited, functioning to take place. Steiner (1993) stresses how this attempt often involves pressurising the analyst into collaborating with a system that relies heavily on omnipotence to put things right. In this situation there can only be *concrete restitution*, not true reparation. He proposes that in psychotic and non-psychotic pathological organisations the sane part of the self is unable to resist, because it fears being harmed by the Mafia organisation if it does not comply. He believes that there is also a more complex situation where the sane self *does* know what it is doing, and is aware that it is wrong, but feels gratified by the activity, either in a masochistic or in a sadistic way. The presence of such perverse mechanisms within my patient made the work with her particularly fraught and dangerous.

Clinical material

Ms B came to the Mental Health Services urgently, in her early twenties, after the conviction of a man who had raped her and several other women. She had given evidence crucial to the conviction, but later told me that she had achieved this by 'not being there'. She presented for help in a suspicious and fragmented state, unable to bear contact with her parents or older brother, with whom she lived. She seemed vacant and preoccupied and complained of hearing voices and seeing terrifying, threatening figures that seemed linked to the rapist. She said that nothing was the same any more. On her admission to the acute ward she suffered diarrhoea, which particularly troubled her and felt out of control. It was as if everything inside her was being emptied out with some force, leaving her depleted, terrified and confused. Psychotropic medication helped to settle her, but its impact was limited.

History

Ms B had one brother, two years older. Their father's work meant he was away from home for extended periods. Ms B experienced her mother as not straightforward, and certain painful realities had to remain secret and unspoken. Ms B and her mother seemed equally unable to face how unwell Ms B was. Instead, this was communicated by increasingly serious self-harm and suicide attempts. Her father was experienced as more straightforward and reliable. Her mother was apparently dangerously ill when Ms B was about four years old; she had feared that her mother would die, and felt consciously responsible for this. As a child she remembered hearing voices saying horrible things to her, which led to her cutting herself.

Perhaps to relieve mother during father's absences, she and her brother would stay with a friend's family at weekends. Being 'sent away' over weekend breaks in her therapy became concretely equated with being sent to this house, where a picture emerged of her being very frightened, shouted at by the woman who was felt to be in charge, and sexually abused by the woman's male partner during the game of 'Murder in the Dark'.

At school, she reported having hurt younger children, and then comforting them. She obtained a degree, but was never able to work to the level of her educational attainment. Before her treatment and in its early years, she had worked part-time in an unskilled job.

After the rape, her mother pressed her to keep it a secret from the rest of the family. Ms B found it intolerable to remain in her parents' house and she moved in with a man who was keen to look after her. Mr B repeatedly disavowed the extent of Ms B's disturbance and the severe risk that she sometimes posed to him. The period leading up to their marriage was particularly disturbed; she cut Mr B with a knife, and a forensic opinion was sought.

I encountered her first when supervising a psychologist colleague, to whom Ms B conveyed intense anxiety in speaking about herself, coupled with a desperate need to be heard and understood. My colleague felt anxious: could the patient bear to explore the rape, as the referring psychiatrist had requested, or would she disintegrate further? As sessions progressed, the patient spoke of a fear that 'they' were listening and that 'they' wouldn't allow her to speak – if she did, she or the psychologist would get hurt. This brought to my mind Rosenfeld's work on pathological organisations. Six months later, my colleague left the service and I began seeing Ms B myself.

An understanding of analytic theory was essential in enabling me to navigate the often emotionally overwhelming, and profoundly disturbing experience of seeing her for twice-weekly outpatient psychotherapy. I felt plunged into a nightmare world.

Assessment and management of risk, so dominant in today's NHS, were writ very large. Containment of intense anxiety was a constant task, yet I was under pressure from my patient to tell no-one else about what emerged in the sessions. Repeatedly I had to break the boundaries of the consulting room to take different forms of action. I felt caught in a bind, prohibited from speaking to others, while under huge pressure to prevent harm coming to anyone. I was being asked to hold what Ms B could not and this was also being played out between herself and her husband, who was finding it very difficult to maintain sufficient internal balance to protect himself from danger.

Survival was always an issue. During our first long break (three weeks) Ms B collapsed with what looked like a stroke but which had no organic basis. At any break in treatment, including weekends, I became unsure whether she or her husband would remain alive. Ms B assured me that she would not harm me and, indeed, I rarely felt in real danger. She seemed able to rebel against the demands to harm me that were coming from the internal gang of 'friends' who constantly told her that I could not be trusted. On occasion she would miss a session and later explain that had she come, I would not have been safe. Other members of the treatment team were threatened, and did feel frightened for their safety.

It was very important that we both knew that I was a part of an institution, with colleagues to whom I could turn for help. She was a patient whose therapist needed to be part of a service with access to a psychiatrist, acute beds, a care coordinator, and out-of-hours support. There were very many crises and complex issues involved in this work, necessitating the care coordination team meeting with Ms B and her husband in order to discuss the situation and how further harm could be prevented, using the care programme approach.

I am going to concentrate on some main themes of my experience of working with her, the impact on me, and how understanding this theoretically and, most importantly, emotionally, enabled this extremely challenging woman and her husband to survive the increasingly violent destructive attacks on herself and her objects – at least until she became so ill that hospitalisation was essential. In the work with me her internal violence frequently crossed the line from fantasy to real physical attacks. Working with her enabled me to have the opportunity to explore some of the ways in which her particular pathological organisation evolved to protect her from realities she found unbearable.

She could sometimes be helped by interpretations aimed to bring into her conscious awareness my understanding of what was happening. She would say with a sense of wonder, 'Now my head is quiet and there is more space', and be movingly grateful. She described how the noises stopped and the figures that crowded in on her receded. However, this development relied on the *presence* of my mind and would be followed by an upsurge in activity of the internal figures and voices.

Sometimes she felt able to fight against the backlash of the 'friends' who would demand violence and taunt her for trusting me, and for 'talking to me' between sessions. At other times, to make herself 'safe', she sedated herself with prescribed anti-psychotics and hypnotics. Alternatively, Ms B turned to alcohol, which would inevitably lead to violence, against both herself and her husband. I thought the alcohol sedated the saner part of her, leaving the mad part free to engage in reckless damage.

The struggle between the part of her that could ask for help and the part that was contemptuous of help-seeking was enacted in struggles between myself and her psychiatrist, Dr C. I was to speak as advocate for that aspect of Ms B that wanted help and felt a victim of her internal situation. Dr C responded to that aspect of Ms B that pushed for punishment. This split caused me a great deal of anxiety and could be exploited by her internal pathological organisation. The ambulance and police services, along with our crisis services, struggled repeatedly to contain the violence. Any lack of firm containment led to an escalation of her violence.

The inevitable limitations in the therapeutic system mirrored experiences in her childhood: her mother had continued to send her to the family who sexually abused the nine-year-old her. Ms B had told no-one of these experiences until they emerged in the therapy. It was then difficult to know to what extent these 'scenarios' represented real or imagined traumatic events. Many elements of Ms B's history emerged in this way as experiences in the consulting room. It was rarely possible for her to articulate these in direct ways. However, I was left in no doubt that, for her, any here-and-now contact with other people was coloured by, and confused with, an internal reality in which memories and phantasies from the past were timeless. There was always a sense of a profound catastrophe having occurred and of intense persecutory anxieties breaking through defensive barriers that had previously kept them just about at bay. The rape with its threat of death had left her struggling for her sanity and urgently in need of someone who could take in these terrifying experiences, without enacting or being over-whelmed by them.

I learned about her 'room': an internal space whose atmosphere I experienced in my consulting room when she retreated into the far corner, lest I hurt her, or she herself was in danger of hurting me. Following my interpreting her need for this room, she could sit back again in her chair, and articulate how relieved she was when I stayed in my room. I thought this referred to my capacity to take in her experience, think about it and put something into words that could safely contain her.

At times she would sit next to me on the floor and take hold of my hand, demanding I held hers. There seemed something possessive and loving about this – like a small child who clings anxiously, not letting go – but it also felt tyrannical. If I interpreted her need for me not just to be interested in her 'room', but actually to be in the same room, she could let go of me and return to her seat. Over time, things began to settle a little.

I learnt there were 'guards' controlling who came in and went out of her room. Their function seemed to be to keep order. They allowed her to invite me into the room and to speak to me. There were other figures too, who were angry and threatened violence. After she had let me know about these internal figures, she would spend the weekend terrified that I was damaged or dead, and that she would never see me again. She would return in a persecuted state, having cut herself and seeing an array of dead figures behind me and my chair. Once, after a colleague had entered my room in error, she put her chair against the consulting room's door. Barricading the door was to prevent the intruder entering again, but also to stop me escaping; to communicate to me how she felt locked into her internal world; how unbearable it was to be asked to leave at the end of her session, and not to be with me always; how unbearable she found it to be aware that I had a separate, normal life from which she was barred entry; how she wanted to keep me locked in with her for ever. Making these sorts of interpretations enabled her to remove the chair from the door. At other times she attempted to prevent me from leaving the building, and colleagues had to intervene. It was only with great difficulty that she could respect my insistence that to work together we both had to be able to come and go freely.

Breaks in treatment invariably led to difficulties. It seemed that we were perpetually coming up to a break or recovering from one. I felt I was constantly subjecting her to intolerable gaps and absences, and that I was never able to offer her enough consistency. I began to hear about increasing violence during weekends with her husband – about knives, about him getting hurt, of her fears that he would leave her. It was clear that they were both often drinking excessively. She begged me to go away with her, so that we could be together for ever, and became very agitated when I refused to leave the room. It became clear that 'to go away for ever' meant our being fused together in death. This was a psychotic solution to the unbearable reality of her objects being free to live their own lives and not being under her omnipotent control. This 'going away together' became a very preoccupying and chilling fantasy. I decided that she needed to continue her treatment as an in-patient for a while, but at the time my request unfortunately met with failure due to a lack of funding.

What follows illustrates the 'to and fro' of our interaction in a session after a weekend.

> She looked at me intently for some time before speaking, as if she needed my help with something. 'Are going away', she eventually said. I tried to clarify: Was it me, going away? 'No', she said, 'I'm being taken over'. She denied this was by her; rather, she was feeling physically ejected by threatening forces.
>
> I clarified that this was what it felt like.
>
> She agreed and then said, 'My eyes are going funny, I can't see you; you're coming and going.' She looked at me in quite a different way, then, speaking in a contemptuous voice, 'She's stupid asking for your help. She'll be dead. Let's choose one to be dead. Let's choose the one who relies on you, *she'll* be dead.'
>
> I said that this new person hated Ms B talking to me because *she* felt pushed out and angry when my patient came to me, wanting to talk to me. 'Yes . . . and I've spoken to you before.' The contemptuous voice went on to say how stupid her husband was for sleeping at night, and not staying on guard against her, because she could really hurt him. 'I am on guard all the time', she said. 'I never sleep.'

The reference from the contemptuous, threatening figure in this session to the danger her husband was putting himself in by going to sleep while she was present set the scene for more worrying developments between the couple. I also felt it was a clear warning to me not to 'fall asleep on the job'. However, on this occasion it became possible for both Ms B and her husband to discuss with the team the risk of escalating violence and their need for extra help in dealing with it. The police too were able to be involved in these discussions.

Then, Dr C, the consultant psychiatrist whom Ms B had by now grown to trust, told her she was leaving her post in some months' time. Following this, Ms B came to me confused and agitated, unable to distinguish reality from fantasy. She said her husband had been hurt and was now gone, being hurt; this was something she or someone had done. I felt a cold horror that this was not just another fantasy, but that he had *actually* been murdered. I felt impelled to telephone him immediately in order to reassure both my patient and myself that he was alive and well. My mind and body were taken over with an image of him lying dead in their home. In my mind were also newspaper headlines about inadequate and irresponsible mental health professionals allowing murders to happen under their noses. Ms B's state of mind had been so entirely projected into me that I had to concretely check out the reality.

Discussion

I have described aspects of my contact with Ms B in order to illustrate the nature of the pathological organisation that dominated her personality, and the ways in which she used her objects. At times it did seem possible for her to make and maintain contact with me and with reality, at least for short periods. She could use me not only as a container into which she could evacuate the confused and terrifying contents of her mind, but she could also use my mind to help put together her own understanding, however rudimentary. However, the problem was that I still needed to be present in person for this to happen; for this reason any absences from me became crises. When she had the containment of regular sessions and access to a mind prepared to think about, and bear, the disturbance in her mind, then her 'security guards' could bring a semblance of order and functioning. These guards represented, I think, a kind of primitive super-ego, enabling some differentiation to be made between good and bad. She could tell me about her internal room, itself implying the existence of boundaries, allowing the awareness that I did not live there. The room was small, but it offered a limited existence that allowed her to function with some degree of reality. When she had the support of her sessions, Ms B was able to face, albeit briefly, the genuine pain at what she was doing to those internal and external objects she felt were good, on whom she could rely and who were prepared to stay with her. Even so, this recognition could quickly be replaced by a more paranoid and persecuted conviction that everyone hated her for what she had done and were out to destroy her. Thus her hold on reality was always precarious and readily broke down whenever there was any threat of loss or rejection.

There were also unavoidable failures in the network that we worked hard to set up. These would inevitably be exploited by the pathological organisation, leading to splits in the therapeutic team. It is always important, in such complex and high-risk cases, to have a manager with sufficient understanding and authority to 'hold' senior professional colleagues who had been drawn into enacting aspects of the patient's pathology, where enactments are inevitably complicated by personal and professional rivalries.

In the last period of her treatment with me, Ms B began to speak fearfully about her father's serious illness. She now believed that had she spoken to her father when she was a little girl, he might well have listened and taken in what was happening to her. He had not had a wall around him; she had experienced her mother as behind an impenetrable wall, unable to receive any projections from her.

Bion (1962) believed that a mother who cannot allow her infant's projections access, conveys she does not want to know or be known by her infant. I came to understand that Ms B believed her mother's wall was erected to keep her out because she was a damaging and dangerous baby – a reflexive situation though, because mother was also felt to be dangerous to Ms B. Both these situations were alive in Ms B's transference to myself and the care team.

I think that prior to the rape, the destructiveness and psychotic aspects of Ms B's personality were more effectively bound. The catastrophe of the rape led to a pathological fragmentation in which she desperately sought something into which she could evacuate this fragmented inner world. Her first psychiatric admission, when she was suffering acute diarrhoea, reflected this. Memories of the earlier childhood sexual abuse, which she had 'forgotten', were forced back into awareness along with the traumatic experience of a mother who had not protected her and who had kept on sending her into danger. Her physical collapse during the first break in the treatment with me demonstrated, both physically and concretely, what a disaster it had been when she lost her containing object. The 'Murder in the Dark' game enacted the disaster, but was also experienced as excitingly gratifying. The lack of early maternal containment and the sadistic but exciting abuse produced in Ms B a personality that became dominated by a perverse pathological organisation. This may have prevented the total fragmentation of her ego, but was compulsively destructive in its attacks on the needed good objects – thus stalling further development and any hope of integration.

Ms B herself had no confidence in being able to repair any of this damage, except by magical means – an omnipotent restitution. She was constantly frightened that she would lose the object she relied on so much. Now, with her father terminally ill, she begged me to visit him and make him well. It was painful to recognise that her resort to omnipotent putting right was now returning in full force under the pressure of her father's illness and near death. The encroaching reality of his loss, along with his valued paternal functioning, which she was just becoming able to recognise, was experienced as unbearable. She retreated to the pathological refuge of a gratifying violence towards herself and her husband, which increasingly involved ambulance and police engagement.

Even with the support of her twice-weekly psychotherapy, the psychic reality and internally experienced catastrophe of her father's impending death could not be faced, so that ultimately Ms B needed to be detained in a secure forensic ward for her own and others' safety. While this led to the termination of her psychotherapy, it did enable her to be recognised as seriously disturbed rather than bad.

When I went to say goodbye to her in the secure ward she was able both to be very upset and to express her gratitude to me for keeping her alive. Even so, we had to face the fact that although she and her husband *were* still alive, something she and I had worked hard for, this was not enough. The sad reality was that her ever-present dangerousness needed the walls of a secure institution to contain it.

I was left with a lot to process, especially a profound sense of sadness mixed in equal measure with relief – the burden of treating her had been so very great.

References

Bion, W. (1957) 'Differentiation of the psychotic from the non-psychotic personalities', *Second Thoughts*, London: Heinemann (1967), pp. 43–64.

Bion, W. (1962) *Learning from Experience*, London: Heinemann.

Freud, S. (1911) 'Psycho-analytic notes on an autobiographical account of a case of paranoia (dementia paranoides)', *Standard Edition*, Vol. 12, London: Hogarth Press.

Freud, S. (1920) 'Beyond the pleasure principle', *Standard Edition*, Vol. 18, London: Hogarth Press.

Klein, M. (1957) 'On the development of mental functioning', *International Journal of Psycho-Analysis*, 39: 84–90.

O'Shaughnessy, E. (1981) 'A clinical study of a defensive organization', *International Journal of Psycho-Analysis*, 62: 359–369.

Rey, H. (1979) 'Schizoid phenomena in the borderline'. In J. Le Boit and A. Capponi (Eds.), *Advances in the Psychopathology of the Borderline Patient*, New York: Aronson.

Rosenfeld, H. (1964) 'On the psychopathology of narcissism: a clinical approach', *International Journal of Psycho-Analysis*, 45: 332–337, reprinted in *Psychotic States*, London: Hogarth Press (1965).

Rosenfeld, H. (1971a) 'A clinical approach to the psychoanalytic theory of the life and death instincts: an investigation into the aggressive aspects of narcissism', *International Journal of Psycho-Analysis*, 52: 169–178.

Rosenfeld, H. (1971b) 'Contributions to the psychopathology of psychotic patients: the importance of projective identification in the ego structure and object relations of the psychotic patient'. In E. Bott Spillius (Ed.) (1988), *Melanie Klein Today, Vol. 1: Mainly Theory*, London: Routledge.

Segal, H. (1972) 'A delusional system as a defence against the re-emergence of a catastrophic situation', *International Journal of Psycho-Analysis*, 53: 393–401.

Steiner, J. (1993) *Psychic Retreats*, London: Routledge.

Chapter 7

Psychoanalysis, psychosis and the NHS

Just pipe dreams or a new beginning?

Brian Martindale

In making new professional beginnings away from London, we psycho-analysts in the regions probably share common aims: those of conserving our psychoanalytic framework of mental functioning and – as many of us have reached the stage where generativity dominates – ensuring the creation of external structures for the development and maintenance of psychoanalytic understanding and clinical techniques that will endure beyond our brief individual sojourn on this planet.

In moving away from London, my choice has been to work full-time in the NHS for a while, in order to pursue my dreams of developing psychosis services with a significant psychoanalytic component.

In the UK, psychoanalysts have made major discoveries and clarifica-tions of mental functioning in psychosis, but have a very poor track record in the NHS of creating enduring structures that make this knowledge clinically serviceable.

As well as creating structures we need to loosen structures created for different historical circumstances. For psychoanalysis, the training struc-tures have been for one small geographical part of the country (London). For psychosis, nearly all contemporary psychiatric services exclude psycho-dynamic thinking. Can we change these systems without throwing the very different babies out with the bath water? In psychosis, we psychoanalysts will not survive one minute if we are not respectful of the many other non-psychoanalytic perspectives and sources of knowledge about psychosis.

Psychosis

I will sketch my own professional development that led me to be making this change, rather late in my NHS career, and to emphasise the systems within which I trained.

My Maudsley training involved supervision from a number of psycho-analysts before I went on to the Cassel Hospital and the Institute of Psychoanalysis. I became a consultant psychiatrist in psychotherapy in 1983 and until 2004, I always had a part-time analytic private practice, mostly of four and five times a week patients as well as supervisees.

My analysis was good enough for me to have faced with a mixture of amazement, curiosity, and distress the fact that I had some well-formed delusions lying behind surface conscious phenomena, such as anxiety states in certain situations. Those who know me will not be too surprised that some of these delusions were related to but, as always in psychosis, disconnected from the painful reality of there being only 24 hours in a day.

I sometimes quip that the success or failure of my analysis depends on whether it is the psychotic me or the reality-oriented me that is in charge whenever I am complaining that in spite of my analysis there are still only 24 hours in a day.

When the Royal College of Psychiatrists was formed in 1975, separate faculties of psychotherapy and general psychiatry were created. Consultant psychotherapists like myself, many of them psychoanalysts, were trained to work with non-psychotic disorders. Psychosis was usually seen to be an absolute contra-indication for offering psychotherapy. However, consultant psychiatrists worked mainly with psychosis in separate departments from psychotherapy and were wary of both personality disorders and psychoanalysts!

There have always been rare exceptions of psychoanalysts who have worked regularly with psychosis – such as Murray Jackson (Jackson and Cawley, 1992), Michael Conran (2008) and Richard Lucas (Garelick, 2008). It is sad that these gifted individuals have been regarded as exceptions, in contrast to some other countries where analytic thinking and clinical work with psychosis are more able to advance hand in hand.

The 1970s and 1980s were also full of expectations that THE biological cause of SCHIZOPHRENIA would be found: a gene, a neurotransmitter, an infection in pregnancy would at last reveal the vital clue. Research showed the effectiveness of neuroleptics and purportedly the ineffectiveness of psychoanalytic psychotherapy in psychosis. An international publication went so far as to suggest a complete moratorium for such treatments (Mueser and Berenbaum, 1990).

A factor was the massive backlash to Laing in the UK (Laing and Esterson, 1964), and even more in the United States to Frieda Fromm-Reichmann's 'schizophrenogenic mother' (Fromm-Reichman, 1948), with their ideas that family disturbance evoked psychosis. Sadly, this led to analysts beating a hasty retreat from the family in psychosis. Avoiding blame is everywhere now in contemporary family work guidelines (Expert Consensus Guideline Series, 1999), with issues of blame still being laid at the door of psychoanalysis (Martindale, 2008).

So we have the paradox in the UK of several decades of psychoanalysts contributing to the most extraordinarily rich developments in understanding psychosis, alongside the rarity of any utilisation of this understanding.

As a consultant psychiatrist in psychotherapy, I was part of this divorce of psychodynamics and psychosis since, for at least a decade, in both my NHS service and my private practice I would consciously exclude patients with a history of psychosis.

When I first took up my current NHS post, not a single member of the otherwise well-chosen 20-strong staff group that I joined had the slightest awareness that psychodynamics had *any* contribution to make to psychosis. It was a very touching moment when, after an afternoon of basic training, a support worker – the least qualified member – was reported to have said, 'at last it all begins to make some sense'.

But is this something about psychosis – are psychosis and psychoanalysis incompatible bedfellows? Well, dynamically yes – and I still struggle to integrate my knowledge that there are only 24 hours in a day – but let's take a wider look.

Unknown to me until the early 1990s, in parts of the Nordic countries, things were radically different. Psychoanalysts such as Yrjo Alanen (1997) in Finland, Johan Cullberg (2006) in Sweden, Endre Ugelstad (1985) in Norway and Bent Rosenbaum (Rosenbaum *et al.*, 2005) in Denmark had long been developing psychosis teams in which psychoanalytic under-standing was at the core. In France it was not dissimilar.

To continue with my personal journey: Murray Jackson and Michael Conran, at the end of their NHS careers, persuaded me with my EFPP experience behind me to go with them to the 1991 ISPS conference (the International Society for the Psychological Treatments of the Schizo-phrenias and Other Psychoses, www.isps.org). They were concerned that as members of a rare NHS species, their valuable knowledge and experience of psychosis had no ongoing NHS container.

It was a very moving experience to hear, at that conference in Stockholm, account after account by persons of different disciplines of quality Nordic psychoanalytically oriented work with individuals, in therapeutic communities, in outpatient groups, with families.

In emphasising the contrasting cultural contexts, the UK situation cannot be attributed only to the effect of psychosis itself on systems. Cultural and organisational aspects independent of the dynamics of psychosis deserve consideration. To emphasise my point, in large areas of Finland, more than half of the patients are being successfully managed without any neuroleptic medication at all, and some 80% are returning to work in areas of high unemployment (Seikkula and Aaltonen, 2006).

Those in the Nordic countries who work in this way – and I do not want to exaggerate as there are many who adopt an exclusively biological approach – have held onto a view of psychosis as a way of dealing with unbearable life issues.

So from 1991 onwards, I have been going through a professional trans-formation leading up to my appointment in 2005 as a consultant psychiatrist (note: not a psychotherapist) to an 'early intervention in psychosis' service in the North-East of England with some 100–120 new cases of psychosis a year, aged from 14 to 35.

Is there ground for hope in the UK for psychodynamics and psychosis? What are my views of the kind of UK systems needed for psychodynamics to have a hope of finding a more enduring place in psychosis, and what do I hope to create in the North East?

1   Firstly, I believe that the UK early intervention framework itself has a great potential for psychodynamics (Department of Health, 2001). Patients will be reached very soon after the development of a psychosis and taken into comprehensive specialist services with low case-loads, and treatment will be available to all for three full years. The service focuses on a stress-vulnerability model as the cause of psychosis, and family engagement should be the norm. These are really radical system changes for the UK and offer wonderful potential soil and space for psychodynamic work, if we can inhabit it. Once the psychosis has settled and major relapse-prevention measures are in place, one realises that one is left with a wide range of vulnerable personalities and families, a good number of whom are amenable to psychodynamic work, as I will exemplify later in this chapter. I would argue that it is vital that psychological therapy departments come to a recognition of this.

2   My second point follows naturally from the first: the need to loosen those structures within psychiatry that separate psychosis and non-psychosis services. I was pleased to co-chair a college interface report, and hope that this will have some influence (Martindale and Interface Group). This report outlines the routes through which general psychiatrists and psychotherapy departments can exchange expertise. I hope that my service will attract consultant psychiatrists and specialist registrars who wish to gain special experience of the dynamics of psychosis, in the same way that I am currently learning many things about neuroleptic medication.

3   What else could happen in the North-East? It is encouraging that in this area there is an increasing number of both psychoanalysts and psychoanalytic psychotherapists. Some work in the Health Service and/ or are involved in the North of England Association of Psychoanalytic Psychotherapy. Then there is Newcastle's Claremont House – the NHS regional psychoanalytic psychotherapy resource centre, which specialises in the treatment of borderline personality disorders, is geographically close to my service and is in the same NHS Trust. It is my hope that discussions may lead to psychoanalysts and psychoanalytic psychotherapists developing an interest in gaining experience and training opportunities in the treatment of psychosis. This may take some years to solidify but would lead in time to a pool of

psychoanalytic therapists able to supervise others at different levels (similar to the different levels at which psychotherapists work with other patients), especially if they gain experience of the contemporary systems or contexts within which psychotic patients are treated. It would of course be essential to build firm links with the leaders of the early intervention services. The three early intervention teams in our Trust cover some 1.5 million people and to my relief the other two have at least one senior staff member seriously interested in the psychodynamics of psychosis.

In the service I started to work a year ago, we now have:

- a weekly supervision group for practitioners who are already well advanced in training or who have trained as psychoanalytic psychotherapists, and who are taking on cases from our service
- acceptance of the idea of a weekly case discussion group for some care coordinators led by a psychoanalytic psychotherapist – funding is now being organised
- acceptance in our business plan of a full-time psychoanalytic therapist as a member of the team
- acceptance of the idea of a group analyst working one day a week to supervise group work for young paranoid persons with major problems in engaging in peer activities.

Some months before I arrived, I was pleased to hear of the creation of a region-wide peer group network for those interested in psychodynamics and psychosis – linked with the ISPS. This is a well-attended group that meets about four times a year to discuss patients and papers.

This is where we have now reached, just south of the Tyne, and I would like to end with some brief vignettes of three consecutive families I worked with in a pilot study I undertook in London. This work was helped by my membership of an APP (Association of Psychoanalytic Psychotherapy in the NHS) psychoanalytic family work seminar. It gave me the confidence to stand up for psychoanalytic family work and perhaps helped me better understand the denigration that took place in the third case.

First case

Twenty-nine-year-old Shanti was found on the railway in denial of her pregnancy. The ward was locked because of her continuing suicidal impulses. In spite of neuroleptics she remained psychotic three months later, garbling statements of ridding herself of the alien and coming through reincarnation to have her baby, as she repeatedly escaped intending to throw herself from the ninth floor of hospital buildings.

I was asked to get involved. With Shanti now six months pregnant, I elected to see her initially with her parents and siblings and, importantly, the ward nursing manager. It transpired that Shanti came from a traditional and caring Asian background and the baby's father was probably a dope-smoking Afro-Caribbean. Whenever Shanti spoke of her worries, mother would say 'Don't worry –we'll take *care* of you and the baby' – I noticed Shanti go silent and treat the mother with non-verbal disdain and contempt, just as the ward manager had described Shanti's attitude to nurses – without her recognising what this attitude was about.

In time, I verbalised what they could not – the unbearable family shame of the circumstances of their first grandchild. It was of course physical care that mother was offering and she, like the ward staff, was completely cut off from being able to offer psychological containment in the selective area. Shanti was discharged within ten days and had her baby. The psychiatric psychosis never returned, although it would have done if I had not provided a regular setting to address further aspects of the family shame related to the impending birth.

I do not bring this as a miracle change – Scandinavian psychoanalysts and others find that a reasonable percentage of patients do not need their psychosis when a suitable container is found early enough after a psychotic decompensation following an overwhelming event.

In my second and third cases, I return to the problem of guilt in families, which psychoanalysts have been blamed for exacerbating. There has been a failure to distinguish between (a) reparative guilt, (b) experienced punitive guilt, and (c) guilt so unbearable that it has to be projected. In my view, whole systems can become organised to concretise (c), with psychoanalysis perhaps not having been able to bear the consequences. Hanna Segal, in another context, said of psychoanalysis, 'Silence is the real crime!'

Second case

In Jack, reparative guilt was available and crucial to recognise. Hospitalised with a manic episode, treated with anti-psychotic drugs, he recovered and discontinued these after discharge. He met his Jill, became engaged but immediately relapsed, 'recovering' as before. Then for 18 months he was worryingly depressed, unresponsive to medication and underwent a trial separation. A frequent refrain made to his wife was that she was not the right woman. I then carried out assessment meetings, including some with his wife.

Jack was an identical twin and broke down soon after the twins' conscious decision to live more separately. Jack told me of a long-held concrete fantasy of marrying a supermodel, not just an ordinary model – then all he would need to do to get the attention of his friends would be to be with this model. In childhood, as an identical twin, all Jack needed was his identical brother's presence to gain the centre of attention of the crowd. He stressed that this attention did not require any effort. However, there were some humiliating aspects to the visibility of the two brothers. At sports day this 'identical' brother would be faster than Jack at events such as the 100 metres. I felt that Jack had never accepted this kind of public exposure of his limits. When climbing and reaching icy mountain peaks with his brother, he would press on – aiming to make his brother feel the inadequate one – sadistically reversing the situation that had been symbolically captured by the athletics events. Importantly, he knew it was cruel.

It was also awful for him that he had had a breakdown, unlike his brother. He now endlessly projected into his wife his limitations, as he had previously done to his brother – saying that Jill was not the right woman. Jill herself was pathologically kind and in the process of seeking assertiveness training at work. I detected in Jill a well-organised delusion that supported Jack's projections; Jill believed that to be assertive would be to do terrible damage to her husband. She was also very depressed by the situation: feeling hopeless about her wish for a family and left out by the treatment being given to her husband.

The point of this vignette is to contrast Jack with Archie's mother in the next case in terms of guilt and treatability in psychosis. Jack was aware and concerned about his cruelty toward his wife and to his brother in the past. He would say with contempt 'she takes my crap'.

Jill was able to get her assertiveness training with me, and Jack had to do some painful work on his cruelty, as well as to mourn his rather enjoyable delusional idea that all he had to do was be present alongside his wife and the marriage would not only work, but be the envy of his friends. After four months of fortnightly therapy, the marriage was functioning very well and this was sustained for a year, when Jack had a brief manic episode that I managed to contain in an outpatient setting, with Jill's help. Now, two years later, Jack continues to work successfully and there is a young child. It would have been fatal to the outcome to have *reassured* Jack in his feelings of guilt.

Third case: *Guilt had a different dynamic in Archie and family*

Archie was 29 and had been labelled as schizophrenic five years before my involvement. A presenting complaint was that his mouthwash had been replaced by street drugs.

Archie's mother relentlessly complained of the treatment inadequacy, ending in the transfer of Jack to another service. The dissatisfaction intensified and mother became hated by the staff as she continued to insist that Archie had inadequately treated schizophrenia. The staff in turn began insisting that he had a personality disorder (i.e. did not need their service).

During the five years there had been no family meetings. To illustrate *unbearable guilt*, I bring this vignette after a year of regular family meetings. We had discovered that Archie had broken down soon after mother's early retirement from a teaching career. She was now at home all day with him (keep in mind the mouthwash symptoms).

This session began with quite a 'good' atmosphere, the family giving examples of how Archie was engaging more with the outside world. Mother seemed to be making a conscious effort to hold onto her usual intrusive impatience for more help – a welcome outcome of our work. Mother said that Archie had received money for something he had done with children and suggested he follow this up.

Working on non-verbal cues I asked Archie if I was correct that he seemed perturbed by the idea of something that he had done being recognised, valued or pursued. Without hesitation he said 'Yes, I would immediately be under pressure to pursue something that was not really "me"' (the street drugs).

Mother did not take this in at all – and carried on saying that 'Archie would like working with children – everyone does' – and how much she had enjoyed it. Archie said this was not his impression of her.

The atmosphere immediately changed – Mother started to get indignant – 'don't try that on – you know it was only in the latter years I did not enjoy work. *You* need to find work that is enjoyable.' Archie tried to say that he had simply been voicing *his* experience that mother had not enjoyed her work. Mother got very uptight indeed and began accusing Archie – 'don't start – you are trying to manipulate me!'

My reason for this vignette is *unbearable guilt*, and this was the point at which we saw a familiar pattern of pressure from mother. Up to this point, I felt that Archie had indeed been trying to do no more than convey *his* experience of mother and to enlarge on his own wariness of work, and nothing malevolent was detectable. The word 'manipulate' had got under Archie's skin. He had felt accused – 'why is everything my fault? What about Saturday?', said Archie – beginning to retaliate – 'you (mother) – simply lost it. You went completely wild blaming me.'

Mother 'What are you talking about? Nothing happened.' She seemed to have no idea. Father thought he had not been there.

Archie: 'You were in a rage, accusing me of being responsible for everything that goes wrong.'

Mother did recall, but said 'I went out of the house and when I came back it was "forgotten", it was nothing – it was water off a duck's back.'

Archie indicated that for him it had not 'been nothing' – he had been very disturbed by mother's outburst – 'you went berserk – and I had done nothing. I was simply telling you that Susie [his individual therapist] had said something about a positive change. You said what a load of rubbish and got into a fury, saying my sessions were a waste of time.'

Mother got very defensive and attacking (presumably feeling exposed); father joined in, recalling he *was* there!

Father: 'Why are you bringing this up? Nothing has been said since Saturday. You are deliberately manipulating the situation, *trying to blame us* – well, we are not going to take it!'

And so it escalated.

You will not be surprised that in contrast to Shanti's family, any attempts by myself to reflect on the process felt like an accusation to mother and her husband. In past sessions when mother had brought depressed feelings, father had subsequently chastised mother for bringing her difficulties.

Since guilt in psychosis has played an extraordinarily powerful part in determining collusive systems of care and their content – in which psychoanalysts have been named and shamed – I thought it would be useful, in bringing these three contrasting cases, to look at the differing role of guilt in the psychosis itself.

In the first case it was a different affect – unbearable shame regarding the pregnancy – that was the key organising affect for the whole family.

In the second case there was sufficient *concern* in Jack of his awareness of dumping his own 'crap' – that allowed him to face some of the causes of his depression and his resistance to facing those causes.

In the third case, guilt was seemingly unbearable for Archie's mother for what she had been doing and for father for what he had not done. Blame was massively and conveniently projected into Archie and the struggling health service. The latter did not have any analytic input to understand what was going on. However, a year of psychodynamic work allowed the family to let us really see what they were burdened with. During that time the dissatisfaction with the service took a less noisy form. Archie was now functioning better than at any time in the previous five years.

I hope that it is clear from these vignettes that in thinking about psychosis, we should not just focus on the individual's clinical material, but think about the complex system in which the psychosis has developed and how it may be helped to be modified. In that way, we can ensure that patients with psychosis – and their families – do not just benefit from the occasional analyst who passes through, but can be provided with the kind of broad-ranging mental health care that is needed.

I hope too, that I have conveyed the usefulness of stepping right outside our own systems and seeing what happens elsewhere in the world. I was fortunate in being exposed to the ways in which psychosis is handled in other countries, particularly the Nordic countries, and for this to have brought me fresh perspectives on what had previously seemed a given – that psychoanalysis and psychosis don't get on too well together – anything else felt like a pipe dream. I would not have moved away from London to work in an NHS setting in the North-East had I not thought that psychoanalytic systems and psychoanalytic thinking had a very important part to play in helping individuals and their families deal with the distressing and disabling effects of psychosis.

References

Alanen, Y. (1997) *Schizophrenia: Its Origins and Need-Adapted Treatment*, London: Karnac.

Conran, M.B. (2008) 'The patient in hospital', *Psychoanalytic Psychotherapy*, 2 (1): 7–19.

Cullberg, J. (2006) *Psychoses: An Integrative Perspective*, London: Routledge.

Department of Health (2001) *The Mental Health Policy Implementation Guide* (pp. 43–61), London: Department of Health.

Expert Consensus Guideline Series (1999) 'The treatment of schizophrenia', *Journal of Clinical Psychiatry*, 60: 8–80.

Fromm-Reichman, F. (1948) 'Notes on the development of treatment of schizophrenics by psychoanalytic psychotherapy', *Psychiatry*, 11: 263–273.

Garelick, T. (2008) Obituary. *Psychoanalytic Psychotherapy*, 22 (4): 245–247.

Gaudillière, J.-M. and Davoine, F. (2009) 'The contribution of some French psychoanalysts to the clinical and theoretical approach to transference in the psychodynamic treatment of psychosis'. In Y. Alanen, M. Gonzalez de Chavez, A.-L.S. Silver and B. Martindale (Eds.), *Psychotherapeutic Approaches to Schizophrenic Psychoses: Past Present and Future*, London: Routledge.

Jackson, M. and Cawley, R. (1992) 'Psychodynamics and psychotherapy on an acute psychiatric ward: The story of an experimental unit', *British Journal of Psychiatry*, 160: 41–50.

Laing, R.D. and Esterson, A. (1964) *Sanity, Madness and the Family: Families of Schizophrenics*, Harmondsworth, UK: Penguin.

Martindale, B.V. (2008) 'The rehabilitation of psychoanalysis and the family in psychosis'. In J.F.M. Gleeson, E. Killackey and H. Krstev (Eds.), *Recovering from Blaming in Psychotherapies for the Psychoses: Theoretical, Cultural, and Clinical Integration*, London: Routledge.

Martindale B. and Interface Group (no date) *Interface between the General Adult and Community Faculty and the Psychotherapy Faculty of the Royal College of Psychiatrists*. Available online at www.rcpsych.ac.uk/pdf/Martindale0706.pdf

Mueser, K. and Berenbaum, H. (1990) 'A moratorium on the use of psychodynamic treatments for schizophrenia', *Psychological Medicine*, 20: 253–262.

Rosenbaum, B., Valbak, K., Harder, S., Knudsen, P., Køster, A., *et al.* (2005) The Danish National Schizophrenia Project: prospective, comparative longitudinal treatment study of first-episode psychosis, *British Journal of Psychiatry*, 186: 394–399.

Seikkula, J., Aaltonen, J., Alakare, B., Haarakangas, K., Keranen, J. and Lehtinen, K. (2006) 'Five-year experience of first-episode non-affective psychosis in open-dialogue approach', *Psychotherapy Research*, 16 (2): 214–228.

Ugelstad, E. (1985) Success and failure in individual psychotherapy with psychotic patients: Some follow up considerations, *Nordic Journal of Psychiatry*, 39 (4): 279–284.

Part 3

Analytic thinking in health service practice

Chapter 8

A4C

The dissemination of anxiety in mental health services

Veronica Gore

The email I opened simply stated 'FYI'. I looked at it perplexed, bewildered and somewhat annoyed. It had come from a close colleague, but what did it mean? There was an attachment regarding a policy change in the Trust about integrated notekeeping. Like so many I had received in the past few years, this was another document about tightening up on policies; more new developments to replace outmoded ways of working. Slowly it dawned on me that FYI meant 'for your information', yet ironically the abbreviation had been far from informative.

This experience led me to think about a pervasive feeling in the NHS of being bombarded on all sides by new policy initiatives. These changes often seem to be divorced from clinical experience, and at times even from clinical common sense. It seemed to me that such changes are linked to the proliferation and use of abbreviations in the mental health services. For many of us in the NHS (itself an abbreviation), such abbreviations as A4C, PFI, BPD, IWL, EIP, DSPD, PICU, CMHT, AOT are familiar, and are generally viewed as a kind of practical shorthand (see glossary at end of chapter). How many of my colleagues, I wondered, find themselves as initially confused as I had been, and have to translate these abbreviations into real words before their meaning can be understood?

Much has been written about the inherent difficulty of the task in mental health work, the anxieties associated with this work, and the social defence systems that are put in place to avoid facing the painful realities involved in the work. In this chapter I shall argue, drawing particularly on theories based on the thinking of Klein and Bion, that this excessive use of abbreviations forms part of a social defence system. In this system, the abbreviations function as fragments of words that are denuded of real meaning. This, I propose, mirrors the attempt in mental health services to minimize the degree of complexity and disturbance in such work. Clinicians and managers are then left bereft of proper words that could form the basis of communication, enabling meaning to be conveyed and anxiety contained.

Isabel Menzies (1960), in her classic study of general nursing in a large teaching hospital, demonstrated how an organizational defensive system was set up so as to avoid the unconscious anxieties that were aroused in the staff when carrying out their task of nursing the seriously ill and the dying. She suggested that this work would be likely to stir up strong feelings of pity, compassion, disgust, fear, helplessness, vulnerability, rage: all of which would cause anxiety if allowed too much into consciousness. From a more psychoanalytical framework, she hypothesized that the work of nursing the sick and the dying would stir up primitive anxieties related to damage done in phantasy to internal objects (internal representatives of parental and other important figures), which would then be experienced as internal persecutors that were themselves irreparably sick or dying. The system she described was based on dividing up patient care into defined tasks. While this functioned to keep the nurses at a distance from these feelings and their associated anxieties, it also reduced their sense of pride in their work and their lively engagement with it.

In mental health work, studies by Donati (1989) and Goodwin and Gore (2000) have demonstrated that similar defensive organizations can occur in the nursing of mentally ill patients. Mental health work is painful. Those who work with the psychologically disturbed and mentally ill are in contact with patients who may have fragmented minds, who are likely to behave unpredictably, to be highly vulnerable, and to be challenged by feelings of dependency, helplessness and chaos. This kind of severe disturbance inevitably stirs up in care staff similarly disturbing feelings such as helplessness, inadequacy and vulnerability, along with fears at times for their own safety. Donati (1989) described three types of defensive manoeuvres observed in staff on a psychiatric ward: (1) stereotyped and depersonalized relationships; (2) rejection of the patient's projection of despair, depression and hopelessness, alongside projection of the nurse's sense of failure into the patient; (3) inhibition of any sign of spontaneous involvement or emotional arousal. This system, Donati argued, functioned defensively to protect staff from their anxieties in relation to the fear of constantly experiencing failure and impotence, loss of professional skills, uncertainty, loss of identity, low self-esteem and madness.

Other writers in this field have discussed the role of the institution as a container of anxiety, with particular reference to anxieties about life and death or, in more psychoanalytic terms, about annihilation (Obholzer, 1994). Obholzer goes on to make the point that all societies fear death and try to find ways to manage this anxiety. To this, I suggest, could be added the fear of madness, which can be thought of as the death of the thinking mind, or the mind in endless torment. One such way of managing the anxiety, Obholzer suggests, is by the creation of a health system that is supposed 'to keep death (and madness) at bay' (Obholzer, 1994, p. 171). He writes, 'Patients and doctors collude in this to protect the former from facing their fear of death and the latter from facing their fallibility', and goes on to say that outrage results when this omnipotent phantasy is shown to be just that. The institution, he argues, can function reasonably well only if it can, in Bion's (1959) terms, 'contain' these toxic projections; these fears about death, disease, pain, madness and annihilation. Containing the projections requires a capacity to know about these underlying difficulties and anxieties, rather than trying to 'manage' them away. He points out that in order for the organization to function by containing and metabolizing these toxic substances, it needs to have the capacity to face external and psychic reality. This involves remaining in touch with the difficult feelings and anxieties inherent in the work, rather than defensively blocking them out of awareness.

In recent literature there has been a recurrent theme describing the impact of the 'new style' management in the NHS, which is seen as one aspect of an 'attack on welfarism' inherent in the market economy health care system. Cooper and Lousada (2005) have described the present nature of the welfare state as a retreat from the 'personal dimension of welfare' and from the importance of emotional sources when making rational decisions about care provision. They propose that the rise in consumerism promotes an omnipotent illusion that we can all have everything that we desire. They argue that the current system of bureaucratic protocols to do with regulation, 'evidence-based practice', inspection, monitoring, 'throughput' and other current trends in health care results in care that is shallow and driven by fashion: not only, they argue, because the current system denies the complexity of ill health and distress, but also because it avoids the recognition that hardship, inequity and misfortune are part of life. They see this as an attack on the real welfare issues involved in health care. David Bell (1997) links this attack to a narcissistic process, first described by Rosenfeld (1971), in which there is a wiping out of awareness of vulnerability, pain, and feelings of inadequacy. Instead, there is an identification with an omnipotent, omniscient being (in psychoanalytic terms 'a phallus'), who knows everything, can cure everything, and does not want to know about limitations, doubt or vulnerability, because such states of mind are viewed as weakness. Bell suggests that the pull to this kind of mentality is mostly derived from the despair inherent in the task of caring for the mentally disturbed. In this narcissistic system, there is an emphasis on blame and accusation rather than on the understanding of mental disturbance.

Of course, new ways of working do need to be introduced when useful developments in treatment occur, and when old or inappropriate ways of doing things are replaced by more effective and helpful treatments. These writers argue, however, that the current over-emphasis on such innovations as 'new style' management (supposedly designed to 'iron out inefficiencies in the system'); greater control of clinicians (who, presumably, otherwise would be likely to underperform); the limited focus on targets, concrete outcomes and rapid decision making; the 'NHS market economy'; and health care as a business leads to a collusive group denial (between clinicians and managers) of the difficulties inherent in the work and a reliance on 'the latest fashions in care which succeed each other with manic rapidity'. Stokes (1994) points out the denigration of ordinary health care when managers and clinicians have increasing pressure put upon them to 'cure' NHS patients ever more quickly and more effectively. Whereas 'care' is a slow process that does not provide the dramatic results desired, 'cure' is an exciting ideal that offers a seductive defence of omnipotent denial in the face of the chronic nature of the problems. Clinicians are tempted to use 'treatment', Stokes suggests, 'as a defence against the inevitable experiences of helplessness and failure when working with the severely mentally ill' (Stokes, 1994, p. 122).

The expectation to 'cure' in unreasonable circumstances puts increasing pressures on managers and clinicians and thereby increases the need for defensive structures to keep at bay unpalatable realities. But not facing reality also leaves staff more prone to such feelings as vulnerability, help-lessness and impotence, which then have to be defended against with increased vigour. Managers can feel that they have to exert order and control over what is chaotic and unpredictable, and to implement policies that are imposed from above over which they have no control, yet for which they are held responsible. This is threatening, as it involves facing feelings of powerlessness and failure.

The current emphasis on quantity and 'throughput' results in very little time for reflection. Not having the space for thinking means that there is no psychic separation between the self and the work. Such a space is essential if reality is to be faced, which includes acknowledging the difficulties inherent in the task and the painful recognition that our impact on the enormity and complexity of the task can only be limited. As Isobel Menzies (1960) pointed out nearly 50 years ago, responsibilities and anxieties that were previously handed up through the system and contained by senior managers are now projected downwards into clinicians and junior managers. Health service managers on 'performance-related pay' inevitably feel that their perfor-mance is only as good as the current week's figures, and if they have not met their key performance indicators (KPIs) they feel under constant threat of annihilation. As the anxieties are passed downwards, clinicians also feel under threat: 'We have to survive!' echoes down the corridors, bringing with it a manic emphasis on 'doing' at the expense of 'reflection'. If the institution in which mental health staff work is no longer a good container because the institution itself feels under threat and cannot allow space for thinking, what happens to the feelings of staff that have been stirred up by the nature of the work? This is when, I would argue, abbreviations proliferate, bringing with them a shortcircuiting of reality and a move towards manic reparation rather than thoughtful and contained mental health care.

It is helpful at this point to consider two different states of mind, along with their associated anxieties and defences, outlined by Melanie Klein

(1935, 1946). She described the capacity to know about reality, to be able to bear pain and loss, vulnerability and doubt, ambivalence, guilt about the limitations of what we can offer, and the capacity to see others as whole people who are separate from ourselves, as the 'depressive position'. In the depressive position the primary concern is for the wellbeing of the other, without setting our own needs aside unduly. The other state of mind involves a constellation of defences; in particular the manic defences to do with manic activity, contempt, denial, omnipotence, control and triumph. Klein termed this state of mind the 'paranoid-schizoid position'. In developmental terms it precedes the depressive position and is associated with fears for the survival of the self and of being annihilated. In a paranoid-schizoid state of mind splitting predominates, with the self and others divided into very good and very bad figures. In this splitting process, unbearable anxieties and unwanted aspects of the self can be got rid of by projecting them into others. In such a state of mind, the self, people and experiences are either idealized or denigrated, and the emotional meaning of things becomes separated from its content. Where there is a prevailing fear about survival, increases in splitting and projective processes take place, such that the world is divided into 'them' (the enemy who is to blame for everything) and 'us' (the good people who are the innocent victims). At such times psychotic processes can take over, in which the very capacity to see and know is fragmented. These fragments are expelled from the self and projected into objects and other people, where they take the form of Bion's 'bizarre objects' (1959) and become terrifying persecutors. The resulting experience is one of intense fear, anxieties about chaos and confusion, panic and depersonalization, along with the experience of the self being in pieces.

We can see from this description that the NHS organization I have been describing is one in which a paranoid-schizoid state of mind predominates over a depressive state of mind, such that there is a defensive retreat from depressive concern, ordinary doubt, ambiguity, ambivalence and the capacity to think. Abbreviations can now be understood as part of this defence system which fragments both words and concepts. This defensive process ensures that neither the meaning of the words nor the disturbance associated with their meaning need be known about – and then realistically addressed. Seen from this perspective, abbreviations are 'part-objects' which function as a manic attempt both to minimize pain and threat and to avoid annihilatory anxiety. Like the dividing up of the nurses' tasks in the general hospital, described by Menzies, they divide up people and services in such a way that the complex lives of whole people and the painful reality of their disturbance do not have to be thought about. The inherent difficulties in the task of caring for disturbed and disturbing patients, who rid themselves of their own disturbance by projecting it into staff, need not be recognized. Paradoxically, staff are then at risk of re-enacting the very disturbances that they are employed to treat in their patients. Thus for both clinicians and managers, abbreviations become a shorthand way of not knowing about the reality of the work. It is noteworthy that for the most part the abbreviations relate to particularly difficult and challenging patient groups – for example, DSPD, PICU, AOT, EIP, BPD – and to those policy changes that have caused staff anxiety about their own survival and the future of their institution (A4C, KPI, PFI).

So the challenge for organizations is to contain vulnerability and disturbance, not to project it or control it. As Armstrong (2005) puts it, if vulnerability can be acknowledged not as a challenge but as 'an occasion for real work'; if the 'unthought known' (Bollas, 1987) in an organization is formulated, it creates a difference. It does not make things any easier, but it discloses meaning, and in particular the emotional meaning and significance of what an organization does.

Sustained contact with painful, despairing, hating, or conflicted emotional states of mind in the self or the other is hard to bear, so what can psychoanalysis offer us to help with this problem? Bion's (1959) theory of containment describes a relationship between the infant and the primary caregiver that either can provide for the possibility of knowing about and tolerating painful emotional states or can inhibit and distort them. He conceives of the young infant as experiencing painful states, not as feelings or thoughts, but as what he terms 'beta elements'. These are raw sensory and/or somatic experiences, like the sensation of falling apart, or being ripped open by hunger pangs. The infant cannot process such experiences in a mental or conscious way, but needs to rid himself of them by projecting them into another person (usually mother), who can firstly experience and process them on the infant's behalf, and then respond in a helpful, appropriate and thoughtful way.

When things go well, the infant has the repeated experience of unbearable body and mind states being taken in and thought about, made mental in character, given meaning and made bearable by another person – the maternal 'thinking breast'. This process begins the development, through his internalization of the mother's containing function, of the infant's own capability of containing and giving meaning to painful and disturbing feelings. 'Beta elements' can only be dealt with by expulsion, but if the concrete fragments of raw experience can be understood with the help of a containing other, they can be transformed into thoughts and feelings, and thus put into words. In this way, Bion argues, the basis for mental capacity becomes established. However, if these distressing and painful feelings are not taken in by mother but are blocked from her mind, perhaps because she is depressed, or ill, or her mind and body are full with another baby, the projection comes back to the infant in an unmodified form, leaving him feeling persecuted by what Bion calls 'nameless dread'.

Without the capacity to symbolize and make sense of these disparate elements of experience, the infant mind may have difficulty in fully maturing. As a child and later as an adult, the more primitive defences, such as splitting and projecting, will need to be employed in order to cope with such threats as fear, rage, frustration or pain. These primitive defences operate by ejecting and propelling the disturbing emotions into someone else. This does away with the immediate threat to the self, but at the cost of losing a part of the mind, or self, which is now located in someone else.

Meaning and reality cannot be maintained as the world becomes increasingly desolate and persecutory. The internal maternal thinking breast is felt to be damaged, the capacity to symbolize is lost and the individual cannot feel supported either internally or externally. Experiences that cannot be treated as ordinary thoughts or feelings to be held in mind and thought about become abbreviated fragments, or beta elements, which have to be disposed of in some concrete, physical way. Ron Britton (1998), for example, described a patient who had to get rid of her unwanted experiences by compulsively flushing them down the toilet.

John Steiner (1993) has elaborated the concept of 'turning a blind eye' in which painful realities are both known and not known at the same time. I would argue that the use of abbreviations is one way that clinicians and managers 'turn a blind eye' to the realities of the work that they do and its inherent difficulties. The disturbance is named, but in such an abbreviated form that the meaning is lost.

To go back to my story at the beginning of the chapter, we could now think that the email from my colleague was a beta element; I had to take it inside me and experience a sense of confusion and irritation before I could think about it, understand its meaning and respond in a helpful way, rather than send it back again unmodified. Abbreviations can serve to avoid both meaning and reality for staff and managers alike. They shore up the omnipotent paranoid-schizoid level of functioning as a means of denying pain, doubt, uncertainty and ambivalence. The extensive use of emailing in the NHS lends itself to the expulsion of beta elements. The click of a mouse sends (or projects) the disturbing news about cuts, activity reports, performance indicators, swiftly on to the next person. In this way, the anxiety about these communications and what they might mean is got rid of and pushed into someone else, as often as not to someone lower down the management chain. I suggest that this may be particularly so when the information pertains to issues that arouse fears about survival, disturbance and madness.

There is inevitably a resistance to becoming aware of the thoughts and the emotional experience that will lead to a psychological or emotional upheaval. The use of the abbreviations 'BPD' to denote 'borderline personality disorder' and 'DSPD' to denote 'dangerous and severe personality disorder' are apt examples of this 'borderline' state of mind, in which the patient's profile is assembled and analysed using procedural and policy shorthand rather than a more time-consuming clinical language. The abbreviations are not usually experienced as systems of representation that operate as carriers of information about human experience; instead they tend to pathologize and caricature, thereby depersonalizing the individual as a whole person. They can only become effective carriers of information when thought is applied to their meaning. Inevitably it is the more frightening, painful or conflicted areas of experience that we have trouble in symbolizing, but failing to do so makes the experiences even more frightening.

We need to be able to put things into meaningful words; to use them in the service of understanding, knowing and making links between people. Britton (1998) describes two functions of containment: firstly to give sanctuary in a safely bounded space, and then to give meaning. He comments (1998, p. 21):

> If a name enshrines a psychic quality – like love, for example – the word provides a container for the emotional experience, putting a semantic boundary around it. It also places it in a ready-made context of significance provided by the place in human affairs of love and the place of the word in an existing language. At the same time, the experience of the emotion gives meaning to the word for that individual. The analytic situation could be described as endeavouring to provide both a bounded world and a place where meaning can be found.

It is my view that the kinds of abbreviations that I have described are not being used as symbols – that is, as shorthand representations of the thing symbolized – but rather as a means of denuding meaning, described by Hanna Segal (1957) as a 'symbolic equation'. Thus they fail to provide us with a meaningful language to reflect on the nature of the work that we do with mentally disturbed people, or to develop the most effective ways of helping the people in our care. The proliferating abbreviations become fragments of words, part-objects with no real meaning, which then function to make experiences emotionally shallow and avoid the realities of the disturbance associated with the services for which they stand. This in turn leads to more splitting and fragmentation and the increasing impossibility of the task. It is only by facing and understanding reality, by using words to convey meaning, that treatments can become responsive and the task realistic.

Glossary

- A4C – Agenda for Change
- AOT – Assertive Outreach Team
- BPD – borderline personality disorder
- CMHT – Community Mental Health Team

- DSPD – dangerous and severe personality disorder
- EIP – early intervention in psychosis
- IWL – Improving Working Lives
- KPI – key performance indicator
- PFI – private finance initiative
- PICU – psychiatric intensive care unit

References

Armstrong, D. (2005) *Organization in the Mind: Psychoanalysis, Group Relations, and Organisational Consultancy*, London: Karnac.

Bell, D. (1997) 'Primitive mind of state', *Psychoanalytic Psychotherapy*, 10: 45–47.

Bion, W.R. (1959) 'Attacks on linking', *Second Thoughts*, New York: Jason Aronson.

Bollas, C. (1987) *The Shadow of the Object: Psychoanalysis of the Unthought Known*, London: Free Association Books.

Britton, R. (1989) 'The missing link: parental sexuality and the Oedipus complex'. In J. Steiner (Ed.), *The Oedipus Complex Today*, London: Karnac Books.

Britton, R. (1998) 'Naming and containing', *Belief and Imagination* (pp. 19–28), London: Routledge.

Cooper, A. and Lousada, J. (2005) *Borderline Welfare: Feeling and Fear of Feeling in Modern Welfare*, London: Karnac.

Donati, F. (1989) 'A psychodynamic observer in a chronic psychiatric ward', *British Journal of Psychotherapy*, 5: 317–329.

Goodwin, A. and Gore, V. (2000) 'Managing the stress of nursing people with severe and enduring mental illness: A psychodynamic observation study of a long-stay ward', *British Journal of Medical Psychology*, 73: 311–325.

Klein, M. (1935) 'A contribution to the psychogenesis of manic-depressive states', *International Journal of Psychoanalysis*, 16: 145–174.

Klein, M. (1946) 'Notes on some schizoid mechanisms', *International Journal of Psychoanalysis*, 27: 99–110.

Menzies, I. (1960) 'A case-study in the functioning of social systems as a defence against anxiety', *Human Relations*, 13: 95–121.

Obholzer, A. (1994) 'Managing social anxieties in public sector organizations'. In A. Obholzer and V.Z. Roberts (Eds.), *The Unconscious at Work: Individual and Organizational Stress in the Human Services*, London: Routledge.

Rosenfeld, H. (1971) 'A clinical approach to the psychoanalytic theory of the life and death instincts: An investigation into the aggressive aspects of narcissism', *International Journal of Psycho-Analysis* 52: 169–178.

Segal, H. (1957) 'Notes on symbol formation', *International Journal of Psycho-Analysis*, 38: 391–397.

Steiner, J. (1993) *Psychic Retreats: Pathological Organizations in Psychotic, Neurotic and Borderline Patients*, London: Routledge.

Stokes, J. (1994) 'Institutional chaos and personal stress'. In A. Obholzer and V.Z. Roberts (Eds.), *The Unconscious at Work: Individual and Organizational Stress in the Human Services* (pp. 121–128), London: Routledge.

Chapter 9

The impact of the archaic on mental health work

Colin Thomas

> There is no effectual way of improving the institutions of any people but by enlightening their understandings.
>
> William Godwin, *An Enquiry Concerning Political Justice*, 1793)

In her *Dynamics of the Social* the psychoanalyst Isabel Menzies Lyth (1989) comes to the depressing conclusion that 'institutions have a natural tendency to become bad models for identification . . . The risk tends to be greater where situations of real danger occur . . . or where there is shared impact of great human suffering' (p. 42).

It is uncontroversial nowadays to propose that the mental health wing of the modern NHS is a place of great suffering and frustration. The impact of disturbance combined with continuous change, political buffeting of all varieties, unrealistic expectations, and a drive by the participants to improve things against a background of underfunding is clear to most of us. No wonder, then, we find such institutions full of 'defences against what is felt unfaceable' (Hinshelwood and Skogstad, 2000). In this chapter I explore some aspects of the unconscious institutional context of the psychoanalyst's work in the public mental health setting. Although management conditions in the NHS are currently very strained, I think there is a sense in which aspects of the universal distress, given the aims of the organization, are inevitable. For example, Menzies Lyth (1988) and others (e.g. Obholzer and Roberts, 1994) have discussed the depression in the organization and the tendency to revert to manic or paranoid-schizoid modes, in part to defend against this depression. I think there is a constant need when working in the organization to take the depression and disappointment seriously and to try to understand as much as possible of its background and intrapsychic context.

The introductory quotation comes from William Godwin's enquiry, influential in the 1790s enlightenment, which elevates truth and reason:

> 'there is no science . . . or art [or morals, or social institutions] . . . that may not be carried to a still higher perfection.

The seeking and espousal of 'truths' about phantasy and reality, and reflection on unconscious psychic realities, are parts of the analyst's ego ideal, and are essential to a searching analytic attitude (Schafer, 1983). In the realm of the modern health organization I also think modesty of aim and purpose, and also less 'ambition' than that proposed by Godwin, are required when engaging with the often disturbed systems. The inevitability of the disturbance, of human limitation, vulnerability, and individual and group enactment will be foci for the analyst amid the often unrealistic clamour to improve things. Furthermore, the enlightenment we may offer, if not tempered with caution about reception, may increase burden and anxiety yet further. Additionally, abnormal and disguised editions of the primitive, or anti-life super-ego (Bion, 1962; O'Shaughnessy, 1999) may undermine efforts to develop and sustain creative work.

This chapter is about the struggle we all have with the archaic unconscious when engaging with an organization such as the NHS. I will first describe the socio-historical context of such work.

There are significant literatures discussing the background to health and mental health policy from which I extract a couple of perspectives.

Baggot (2000) draws attention to public health policy lacking coherence because of the range of competing perspectives emphasizing different priorities and modes of intervention. For example, the collectivist state is not seen as a benign or even neutral force, but as a hostile entity that coerces and disempowers citizens (Baggot, 2000; Hayek, 1976, 1988). He draws out three sorts of framework for analysing the process and outcomes of health policy: firstly as the product of competing political ideologies – that is, within and between different political institutions, and between different interests articulated by pressure groups; secondly as emerging from the interplay of ideas and knowledge and implemented on the basis of advice from so-called experts (in reality, interested parties); thirdly as shaped by public perceptions of risk by experts with a tendency for 'risk expertise' to promote a greater regulation of human activities on the basis of vested interest. He quotes Castel's (1991) arguing that there had been a shift in emphasis over the past century from dangerousness (more individually assessed) to risk, and that this represents an erosion of professional power by administrators. Sometimes this is perceived as an attack on the professions, which have lost control of health surveillance and the flow of information and resources. Modern ideologies of prevention are seen as oppressive, restricting freedom of thought and choice (Stone, 1989).

Blank and Burau (2004) place more emphasis on the providers of health care, who instil a demand in the public – which I would argue is already latent in them – for a do-everything approach (Fuller, 1994). In this model, providers need restraint from government and executive institutions, rather than mere control, lest they create an illusion of largesse doomed to perpetual disappointment. Public expectations and demands for health care

are potentially insatiable. Despite competing views about the political and social context of public provision, the creation of an NHS in 1948 is generally regarded as a major public health achievement. However, as Baggot, quoting Lewis (1992), further comments, many were concerned that from the beginning it was a 'sickness' rather than a health service.

Within this socio-historical context there are, I would argue, a range of potentially confusing personal identifications for both givers and receivers of services. As Bion (1961), Menzies Lyth (1989), Obholzer and Roberts (1994) and many others have pointed out, maintaining a well-functioning group life around such a dynamically complex mix is bound to be disappointing and fraught. It is better, in my view, to assume from the outset that we are dealing with intrinsically conflicted systems, where the interactions between personalities and different agendas are just as likely to be explosive or blocked as they are to be co-operative and/or running efficiently.

Amid the competing ideologies (themselves originating in unconscious shared phantasy and belief), the largest background condition affecting the nature of our engagement with our institutional work remains the impact of our own primitive unconscious. This we share in a constant dynamic relationship with our colleagues and clients (both staff clients and patient groups). Our capacity to reflect on this shared unconscious dynamic affects the reception and utility of our interventions whether we are clinicians, supervisors, managers, or all three.

I shall now describe some of the pitfalls for the analyst working within the mental health organisation. Jane Milton (2000) warns psychoanalysts of a potential for unconscious drift to the moral high ground with individual patients. From my experience this is also a danger for us in the institutional sphere. For example, through the forces of institutional transference, we may feel compelled to provide something helpful to hard-pressed staff and find ourselves unconsciously colluding with a view that 'The Management' is destructive to the work being done with patients. Under the pressure of splitting, we can all lose touch with that part of ourselves that unconsciously hates the intractable work or the demanding patients (Winnicott, 1949). 'The Management' then becomes a convenient container for such feelings, and the psychoanalyst may find he has unwittingly assisted group splitting. As psychoanalysts, then, it is important to remain open to our own internal pressures to act out, and to become 'disturbed' by the organization. An analytic colleague once put it that she felt one of our functions in the institution might be to 'break down' from time to time by becoming irrationally perplexed or outraged, but then to use the 'breakdown' to understand more about the context of the work.

I think what my colleague meant was that when working in these heated contexts, the analyst needs not only to be able to feel the primitive transference that is affecting the staff, but also to contain and process this dynamic, via his or her countertransference responses. Only then can this dynamic be properly understood and reflected on, along with one's own unconscious contributions to it.

The theoretical roots of these ideas originated with Freud and were extended by later psychoanalysts such as Klein, Isaacs and Bion. Freud realized that when the psyche was under pressure, not only did it develop a variety of internal strategies to avoid, eject, rearrange or remodel uncomfortable perceptions of reality, but these strategies were influenced by pre-existing internal factors (Freud 1923, 1924). In the face of unacceptable psychic pressures, Freud described how the ego could become split in the process of erecting its defences, or that parts of the psychic apparatus, or its awareness functions, could become lost (1923, 1924, 1938). Unconsciously, and under pressure from impulse, phantasy or overwhelming stimulation, the ego employed mechanisms such as repression or denial, together with more wholesale disruptions to its perceptive and integrative functions. These mechanisms served to reduce or remove the painful psychic impact of the original impingements and memories. In 'Group Psychology and the Analysis of the Ego' (1921), Freud began to explore the powers that *groups* have in distorting or channelling uncomfortable aspects of reality. He noted how a group could amplify, for example, the power of words, magical ideas, impulsivity or affects. Perhaps most significantly, he noted that the emotional bonds between group members and with the group leader became amplified through archaic identifications to do with sibling and parental figures (Chapter 7, 1921).

Klein's studies in child analysis had revealed to her through the play transference, a pre-Oedipal and Oedipal world full of violent relationships (Klein 1932). Her colleague Susan Isaacs (1948) later developed these observations into a wider exploration of unconscious phantasy, which was seen as the correlate to all conscious life and a constant counterpart to what we perceive. In this, she foreshadowed Klein's later work on projective identification. In 'Notes on some Schizoid Mechanisms', Klein (1946, p. 2) writes:

> The psychotic anxieties, mechanisms and ego-defences of infancy have a profound influence on development in all its aspects, including the development of the ego, super-ego and object-relations . . . and thus from the beginning object-relations are moulded by an interaction between introjection and projection, between internal and external objects and situations.

What Klein termed 'projective identification', based on her observations of these primitive levels of infantile phantasy within the individual child, came to be elaborated as an important conceptual instrument that could serve to illuminate how primitive mechanisms make their presence felt not only in individual relationships but also in the group context. According to Klein, in the struggle with the primitive transference (the first transference being to the parental figures themselves), we do at some point have to deal with the problem of guilt for the real and imagined damage that we have done, once we become aware that the hated and attacked figures of the internal world are the same ones that we love and absolutely depend on for our survival. The attempts to deal with such damage and the guilt it engenders can involve the production of radical defences – the 'manic defences' – some of which can involve excessive reparation or a turning away from the needed objects in contempt, superiority or triumph. It follows that there will also be socially shared structures that serve to lessen the anxiety connected to intense guilt by universalizing it. In John Steiner's interpretation of the Oedipus myth, for example, a universalizing (sharing) of the blindness to the Oedipal crime is posited as flowing from and defending against shared guilt (Steiner, 1985).

Bion (1962) developed a theory of 'alpha function', in which 'pre-thought' elements are able to assume a form suitable for being consciously thought about, after they have been contained and bound firstly through the processes of maternal reverie and later through the triangular structure of the Oedipus situation. These bound elements of thought become elaborated into increasingly higher levels of thinking structures – which then further act as prototypic organizers of later experience, including the capacity for scientific reasoning and shared phantasy (Bion, 1963). Experiences are thus enabled to become more organized internally, as well as becoming capable of being shared or observed.

In discussing the functions of such myths as 'Oedipus' and 'Eden' as prototypic, that is, universally shared 'models' of mental life, Bion (1963) suggested that these myths were based on primitive or archaic structures emphasizing elements such as omniscience, punishment, loss by expulsion or blinding, the seeking of truth or knowledge through exercising curiosity. Bion (1961, 1963) proposed the idea of a *redemptive future* in his basic assumption theory and cited the Eden myth as one of the more significant of the unconscious group motifs. Bion (1961) has pointed out how readily groups can generate and participate in a shared myth which influences, and is influenced by, individual phantasy. We could speak then of group phantasies being influenced by shared conscious and unconscious myths, which incorporate universal archaic elements, fears and defences. Larger-scale group relationships tend to breed an even greater intensity, via the mechanism of multiplying shared phantasies with their associated primitive defences.

I think it may well be that it is this intensified fear arising out of the archaic pressure in group life that most promotes the longing for a defensive Eden, the wish to build an Eden in practice, or indeed to find a messiah to give hope for the future. Such unconscious phantasies, sometimes magnified through group pressures to identify, or identify *with*, heroic, redemptive figures, incorporate the wish to find somewhere in external reality a place (as it is unconsciously imagined childhood once was) free from disturbance and corruption: 'The happy highways where I went, And cannot come again' (A.E. Housman, *A Shropshire Lad*, 1896).

In his poem 'Vespers' (1940) and an essay on *The Pickwick Papers*, W.H. Auden discusses the dishonesty of both the pursuer of Eden, and his apparently opposite (but similar) antitype, the Utopian. The latter dangerously projects his Eden, where all was thought possible (we would nowadays think this to be associated with childhood phantasy), into an idealized future free from 'contradictions'. Idealization, I think, becomes proportional to the lurking dangers. A senior manager recently said to me, 'All our problems with this service will be resolved, once it is completely clarified exactly what everyone is doing.' I would argue that idealized, or Utopian, structures such as clinical governance systems, institutes of excellence and efficiency, comprehensive NICE guidelines, to name a few, have been unconsciously devised on a mythic group ideal. Sadly, they can only perpetuate anxiety, disappointment and guilt if the archaic phantasy level is not taken into account.

The concept of the 'defensive organization' has been widely explored in the consultancy literature and by many psychoanalytic thinkers. It is my view that fluctuating social defensive structures are always a background condition in the functioning of the group, as is the archaic drama of already processed, or becoming processed, elements that they help to organize. The individual within the group setting inevitably utilizes the projective field that the organization provides as an opportunity to project, to act out, and to establish meaning through the shared group phantasy. The group member also makes use of its defensive organization in the service of the shared group phantasies, sometimes at the expense of a more personal reality.

Group structured phantasy and the defensive organization can also act as a mirror to the personality structure, since it is built on individual and group shared internal phantasy, combining in relationship patterns within the group. Turquet (1974) used the concept of 'organization in the mind', later developed by Shapiro and Carr (1991) and Armstrong (2005) to describe the diverse fantasies and projections that group members may share in various degrees, amounting to a 'mental image' of the organization. In other words, we unconsciously create our own structures, and we do this together in the group to reflect both individual phantasy and group phantasy, along with a wide variety of defences and transference arrangements. We may therefore get the 'managers' (parent figures) we unconsciously feel that we need in order to represent, or act out for us, specific archaic internal positions or roles whose significance to us is denied. We then have these group-sponsored proxies capitulate in, or act out, their required role for ourselves *and* the group in the external structure (Sandler,

1976). These secretly assigned roles may well have valence for the particular personalities to which they are assigned and may be at odds with officially designated roles. A criticized and disliked manager, for example, may become the unwitting agency for the group in preventing organizational developments that have been demanded by the group, but about which they actually feel guiltily ambivalent.

I have noticed in this regard an interesting fate for psychoanalytic thinking in the group. While this may officially be ignored, or even denounced as time-wasting, those engaging in it are also unofficially given permission by the group to use it. This may be because anti-life, super-ego-driven forces in the group, which undermine its creativity, are unconsciously felt to have a greater chance of being scrutinized if someone else – such as the psychoanalyst – is free to take on that role. Thus through 'choosing' opinion leaders that the group can persecute on one hand while on the other having the group's defensive *status quo* challenged, group learning can be promoted. From this point of view, psychoanalysts must be careful of assuming that we are 'not wanted' and ask instead: what is 'required' of us by the group?

Ignes Sodre (2000, 2004) described a manic defence that she termed *Non-Vixit*, so named after a scene in which a friend who caused Freud internal disturbance and guilt was made to completely de-materialize in one of Freud's dreams (Freud, 1900). The existence of this disturbing friend was consciously negated, but as a result became even *more* potent and *more* widely alive in his *unconscious* effects, thus needing to be exterminated in order to maintain the *status quo*.

In organizations and institutions, there can be similar attempts to extinguish the primitive in ourselves and in the group by expulsion or confinement. In mental health settings, we call this confinement by such names as 'the ward', or 'the CMHT' – and these become places where the disturbance can break through and become manifest, haunting us in ways that then feel persecuting. Removal methods, based on the manic defence, may be enacted under 'reorganizations', or 'service re-designs', or 'management re-design', in a vain attempt to assuage the problem. As well as being experienced as disturbing, an institution driven by the manic defences can feel very disappointing. It can feel like a frustrating, depressing and lonely place for those seeking more personal meaning. The excitement of periodic group and individual conflicts (often a group enactment of mutually felt frustrations), may then be unconsciously sought by the group as an antidote to this loneliness, in just the same way that manic acting-out operates in an individual who is struggling with emptiness and depression.

The phantasy configurations that cause most difficulty in organizational life are, in essence, the same ones that cause difficulty for the individual and in each case the pressure to enact, or act out, is high (Feldman, 1997; Obholzer and Roberts, 1994; Tuckett, 1995). Under the sway of unconsciously shared archaic scripts, enactment affords the temporary reassurance of reducing the gap between internal phantasy life and what is actually found in the external situation. In my experience, configurations that involve members of the group, and then the group as a whole, and that deal with the unconscious psychic realities of the 'primal scene' (Britton, 1998), of unresolved loss, of frustrated longings, and of other psychic traumas (including castration and annihilation fears), have the greatest power to organize the group phantasy and transference, just as they organize individual development. Group phantasy life can thus become very disturbed around configurations that stir up intense unconscious longings and fears. Facing these deeper phantasies is very frightening and can lead to projections into particular individuals within, or outside, the group who are now seen as the sources of jealousy, envy, humiliation, deprivation, hostility, greed or shame.

I shall now give an illustration of these theoretical concepts with an example taken from work with groups in the mental health organization.

My consultation was twice weekly to a staff team working with chronic-ally disturbed clients, most of whom had recurrent psychotic episodes. I had been seeing them over a period of several years since the unit had been relocated to a community residential base. It was my impression that new relationships were emerging of a more containing nature than had formerly been experienced in the more traditional hospital-based care environment. After a considerable struggle and detailed discussion in the group, some staff felt that they themselves were beginning to come more into contact with their own deeper personal issues. They were becoming aware that certain repetitive defences had for many years helped them avoid, in the interests of psychic survival, many conflicts, including the awareness of profound loss.

I discussed with analytic colleagues my feeling that I was in risky ambiguous territory. We reflected together that despite the sense of difficulty and struggle, the group had valued and gained meaning from this kind of painful exploration of their difficult work and relationships. Some staff in the group (and their patients) had, over a long period of time, allowed themselves more conscious contact with depressive pain; this included some dashed expectations about an imagined new lease of life for patients in the improved environment. The staff team began to encounter and struggle with feelings connected with loss, both in connection to relationships with clients and within ourselves. I began to feel that the staff group was becoming a creative place, where the important issues of life were now allowed to be explored in more detail, and that the impact of the painful work of relating to traumatized patients, and to each other, was becoming more understood. Some members of the group, not yet particu-larly qualified in mental health work, were also becoming ambitious for further knowledge and training. Many of the group had received, or were now receiving, additional training elsewhere and where there were some basic educational gaps, we arranged some training.

In our fourth year of working together, one of the more ambitious group members began to absent herself from the group. She took an additional course, which clashed with the times of the group. I noticed, incidentally, that I had been fond of this group member, feeling that she had made a large personal and creative contribution to the group's exploration of the work.

Soon afterwards, I discovered that a formal grievance process had been started by this absentee group member against the local managers of the unit, one of whom sometimes came to the group itself, although he had not yet mentioned the grievance. The basis of the criticism, an intensely felt and argued one, was that some of the physical care and hygiene needs of the patients in the unit had been neglected. This criticism was now putting managerial colleagues under great pressure and causing enormous ripple effects in the unit's wider hospital-based senior management, some of whom had always been ambivalent about the existence of the unit.

It was possible to recruit evidence to the substance of the grievance, because some of the residents did have significant ongoing difficulties with general hygiene and self-maintenance related to their ongoing psychological difficulties. It was my impression, though, that on the whole management were not neglectful of such issues. Nevertheless, our group member dug in and took them on, initially with destructive effect, to both herself and the unit's work.

I think this kind of process is very complex, involving, as it does, the projection and enactment of archaic elements, not least of which was the aggrieved group member's own inevitably intense ambivalence about the difficulties of the work. Management suspicion was provoked and this was followed by attacks on the unit in which she had been a dedicated member. While this incident might be understood in many ways, I shall choose one or two that particularly struck me. In all the tension of the battle unfolding after the establishment of the grievance, it took me some while to remember – and local management also appeared to have forgotten this in their 'battle' – what a helpful person this woman had been, how much I had liked her and how she'd had a genuine wish to see the situation of her patients improved. Prior to becoming entrenched in this negative view of management's concern for patients, she had used the group, which had in reality been provided by management, to help open up the group discussion on some of the most sensitive and difficult issues.

My view now, in reflecting back on this painful episode, is that her own role in furthering and deepening the group's discussion about relationships in the unit, including the attachment to myself as the group's consultant (with all the transference issues involved in that), had involved her in more depressive pain than she could bear. This group context was therefore unconsciously attacked by means of a grievance process; a process that was to do with the issue of failure of care by management. In this way she could not only deny the pain about what she had experienced as *my* failure of care of her in the group, but simultaneously express it very forcibly through a group enactment in which the group and I were put under threat by management.

Thus the enactment involved in phantasy the transference parents who were seen to be responsible for *failures* of care, but included myself in unconscious phantasy. I provided a place where failures of care, including failures in patients' earlier lives and, where appropriate, the feelings about our own losses these stirred up, could be explored. Somewhere it was felt that I was not protecting the group members from, as it were, an 'unhygienic' exposure to depressive pain and anxiety. In thinking about what the staff member had chosen to bring regarding aspects of her own history, it became clear to me that she had valence (in Bion's terms) as a conduit to receive the group's projections, and to take on the role of being projectively identified with issues relating to failures of care. Her grievance then enabled the local management to vent a similar grievance in relation to senior management about the inadequate original practical provision for the unit. The issues were indeed for everyone.

Some eventual resolution was achieved, and the member of staff around whom the grievance had become organized was able to move into a more creative period in her life. I was able to make some limited interpretation to the group about the wider meaning of the process for us all, in terms of our being faced with such difficult and almost intractable tasks. Among the issues that we were then able to explore further to good effect in the group were the frustrations associated with trying to improve things against a backdrop of great damage; the feeling that this might fuel a sense of group omnipotence versus humiliation; that creative developments were always precarious; and that if the group was creative there was always unconscious envy at work from several directions and origins.

This scenario that I have just described is typical of NHS configurations at the present time, where the giving of sustained care is under severe strain due to a combination of financial restraint and the actual difficulty of the work. I have come to recognize that complaints and grievances have particular power in mental health care systems in promoting archaic enactments. It is commonplace, as here, that a fight can break out within or between the different factions, leading to a kind of 'plague on both your houses'. This is born, I think, out of the frustrations of the task, the difficulty in sustaining creative couples (who act as containers for the work), the failure to hold on to a 'third' position from which what is going on can be observed non-judgementally, and the difficulty in repairing and forgiving the inevitable and extensive nature of the archaic processes and phantasies that can ensue and escalate in such contexts.

Concluding remarks

What can be described as the omnipotent and seductive optimism of successive governments regarding mental health service aims is permeated with the belief that anything and everything can be improved for everyone, rather than having to face the painful reality of limitation. This optimism, based as it is on the manic defences, continues to foster an amplification of the archaic and persecutory elements in mental health systems. Those that 'manage' the organization in the external sense attract all the associated group transferences that follow on a largely unrealistic and idealized group-sponsored care promise. This group transference interacts with all the other individual transferences that might then be further played out and fostered in the disappointed and frustrated workforce, sometimes with destructive results. Inevitably, there is pressure for intense group and individual enactment. The 'thinking' processes that might de-intensify the most pressured or destructive group phantasies and enactments are not enabled to gain ground. The reflection needed on the presence of the primitive unconscious processes and defences is not given time and energy; energy is instead recruited into the excitement of the unconscious group enactments.

Even so, it is my belief that the psychoanalyst has a role in consulting to the health system, via engagement with and reflection on the unconscious archaic organizational process. Participation in the attempt to understand some of this may help space become available for more realistic and compassionate thought.

References

Armstrong, D. (2005) *Organization in the Mind*, London: Karnac.

Auden, W.H. (1940) 'Vespers' (5 of 'Horae Canonicae'). In *The Shield of Achilles*, London: Faber and Faber.

Auden, W.H. (1948–1962) *The Dyer's Hand*, New York: Random House, 1962, republished Vintage, London, 1989.

Baggot, R. (2000) *Public Health: Policy and Politics*, London: Macmillan.

Bion, W.R. (1961) *Experiences in Groups*, London: Tavistock Publications.

Bion, W.R. (1962) *Learning from Experience*, London: Karnac.

Bion, W.R. (1963) *Elements of Psycho-Analysis*, London: Heinemann.

Blank, R.H. and Burau, V. (2004) *Comparative Health Policy*, Basingstoke, UK: Palgrave Macmillan.

Britton, R. (1998) 'Poetic space and the other room'. In *Belief and Imagination*, Chapter 10, London: Routledge.

Castel, R. (1991) 'From dangerousness to risk'. In G. Burchell, C. Gordon and P. Miller (Eds.), *The Foucault Effect: Studies in Governmentability*, Hemel Hempstead, UK: Harvester Wheatsheaf.

Feldman, M. (1997) 'Projective identification: The analyst's involvement', *International Journal of Psychoanalysis*, 78: 227–241.

Freud, S. (1900) 'The interpretation of dreams', *Standard Edition*, Vol. V, London: Hogarth Press.

Freud, S. (1921) 'Group psychology and the analysis of the ego', *Standard Edition*, Vol. XVIII, London: Hogarth Press.

Freud, S. (1923) 'The ego and the id', *Standard Edition*, Vol. XIX, London: Hogarth Press.

Freud, S. (1924) 'The loss of reality in neurosis and psychosis', *Standard Edition*, Vol. XIX, London: Hogarth Press.

Freud, S. (1938) 'Splitting of the ego in the process of defence', *Standard Edition*, Vol. XXIII, London: Hogarth Press.

Fuller, B.F. (1994) *American Health Care: Rebirth or Suicide*, Springfield, IL: Charles C. Thomas.

Godwin, G. (1793) *An Enquiry Concerning Political Justice and Its Influence on Morals and Happiness*, Ontario, Canada: Toronto Press, 1946.

Hayek, F. (1976) *The Constitution of Liberty*, London: Routledge.

Hayek, F. (1988) *The Fatal Conceit: The Errors of Socialism*, London: Routledge.

Hinshelwood, R.D. and Skogstad, W. (2000) *Observing Organisations*, London: Routledge.

Isaacs, S. (1948) 'The nature and function of phantasy', *International Journal of Psycho-Analysis*, 29: 73–97.

Klein, M. (1932) 'An obsessional neurosis in a six year old girl', *Psychoanalysis of Children*, London: Hogarth.

Klein, M. (1946) 'Notes on some schizoid mechanisms', In *Envy and Gratitude*, London: Hogarth Press.

Lerner, L. (1972) *The Uses of Nostalgia: Studies in Pastoral Poetry*, London: Chatto and Windus.

Lewis, J. (1992) 'Providers, consumers: The state and the delivery of health care services in twentieth century Britain'. In A. Wear (Ed.), *Medicine in Society: Historical Essays*, Cambridge, UK: Cambridge University Press.

Menzies Lyth, I. (1988) *Containing Anxiety in Institutions: Selected Essays*, London: Free Association Books.

Menzies Lyth, I. (1989) *Dynamics of the Social: Selected Essays*, London: Free Association Books.

Milton, J. (2000) 'Psychoanalysis and the moral high ground', *International Journal of Psychoanalysis*, 81: 1101–1115.

Nitsun, M. (1996) *The Anti-group: Destructive Forces in the Group and Their Creative Potential*, London: Routledge.

Obholzer, A. and Roberts, V. (Eds.) (1994) *The Unconscious at Work*, London: Routledge.

O'Shaughnessy, E. (1999) 'Relating to the superego', *International Journal of Psychoanalysis*, 80: 861–870.

Sandler, J. (1976) 'Counter-transference and role responsiveness', *International Journal of Psychoanallysis*, 3: 43–47.

Schafer, R. (1983) *The Analytic Attitude*, London: Karnac.

Shapiro, E.R. and Carr, A.W. (1991) *Lost in Familiar Places: Creating New Connections between the Individual and Society*, New Haven, CT: Yale University Press.

Sodre, I. *For ever wilt thou love, and she be fair: On Quixotism and the golden age of pre-genital sexuality* (unpublished draft).

Sodre, I. (2000, 2004) 'Non Vixit', a ghost story, Institute of Psychoanalysis (2000), republished in R. Perelberg (Ed.), *Dreaming and Thinking* (2004), London: Karnac.

Steiner, J. (1985) 'Turning a blind eye: The cover up for Oedipus', *International Review of Psycho-Analysis* 12: 161–172.

Stone, D. (1989) 'At risk in the welfare state', *Social Research*, 56: 591–633.

Strachey, J. (1934) 'The nature of the therapeutic action of psycho-analysis', *International Journal of Psycho-Analysis*, 15: 127–159.

Tuckett, D. (1995) 'Mutual enactment in the psychoanalytic situation'. In J.L. Ahumada, J. Olagaray, A. Kramer Richard and A.D. Richard (Eds.), *The Perverse Transference and Other Matters*, Northvale, NJ: Jason Aronson.

Turquet, P. (1974) 'Leadership, the individual and the group'. In A.D. Coleman and M.H. Geller (Eds.) (1985), *Group Relations Reader 2*, Washington, DC: Rice Institute Series.

Winnicott, D.W. (1949) 'Hate in the counter-transference', *International Journal of Psycho-Analysis*, 30: 69–74.

Chapter 10

Confidentiality matters

Anne Ward

> What I may see or hear in the course of the treatment or even outside of the treatment in regard to the life of men, which on no account one must spread abroad, I will keep to myself, holding such things shameful to be spoken about.
>
> (From *The Hippocratic Oath*)

> It is the responsibility of the individual registrant to keep strict standards of confidentiality in all Records and Notes about a patient, and under all circumstance, vigorously to resist identifiable disclosure of this material against his/her clinical judgement.
>
> (In *Guidelines on Notes and Records, British Psychoanalytical Council*, September 2005)

Medical students 'know' that patient confidentiality is paramount except where there is significant risk to self or others. Psychoanalytic trainees are usually older and more experienced; correspondingly the issues often seem less clear although there is usually agreement that the principle itself is unambiguous. However, it is only in the murky world of practice that the subject really comes to life. And in this respect at least, the multidisciplinary world of psychiatry, in a risk-averse, information-seeking, electronic age, can be murkier than most. Add to this the potentially competing loyalties of senior clinicians who are also effectively part-time managers and the situation can be even more complex, particularly in the recent past when financial issues have assumed such priority. In the midst of what often feels like ongoing chaos, the preservation of a psychoanalytic stance regarding confidentiality seems an arduous, sometimes unobtainable, but essential goal.

In this chapter, I offer some examples of conundrums arising in routine practice in an NHS psychotherapy department that have set me thinking more than usually hard about this issue; for example, whether confidentiality may be confounded with secrecy, or the duty of confidentiality exercised in a perverse or harmful manner. The situations described are not intended as exemplars – indeed, they are mostly situations in which hindsight might have suggested a different course, and consultation not infrequently did so. However, they are illustrative of what we increasingly have to grapple with. All case histories have been fictionalized.

Confidentiality or collusion? *A psychotherapeutic group in a psychiatric institution*

Prior to attending our psychotherapy group, Ms B had an affair with her community psychiatric nurse (CPN) (Mr X) at another hospital. After he left her she became hospitalized with depression, but kept the affair confidential until she felt the information was 'forced' out of her by the nursing staff, and Mr X was subsequently suspended. Following this, she refused to have anything more to do with her local services, and was now being treated in our group with the back-up of her GP alone. The complexity of this became apparent when she disclosed her suicidal intent and her propensity to self-harm. However, as she settled into the group these threats abated and, without its being consciously registered by the group, the CPN crept back into her life, while remaining suspended. It took a new group member to highlight the ongoing affair, but this new member stayed only briefly in the group while Ms B and Mr X continued to remain together. Things slowly escalated, and the sado-masochistic nature of the relationship became increasingly apparent, with Ms B reporting that Mr X had been violent towards her. Although seemingly upset, it gradually became clear that she had no intent of ending the relationship, to which she was apparently enthralled.

Another new member, Ms A, was openly shocked by what she heard, and stated her belief that Mr X should be reported. To compound matters, Mr X was (reportedly) undertaking a humanistic counselling course that would enable him to work with clients. Ms A wrote a letter to the group therapist, delivered by hand on the first day of the summer break, prefaced by her insistence that the letter should not be discussed with the rest of the group, and asking that the letter be shredded if the therapist could not keep her confidentiality. The therapist later learned that the letter had reiterated Ms A's view that Mr X should be reported to his professional body. On this occasion though, she wrote to Ms A explaining that she could not in these circumstances read the letter and inviting her to reconsider her stricture on confidentiality. Ms A herself had been accepted in the group on condition that she had access to her community mental health team (CMHT) in an emergency, without having to go through her GP (lessons having been learned with Ms B). She too had been suicidal and an inpatient. Her CMHT had allocated her a care co-ordinator, who offered her regular appointments, but Ms A professed to distrust this person, informing the group that she could only speak freely if her confidentiality was guaranteed, i.e. that her care co-ordinator would *not* be informed of what she might say.

'Confidentiality', along with 'conflicting loyalties', inevitably became an issue in the group. It was clear that the Nursing and Midwifery Council (NMC) needed to know about the situation, but to report it seemed like a breach of group confidentiality. The Trust Caldicott Guardian, as well as the group therapist's supervisor, made a decision to inform the NMC that allegations of violence, arising during the course of therapy, should be investigated if Mr X applied to work again. The group members were informed of this decision and the implications discussed. Ms B neverthe-less continued in the relationship. The stories of violence continued to escalate until the group therapist concluded, regretfully, that Ms B was too entrenched in a perverse structure to benefit from further therapy. Ms A was not given the absolute guarantee of confidentiality that she was demanding, but has been able to work around this and is gradually more trusting of the group process as a container for her anxieties.

I am still unsure about how I (the therapist) handled this, but a positive feature of working in the NHS is the shared expertise, and I did have other minds to call on. No-one had ready answers – they had not encountered these particular situations before, but they were prepared to help me think about them in an informed way. From an analytic perspective, there was a complicated dynamic at work, with issues of 'confidentiality' being used both to undermine and to preserve the group structure. It was no accident that the majority of group members had suffered abuse in the past, some of it quite gross, so that boundary violations were played out both in and between the sessions, with issues of 'confidentiality' being frequently used in the service of resistance.

Electronic ease

Another area where issues of confidentiality can present particular chal-lenges is in the management of shared cases. This is made both easier and more perilous by the explosion in electronic communications. There are general principles, but when these are breached, it can frequently reflect both systemic and dynamic disturbance.

Individual therapy in the electronic age: Enactment or safeguard?

Mr D suffered from a paranoid psychotic illness. He had, however, benefited from a long-term structured therapy to the extent that he was apparently no longer symptomatic. His previous therapist had written a long report, seen and agreed by the patient, specifically recording that this agreement might have affected his report. The patient was now expressing a wish to explore his past, in a psychodynamic therapy, with a view to understanding and managing whatever contribution his background had made to his illness, and thus decreasing his vulnerability to relapse. At the time of assessment for psychodynamic psychotherapy, he was not on any medication. Mr D settled into therapy, bringing past and current issues to the sessions, tolerating silences and seeming to free associate. However, the therapist (myself) often found it difficult to be in the room with him, becoming aware of hostile thoughts and feelings that were initially confusing and hard to understand; for example, feeling trapped, helpless and hateful, while time stretched out endlessly ahead. Although this was understandable in that Mr D was recounting a horrific saga of neglect and abuse, it was not quite enough to explain the atmosphere in the room. The therapist gradually realized that a psychotic process was being enacted in which Mr D was filling the room with the horror of his internal world, such that it felt a paranoid and increasingly deluded place.

The therapist was not in regular contact with Mr D's care co-ordinator, the latter having decided, as she saw it, to preserve confidentiality. Thus she did not discuss Mr D's therapy with him, nor did she inform the therapist of what later proved to be significant decisions about Mr D's psychiatric treatment. Issues of safety loomed, and the therapist decided to check out the patient's records – as it happened, electronically, which made it that much easier. In retrospect, this was both a grasping for reality and an escape from something toxic in the room; perhaps too, it represented a cry for help from the multidisciplinary team. However, it complicated the situation further as Mr D's electronic notes recorded instances of medication prescribed some time earlier that the therapist was almost certain he was not taking. So Mr D had been secretly duplicitous, and the therapist had compounded this by going secretly behind his back, albeit with the conscious reasoning that he was at risk.

Feeling uncomfortable about her 'enactment' the therapist asked Mr D straightforwardly if he knew that he had electronic records. It transpired that he did not; he was quite shocked, and this opened up a new phase in the therapy, with Mr D engaging more fully with his CMHT and choosing to restart his medication. The therapy was extended to allow this phase to run its course, and Mr D went on to make some convincing changes in his life that he felt were not simply due to the medication. As was his right, he requested copies of all final correspondence about him. The therapist agreed, but said that she would be writing a report for the notes that Mr D would not be given access to. Despite the increased openness generated by the electronic records episode, the therapist was left with the uncomfortable knowledge that she would be writing one thing in the letter seen by Mr D, and something much more complicated, that she did not want him to see, in her report for the group therapy that was now being suggested. This was scarcely in the spirit of 'copying patients into correspondence', nor was it in the spirit of preserving the patient's right to a private intercourse. Indeed, it felt like an unsatisfactory compromise born from a not quite coherent set of policies and practices.

Would this have evolved differently had we been limited to paper records? Certainly my patient considered it a breach of confidentiality for the Trust to have moved his records to the electronic system without an explicit discussion of this with him. Less clear, but I think implicit, was a sense of my having violated his privacy, particularly relevant given his history of abuse. There was also the question of my lack of connection with his CMHT: would better communication between us have avoided this situation arising, or would it have been a breach of confidentiality of yet another sort? I was initially pleased by his care co-ordinator's stance, but with hindsight I have wondered whether my ready acceptance of this lack of communication between us sprang from my own mistrust in the system, accentuated by my patient's own paranoid beliefs – yet this also felt like a reality in the NHS of the present day. What helped greatly was the consultant psychiatrist's low-key but prompt response, and minimal recording on the electronic system – more or less a record of medication agreed. Also invaluable was the continued interest and opportunity for discussion with the previous supervisor. This highlights another feature of working analytically in the NHS, namely the cross-fertilization with other therapeutic approaches, enriching rather than diluting our own.

Legal liabilities

There has always been a tension between the individual's right to privacy and the larger community's right to protect itself. This is seen in medical practice when, for example, a 'notifiable' disease is diagnosed, or a patient with imperfectly controlled epilepsy continues to drive. In psychiatric practice, a lawyer may – with the patient's permission and in some cases without – request copies of their records. This is more problematic in psychotherapeutic and particularly psychoanalytic practice, as exemplified by Hayman (1965). In many states of the USA, the Tarasoff Rule (1976) holds 'that when a therapist determines, or pursuant to the standards of his profession should determine, that his patient presents a serious danger of violence to another, he incurs an obligation to use reasonable care to protect the intended victim against such danger' (p. 431). . . . 'The protective privilege ends where the public peril begins' (p. 442). In the 30 or so years since, no analogous case has arisen in the British courts,[1] although the Tarasoff rule has been widely considered as good practice for psychiatrists and taught as such to trainee psychiatrists.

A psychoanalyst (almost) subpoenaed: 40 years on

Ms C was in her early 40s when she gave birth to her first child, a boy. She had been assessed by the Psychotherapy Department previously, but was felt to be avoidant of addressing her difficulties and did not take up the offer of treatment. On this occasion, she came to the attention of the psychiatric services having taken an overdose three months after the birth of her baby and was referred back to the department for further assessment. When seen, she presented as more borderline than avoidant, and the assessor was left with the uneasy feeling of not having contained her in the assessment. Indeed, Ms C rang the department that night looking for the number of the hospital's Emergency Clinic. Responding to the sense of urgency, as well as to concern for the safety of her young baby, she was allocated to the next senior house officer (SHO) who had a vacancy to see her for therapy. She rapidly overwhelmed him with accounts of her violent relationship with her partner, in which it seemed to us in the supervision group that she could be provocative in quite a cruel way.

The SHO was relatively inexperienced in a dynamic model and, although he could describe his countertransference quite vividly in supervision, had difficulty in using it in sessions. He was also sitting exams, and about to take four consecutive weeks off, despite my expressed concern as his supervisor that this might be problematic for his patient. As soon as he went on leave, there were phone calls from the Social Services, the Emergency Clinic, the police and Ms C's lawyer. Apparently the relationship had now taken a more violent turn and Ms C was seeking to have him thrown out of her house. The lawyer called, asking for a record of the therapist's process notes, and I had an uneasy image of my SHO using his 'Blackberry' during supervision. I realized that I did not know what he was recording on it, nor was I aware at the time whether there were guidelines for recording patient data on such a device; nor did I know whether he had – as initially instructed – kept minimal paper records as well as his process notes. I was, however, almost certain from our regular supervisory discussions that the patient had not been detailing instances of her partner's long-term abusive behaviour – if anything there were records of her own regret at how she had treated him. The Trust's head of psychotherapy advised me that the lawyer was probably entitled to demand the process notes if the patient had consented. I was, nevertheless, concerned at how informed that consent might have been, as it seemed that the patient had convinced herself that the records of abuse really did exist, suggesting that she was operating in quite a disconnected state of mind. After having consulted with a clinical colleague, I suggested to the lawyer that such notes might not be of particular help to her client's case, and she accepted this, albeit reluctantly, settling for a more general statement about the therapy. The patient had, in my view, engaged in a 'flight into health' in order to prove that the problems were all in her partner rather than in herself. She won her case, her more borderline presentation appeared to settle, and she scored highly on our post-therapeutic outcome measures. I remained unconvinced that therapy had done much for her, but I was relieved that at least her baby would be out of the constant warring, at least for the present.

This case brought Dr H's stance to mind, described in a 1965 paper in the *Lancet* (Hayman, 1965). Dr H obeyed a summons to attend court, but refused to give any evidence including whether or not the person in question was her patient, thus risking imprisonment for contempt of court. As it happened, her evidence was not crucial to the case and I have often wondered, without in any way wishing to detract from Dr H's courage, what would have happened had it been essential. There was a similar outlet in the case above, as the lawyer already had a shrewd suspicion, without it having been spelt out, that our evidence would not help her case. Nevertheless, the same question arises – what if she had insisted?

A comprehensive and thorough discussion of issues of confidentiality in psychoanalysis in seven international jurisdictions is to be found in Garvey and Layton (2004); however, having consulted this, I was still without any clear guidelines: 'The situation in each jurisdiction has yet to be resolved satisfactorily' (p. 57). The British Psychoanalytical Society Handbook (internal document, 2004), as well as the British Psychoanalytic Council *Statement on Confidentiality* (2005), highlight that current legislation in this country makes no distinction between factual recorded and working clinical notes, and warns that all notes could be subpoenaed. As in the other cases I have described, what was of most help was the combined psychoanalytic and psychiatric/managerial input that was available to me, as an NHS analytically oriented psychotherapist and psychiatrist.

Discussion

In the course of writing this chapter it occurred to me that I might be breaching the most recent confidentiality guidelines by including case material, despite it being fictionalized. Yet not to do so would be to lose the complexity and confusing nature of such situations. This debate is reflected in a series of recent articles (Kantrowitz, 2004a, 2004b, 2005; Furlong, 2006) as well as in guidance from the Royal College of Psychiatrists (2006) and advice on the General Medical Council website. The latter is not written with psychiatric/psychotherapy patients in mind, but an *International Journal of Psychoanalysis* editorial has addressed this issue (Gabbard and Williams, 2001). Despite this wealth of debate and guidance I was left – yet again – with a sense of conflicting directions. The resolution of this conflict arose from using what can be so richly available in the NHS setting, a combination of analytic thinking and the input of the Trust Caldicott

Guardian, the latter offering to read and 'vet' my material from the data protection viewpoint.

As we move towards more managed care in the NHS, managers are requesting an increasing amount of information in order to justify longer-term treatments in particular; it can be all too easy to comply with this request without thinking what it might mean for the patient and the treatment relationship. At a recent meeting, a clinician had to argue quite hard to gain agreement that a patient's admission summaries would not automatically be seen by lay members of a tertiary referral panel. However, prior to his raising an objection, it had not seemed possible to think about this.

> It is arguable that . . . confidentiality has been such a central aspect of the practice of medicine and psychiatry that its importance is often taken for granted, its maintenance frequently less than rigorous, and the degree of its erosion in recent years underestimated.
>
> (Garvey and Layton, 2004a, footnote p. 2)

The NHS is staffed not only by clinicians, managers and patients but also by large numbers of ancillary workers, such as electricians, technologists and domestic staff, who are not – as far as I am aware – bound by any duty of confidentiality but who see the patients coming and going and have access to our offices, where they may well come across confidential material, despite our ongoing vigilance. Even with perfect security, the patients' faces are on display as they come and go from appointments. There are also storage problems and costs associated with scanning/microfilming old records, which means that these are not always stored as securely as policy dictates, but perhaps may be left visible in the secretary's office. Our secretarial staff speak to the patients, type reports, and very quickly pick up an atmosphere if a therapist is stressed. How much do they need to know about what goes on in the therapy? What if a patient is potentially violent, or particularly upset and liable to be abusive on the phone? One might think in terms of a leaky container, where the leaks serve to release an otherwise intolerable pressure, but which must preserve a critical capacity to hold, without which it breaks down altogether. Armstrong has written about the changing nature of communication and its effect on organizations (Huffington et al., 2005). He suggests that what might previously have been regarded as a defensive splitting and fragmentation within organizations in order to avoid anxiety and pain might now need to be reinterpreted. Such a defence system may instead reflect a fragmentation that has been induced by powerful global and split-second technology. Defences against such fragmentation may well be necessary for survival and need to be worked with, rather than pathologized.

A closing vignette illustrates some of these issues.

Ms T was referred for a psychotherapy assessment suffering from low mood and troubled by events in her past life. The referrers were inexplicably tardy about supplying any background information, apart from that there had been domestic abuse. Ms T cancelled a number of appointments and did not return her pre-assessment questionnaire before finally attending. It turned out that the referrers were probably protecting Ms T's confidentiality as it emerged that her 'ex' was in prison for killing someone after he had left her. What was so striking was her subsequent – apparently chance – employment in the firm of solicitors that defended his case. Unbeknown to her boss, her ex's file was placed on her desk and she was asked to deal with his correspondence. Similarly, it transpired that her brother was a patient of this hospital, and she mentioned working here in the past, suggesting that she might also have had access to his records. The psychiatric diagnosis was post-traumatic stress disorder. The psychodynamic evaluation was far more complicated and encompassed extreme violence and boundary violations, of which her ex's story was but a part. It was uncertain whether or not Ms T would return for her follow-up appointment. In my view, her reluctance was, at least in part, generated by our need to spend so much time gathering those same facts that she had already divulged in another part of the Trust and which were not yet on the electronic record system. It had felt traumatic for Ms T to be recounting her tale yet again, although it was a trauma she seemed unable to leave behind her. If she did return, it seemed very likely that issues of confidentiality would be of particular complexity in this case.

There is a final question, and one that I believe has no ready answer. We frequently see patients who have been victims of child abuse, and who disclose this fact with the apparent ease of a much-rehearsed narrative. Thus there is often a multidisciplinary awareness of an abusing older adult, a stepfather, or maybe an older brother, who may have moved on to another relationship and now be the father of vulnerable younger children. Typically, this information is recorded in the notes, and we move on – sometimes to therapy, sometimes not. At times, however, the abuse information results in a rush of concern. I have been witness to Social Services being called in after one such assessment, with the police also becoming involved and the family – according to the patient, who had returned in fury – destroyed. It was perhaps a rather heavy-handed response on the part of services, but the 'suspect', her stepfather, was a teacher of young children and thus a risk. Furthermore, as far as I understand it, the response was in keeping with the provisions of the Children Act 1989. A more therapeutic approach would almost certainly have been to engage the patient in therapy and to hope that she could, in time, confront the situation from within; in the meantime, however, there were still children at risk.

We are not infrequently confronted with variations of such dilemmas and I have yet to hear a really satisfactory debate on this issue. To conclude where I began – it was once much clearer when we were able to respond according to the certainty of the Hippocratic Oath: '*What I may see or hear in the course of the treatment . . . I will keep to myself*'. Now none of us can be so sure.

Acknowledgements

I would like to thank Dr Humphrey Needham-Bennett, recent Trust Caldicott Guardian, for his interest and advice, as well as my colleagues and supervisors for ongoing support.

Note

1 Although there may be Tarasoff-style legal implications for the UK in a European Court of Human Rights' (2000) ruling on Osman vs UK (see Gavaghan, 2007).

References

Bollas, C. and Sundelson, D. (1995) *The New Informants: The Betrayal of Confidentiality in Psychoanalysis and Psychotherapy*, Northbrook, NJ: Jason Aronson.

British Psychoanalytic Council (2005a) *Guidelines on Notes and Records*. Available online at www.psychoanalytic-council.org (accessed 16 September 2008).

British Psychoanalytic Council (2005b) *Statement on Confidentiality*. Available online at www.psychoanalytic-council.org (accessed 16 September 2008).

Edelstein, L. (1943) *The Hippocratic Oath: Text, Translation, and Interpretation.* Baltimore: Johns Hopkins Press.

Furlong, A. (2006) 'Further reflections on the impact of clinical writing on patients', *International Journal of Psychoanalysis*, 87: 747–768.

Gabbard, G. and Williams, P. (2001) 'Preserving confidentiality in the writing of case reports', *International Journal of Psychoanalysis*, 82: 1067.

Garvey, P. and Layton, A. (2004a) *Comparative Confidentiality in Psychoanalysis*, London: International Psychoanalytic Association.

Garvey, P. and Layton, A. (2004b) *Patient records and confidentiality*. In P. Garvey and A. Layton (Eds.), *Comparative Confidentiality in Psychoanalysis* (pp. 37–55). London: International Psychoanalytic Association.

Gavaghan, C. (2007). 'A *Tarasoff* for Europe? A European Human Rights perspective on the duty to protect', *International Journal of Law and Psychiatry*, 30: 255–267.

General Medical Council (2004) *Confidentiality: Protecting and Providing Information*. Available online at www.gmc-uk.org/guidance/current/library/confidentiality. asp (accessed 25 May 2009).

Hayman, A. (1965) 'Psychoanalyst subpoenaed', *Lancet*, 16 Oct., 785.

Huffington, C., Armstrong, D., Halton, W., Hoyle, L. and Pooley, J. (Eds.) (2004)

Working below the Surface: The Emotional Life of Contemporary Organizations, London: Karnac.

Kantrowitz, J. (2004a) 'Writing about patients: I. Ways of protecting confidentiality and analysts' conflicts over choice of method', *Journal of the American Psychoanalytic Association*, 52: 69–99.

Kantrowitz, J. (2004b) 'Writing about patients: II. Patients' reading about themselves and their analysts' perceptions of its effect', *Journal of the American Psychoanalytic Association*, 52: 101–123.

Kantrowitz, J. (2004c) 'Writing about patients: III. Comparisons of attitudes and practices of analysts residing outside and within the USA', *International Journal of Psychoanalysis*, 85: 691–712.

Kantrowitz, J. (2005) 'Writing about patients: IV. Patients' reactions to reading about themselves', *Journal of the American Psychoanalytic Association*, 53: 103–129.

Royal College of Psychiatrists (2006) *CR33 Good Psychiatric Practice: Confidentiality and Information Sharing*, London: RCP.

Tarasoff v. Regents of the University of California (17 Cal.3d [1976]).

Chapter 11

Why do a psychoanalytic training?

Christopher Phillips

On the face of it, it is difficult to see the relevance of training in adult psychoanalysis for a child and adolescent psychiatrist working in the modern NHS. It is long and expensive, taking a minimum of four years and at its most intensive stage at least 20 hours a week, entailing as it does at the British Institute of Psychoanalysis a personal five-times-a-week analysis, two concurrent patients in five-times-a-week analysis, two one-hour supervisions – not to mention the time taken in session write-ups, and travel to and from home, place of work, consulting room, analyst's consulting room, and the Institute – all of which may be in different locations, and if you live some distance outside London there are train times to be taken into consideration. Add to this the fact that I don't actually *practise* psychoanalysis in the NHS, and as a consultant these days I don't even practise once-a-week psychoanalytic psychotherapy with young people, and the task of justifying my training to a sceptical, time- and money-conscious NHS manager seems at best Herculean, and at worst impossible.

Yet I find myself drawing on my analytic training day-in and day-out, while working each day in the NHS as a consultant psychiatrist. So it seems important to say why it should it be that something I find so useful in my working life often seems so hard to justify to someone else who, like me, wants to deliver the best possible health service they can to their patients.

What do I mean when I say I draw on my training every day? What is it that the analytic training has given me that is useful outside the analytic consulting room? Why should anyone working in the NHS undertake such an arduous training, unless his or her intention is to leave and go into private psychoanalytic practice?

Psychoanalysis has been described as a clinical method, a body of knowledge and an instrument of research, but fundamentally it places the subjective experience of the individual centre stage in all its deliberations. This includes the subjective experience of not just 'the patient' but also 'the clinician'; and, even more fundamentally, how one affects the other. The training comprises among other things a systematic exploration of personal experience: one's own and one's patients'. It demands that one continually ask such questions as 'what am I thinking and feeling, and why might I be doing so?' 'How much of what I am thinking and feeling (and doing) is being engendered in me by the presence of this other person?' I could at this point start to talk about the psychoanalytic concept of countertransference in clinical work, but instead let me describe a recent experience.

I am feeling rather bored at a junior doctor's presentation in a journal club I am chairing. I find myself increasingly frustrated at the rather dull presentation. I think, 'I can accept this boredom and go dutifully through the motions. Or maybe I can protest and tell everyone that I'm bored.' The junior doctor's delivery is in fact rather dull, monotonous and somewhat pompous. I could tell her this (as tactfully as possible – if I don't want to cultivate a reputation as a nasty piece of work), but I'm aware that this is hostile of me, and I'm not here to hone anyone's performance. But is my boredom just of her doing, or is it of my own, or of others in the meeting? The subject is quite interesting, so why am I bored? Although it is quite a polished PowerPoint presentation, there is an atmosphere in the room of others being bored too, as of everyone 'going through the motions'. I notice I've thought about going through the motions several times; 'There's no *life* in this', I find myself thinking. I associate to ideas of 'deadliness' and vaguely connect it to the repetition compulsion. 'There's no spirit of enquiry here', I find myself thinking, and then realize that I'm expecting everyone else to be doing the enquiring. So I start asking questions of the presenter and the audience. Genuine questions, however; not ones that I know the answers to and am asking in order to *impart* my knowledge, but questions that I would like answers to for myself, on areas that I think the juniors ought to be enquiring about. I tell them I don't have the answers myself but maybe they do, and if they don't, they need to find out from somewhere else, because they seem like important questions to me. Gradually the meeting starts to get some life in it. We all begin to become more curious about the article, the soundness or otherwise of the methodology, the validity of its conclusions from a statistical point of view, and so on. The debate gets quite lively, and we're actually having an interesting discussion, not just about the paper, but about kinds of knowledge.

On this occasion, I and the presenter get rated 8.5 out of 10 with 'an interesting topic' and 'a stimulating discussion' as two of the feedback comments.

I may sound self-congratulatory in this account but I have given the vignette, along with a few of my passing thoughts at the time, because it illustrates how I was automatically employing my psychoanalytic training not in an analytic treatment setting, but in a teaching situation. No doubt a group analyst, a sociologist, an educational psychologist or a management consultant would have their own very different way of describing or explaining what went on here, but from my point of view, and employing the language of psychoanalysis – I was reflecting on my immediate experience at the time; I was trying to sort out what came from me and what from others in the room; I identified projected aspects of my own mental functioning (my curiosity, my ignorance and lack of knowledge); I had vague associations to repetition and the repetition compulsion, and how it is against liveliness and creativity; and I thought I should try to come up with something that might help us all to stop 'going through the motions'. This led me eventually to make interventions that the meeting clearly found of some service to them and produced some interest and liveliness, and which, incidentally, I hadn't expected from myself at all. We all learned something new, I think.

Did I need to do the training to achieve this? I think I did, actually. And certainly some of the concepts I am referring to are peculiar to psycho-analysis, such as the 'repetition compulsion' and 'countertransference'.

In a more clinical vein, I would like to illustrate very briefly how I utilize a couple of psychoanalytic concepts in a rather broad and general way in thinking about my work with adolescent anorexic patients.

There is not space here to provide anything like a full clinical picture, but in my experience, the majority of these patients begin dieting because of a chronic and deep sense of dissatisfaction with themselves. They have a low opinion of themselves and rubbish, minimize and devalue their abilities. They have low self-esteem, low self-worth and they develop the belief that things would be a lot better for them, and they would feel better about themselves, if they were *thin*. Why being thin offers itself as a solution to the way they feel is an interesting question, but is linked to their belief that they are unhappy because they are fat and overweight. They want to improve themselves, their sense of themselves, and for life to be better for them; so that although they may be low in their mood, dieting is under-taken in an effort to regulate their self-esteem and improve their mood. Initially, they do not consciously want to starve themselves to death in an overtly suicidal fashion, although later in more chronic cases suicidality may enter the picture.

Prior to dieting they have often been driven to achieve academically, in sport or at ballet for example, in a desperate effort to prove to themselves and others that they *are* worth something; but no achievement is good enough to satisfy the merciless, undermining critic within. This hostile perfectionism subsequently comes to be applied to their dieting and pursuit of thinness, and for many patients, no matter how thin and underweight they become, it is *never thin enough*. This latter problem is why the con-dition can be so malignantly destructive, with such low weights attained.

Although there may be perceptual disturbances of body image, emo-tionally speaking, anorexic patients overvalue thinness, as well as having a morbid dread of being fat. Being thin becomes an idealized condition, being fat a dreaded and hated one, and possession of this idealized state or condition is seen as the solution to their emotional pain. Often this is also linked with notions of compensation, in that although they feel they can do nothing well; at least they can lose weight well. Thus their thinness and underweight state is experienced as a significant achievement attained for no one but themselves, and which, to some understandable extent, they do not want to relinquish.

In this constellation of emotional phenomena – the low self-esteem; a striving not so much for realistic attainments as for perfection; the denigration or dismissal of abilities; the hostile self-criticism; the mean and cruel deprivations anorexic patients subject themselves to; and so on, one can see in operation, I believe, an extremely harsh and cruel super-ego. In support of this suggestion is the intense sense of guilt that anorexic patients report when they transgress their self-imposed rules about what they can or can't eat. They aren't merely afraid of becoming fat through eating, but feel intensely and painfully bad and guilty if they succumb to the urge to eat, eat more calories than they have stipulated for themselves or eat a particular forbidden food.

There has been considerable elaboration and development of the concept of the super-ego, particularly by Kleinian analysts, since Freud first coined the term in the last of his major theoretical works, 'The Ego and the Id' (1927). This was a complex and difficult moment in Freud's theorizing in which he was bringing together his theory of instincts with a completely new structural theory of the mind. The concept as used today has evolved, deepened and broadened from Freud's original idea that the super-ego had its origin in identification with the father. Kleinian analysts, for example, would no longer fully subscribe to Freud's formulation as proposed in 'The Ego and the Id', since they would claim that the super-ego is present in rudimentary form from birth. Nevertheless, Freud's original conception remains fundamental to understanding and to using it clinically, and I want therefore to quote one or two pertinent extracts.

> Its relation to the ego is not exhausted by the precept, 'you ought to be like this . . .'. It also comprises the prohibition 'You may not be like this'.

> How is it that the super-ego manifests itself essentially as a sense of guilt (or rather as criticism – for the sense of guilt is the perception in the ego answering to this criticism) and moreover develops such extraordinary harshness and severity towards the ego? If we turn to melancholia first we find that the excessively strong super-ego which has obtained a hold upon consciousness rages against the ego with merciless violence [something equivalent, I am suggesting, occurs in severe cases of adolescent anorexia], as if it had taken possession of the whole of the sadism available in the person concerned. Following our view of sadism, we should say that the destructive component had

entrenched itself in the super-ego and turned against the ego. What is now holding sway in the super-ego is, as it were, a pure culture of the death instinct.

I do not want to be drawn into the controversial area of the validity or usefulness of the concept of the death instinct, but I quote this last passage as it conveys Freud's notion of how deadly the super-ego can be (developed a lot further by Wilfred Bion and others in the idea of the 'ego-destructive super-ego'). It conveys also what I often feel I am struggling against when trying to work with anorexic patients – an implacable force within them set against their abilities, their creativity, their development, and ultimately their life.

But there is another way of thinking psychoanalytically in general terms about these patients, employing one of Freud's earlier concepts first delineated in 1914, nine years before that of the super-ego. This is to employ the concept of *narcissism*; in particular the subsequent refinement of the concept – *destructive narcissism*.

This may sound like a contradiction of what I said above about anorexic patients having low self-esteem due to their harsh and cruel super-ego – for narcissism is fundamentally concerned with an *over*-valuation of the self, a falling in love with oneself, an inflated sense of one's worth. However, there is an equally important characteristic to narcissism which is a turning of one's libidinal interest, love, energies (or whatever) away from involvement with others to primarily relating to or being interested in oneself. In anorexia one sees this in operation powerfully not only in the rejection of food but in a whole anorexic attitude of turning away from, or against, attempts to help.

Anorexic patients have a completely preoccupying, and sometimes an almost exclusive relationship with their body; with how their body looks to themselves and to others. They feel it, they squeeze it, they pinch themselves, look at themselves constantly in the mirror, all in order to determine how fat or thin they are or are not. Yet despite these investigations they remain convinced, whatever their weight or appearance, that they are both fat and ugly, and that they not only need to lose weight but compulsively *must* lose weight.

I have found it very important clinically to address both the super-ego aspects and the narcissistic aspects of this disorder when working therapeutically with these patients.

So, for example, it was not until I pointed out to one young man who was at death's door, and so underweight that he could not walk because of muscle wasting, that secretly he felt incredibly superior to all of us because of his deadly achievement, that he finally turned the corner towards recovery and started to eat and regain weight. I did also acknowledge how hard it was going to be for him to give up being king of the world, albeit soon to be a dead one, and to be an ordinary, everyday, run-of-the-mill person.

Of course, I can't claim it was solely this change in my line of interpreting that was the key to his change of mind about eating – he was subject to many other therapeutic influences within an institutional setting – but I remember vividly how his progress coincided with me realizing I should be addressing his narcissism and not his super-ego conflicts. Did I need to do the training to work in this way with this boy? What do you think?

References

Freud, S. (1914) 'On Narcissism: An Introduction', *Standard Edition*, Vol. 14, pp. 67–102, London: Hogarth Press.

Freud, S. (1927) 'The Ego and the Id', *Standard Edition*, Vol. 19, pp. 1–66, London: Hogarth Press.

Chapter 12

Psychiatrist or psychoanalyst?

Do these disciplines combine or conflict?

Siobhan O'Connor

In my job as consultant psychiatrist I have worked in different settings while continuing private practice in psychoanalysis. In my current post, I have responsibility for two home treatment teams. The teams offer an alternative to acute admission and take patients out on early discharge when they are still requiring intensive input. The service is the equivalent to a ward at home, with visits twice a day.

My work has always focused on the more severely disturbed, most of the patients being those who present with acute schizophrenic or manic depressive psychoses. At the start of my previous post, in a psychiatric intensive care unit (PICU), I was asked sceptically whether I hoped to 'do psychotherapy' with the patients. My colleagues in psychiatry had no idea of the extent of training we get in psychoanalysis and how this affects the work we do. I did not try to explain that my modest aim was simply to take on the job to improve the psychiatric treatment for patients whom I had seen when I had covered for the consultant on leave. It was also a ward where I would be the only consultant, and I might be able to influence the culture in which the team worked.

My experience of the PICU made me aware that my training of junior doctors in their six-monthly rotations had quite an impact. Most of them chose the job because they wanted experience of a PICU, not knowing they would also get the experience of being supervised by a psychoanalyst. They discovered, in supervision with me, how emotional aspects can lead to departures from good practice in the more strictly 'medical' aspects of our work. They had a different type of supervision.

In addition, they could see how normal or even low-dose medication did work for the most severely disturbed, if one combined this with a more reflective approach. Research in psychopharmacology has shown that there is no benefit to be gained above the recommended dose of medication (Farde *et al.*, 1988; Van Putten *et al.*, 1993). So why are so many patients put on high dose with no obvious benefit? My struggle with persuading nurses and patients of this led to my first paper (O'Connor, 1998).

The role of the consultant psychiatrist

The psychoanalytic literature on the psychoses focuses attention on the transference and countertransference. Of the many debates about theory or technique, one was that of the emphasis given to phantasy versus reality, in terms of aetiology.

The focus is, of course, on the transference relationship with the treating psychoanalyst. How different is the situation for the psychiatrist in a setting where there is not a provision of formal psychotherapy. There is no psychoanalyst interpreting the hostility and bringing it into a different transference relationship. The transference is as Bion described, 'premature, precipitate and intensely dependent', but with the added influence of a reality that has its effects on both patient and clinician (Bion, 1957).

Consider, for instance, how the psychiatrist, instrumental in sectioning a patient, inevitably remains a figure with the power of the legal system. How different then is the communication between patient and clinician. The patient's projection is one of an omnipotent persecutory object who entraps or engulfs the patient. The psychiatrist cannot escape the role of persecutor, for he has restricted the patient's freedom and autonomy. How does he, at the same time, make contact with the patient and encourage separation or individuation? Making contact is the first step, but it is my view that the psychiatrist has to accept the inevitable persistence of a delusional transferential relationship.

My first clinical example will illustrate how the briefest of encounters encapsulates many aspects of what I do to bring psychoanalysis into my work, as clinician, supervising consultant, and trainer of junior doctors.

The setting was one in which I had agreed to act as locum consultant to a PICU for a period of three weeks before the new consultant took up post. The senior registrar had been working for many months in the ward and was well able to manage the clinical demands, but his training requirements were such that he needed a supervising consultant. I sat in on the ward round with an agreement that he would manage it, inviting me to speak at the end of his interviews.

Case example

Mrs R, a 40-year-old patient with a history of schizophrenia, was presented. She had been transferred to the PICU from another ward where she had been violent in her behaviour. The nurses reported that in the week since transfer she appeared suspicious, had made threatening comments, and there had been one episode of aggression. She had made comments suggestive of active hallucinations. They were sure that her paranoid delusions were ongoing, and that the threat of violence remained, but there was little content in her speech, apart from a suggestion that she was being poisoned. It was not enough to be sure of definite delusions. When brought in for interview she behaved in a polite, co-operative way, denying any problems, expressing her wish to be discharged. The senior registrar tried to elicit paranoid ideation, but she insisted that she was fine now; she knew she had been upset when she was admitted, but she put it down to marital problems in which she had lost her temper and had hit her husband.

The senior registrar then politely asked her if he could interview her husband. She said no, that it wasn't necessary. She made excuses as to how he was so busy, and the problem was over anyway. Getting little response from her, he invited me to speak.

I introduced myself and I started with my understanding of the situation. I rarely ask questions except to clarify. My style is in marked contrast to the many questions usually asked by psychiatrists, but as consultant I can come in after others have done the basic fact-finding. Patients usually respond by entering into conversation, even if only to correct me. I said that, as Dr S had mentioned, we were planning to interview her husband. She interrupted me, 'That is not my husband'. 'Oh,' I said, a little surprised. I gathered myself quickly and said 'You mean that man who visits the ward is not your husband?' 'No he is not, he is an impostor.' I noted to her the strangeness of this for, as I said, I assumed the nurses believed him to be her husband. Following her complaint about him being an impostor, she went on to complain about being in the PICU, mentioning her mother's appearance in her room, giving her beans for food. At this stage, not knowing whether her mother really visited bringing her food, I was totally reliant on her account of her experience of the ward.

I tried to explore the nature of her contact with her mother. I asked her if the nurses had seen her mother when she came with food. 'No, she just appears in the room.' As I talked with her, seeking clarification for some of the things she was telling me, she gave me a rich account of hallucinations and delusions, with omnipotent spirits who made these things happen. I asked her to explain some things further, such as how her mother was bringing her good food, yet she was also being sent by evil spirits. She told me that this was the nature of the spirits; they could be good or evil and could turn one into the other.

Following the interview, in which Mrs R had demonstrated her florid psychotic ideas, I was now surrounded by people who had not made such contact. I had to find a way of managing the feelings that might be engendered by this encounter. I knew from experience how powerful the reaction might be, and knew that a focus was needed. It was quite a different situation to one in which I work with my own team. They become accustomed to my approach, able to value it, as something that we offer as a team.

I decided to explain to the senior registrar what I thought had happened. I noted that his polite request to interview this patient's husband was a denial of reality. In her delusional transference he was inevitably the persecutor who had restricted the patient's freedom. As far as she was concerned, he was being false, and she was politely going along with him, playing his false game. I had not denied being a persecutor in my statement that we were planning to interview her husband. His polite request was a denial of the genuine situation, for he would interview her husband against her will if he felt it necessary. I was trying to show how important it was to accept her psychic reality, to become the container of projections. I find that patients, and many others, generally have an exaggerated view of the power of consultant psychiatrists. This 'powerful object' is seized upon in psychoses, and we become easy receptacles for their projections.

The senior registrar was interested in teasing out the detail with me, reminding me of modern approaches to patients in which one had to respect their rights. I pointed out that in the face of violence, with a risk to herself or others, it was the case that we had to consider whether to override the patient's right to privacy or confidentiality. I suggested that the patient knew this, and that this was a reality that he could not deny. He was a thoughtful and experienced clinician. We teased out the reality and he acknowledged that it was true that he would override her refusal if he felt it necessary.

When I said to Mrs R that the nurses believed the man to be her husband, I allowed for her projection in her belief that the nurses were confused, not she, without me colluding in her delusions. I believed her psychic reality and she felt encouraged to elaborate on it, including her complaint at one point that I already knew all of this. This was further evidence of her belief that I was an omnipotent being. Without denying that 'I knew it all', I said I wanted to hear her experience of it all.

I shall describe my further contact with this patient to illustrate how poignant it is to have made contact and yet know that it can only be brief.

In my third and final week in this ward, Mrs R was being brought to the ward round following a decision to change her medication. There had been no change, with further violent episodes. Her attitude remained one of there being nothing wrong. I spoke to her briefly at the end. As I came to the end of the interview she asked if she could leave now. I clarified that she could leave but back to the ward, not home. 'So I am dismissed?' Feeling the impact of those words, I said again that she could go now, but back to the ward. She got up slowly and walked towards the door, turning in a regal manner, bowing slightly, her hand on her breast, and she asked, 'But am I dismissed from your heart?' I felt quite thrown by this comment and answered no, that I would be thinking of her.

When she left, I commented to the junior doctor beside me on how touching was her comment. She said that she felt puzzled by all that had gone on between us, for she could only see a patient who had demonstrated her delusions and hallucinations to me. She couldn't see how I had done it, but she had also not seen her final comment as touching, in the way that I had. Although I was quite stunned and saddened by what she said, I was also reminded of what I often say about the medical model acting as a defence against the emotional impact of what we do.

Following the first interview, the senior registrar said that he welcomed my observations, a rare opportunity of having his interview observed. It is rare in psychiatry to report what one says to the patient, unlike the usual supervision in psychoanalysis. It is not uncommon for me to observe a junior and pick up on a style that denies the psychotic reality of the patient. One such example was when my junior doctor was interviewing a severely depressed man who had delusions of guilt and feelings of worthlessness. He asked him how he thought we, as a home treatment team, could help him. I was quite shocked by that question. The man said he didn't know. Later, I pointed out to my trainee that of course the man thought he was so guilty and worthless he could not be helped, and his asking him the question suggested that he didn't know either how to help him. The question itself was enough to increase the man's feelings of hopelessness.

I told a consultant colleague about this, remarking that I thought this type of question might have crept in with an approach of seeing patients as 'clients' or 'users'. She suggested it was the way the question was asked. She often asked the same question. I hesitated, but told her that I thought no matter what way it was asked, it had the same impact.

Making contact with the family

In my work with the home treatment team, I have mainly a supervisory and consultative role. I supervise the formal presentations of psychiatric history, and become more involved to solve diagnostic issues. At the same time I am listening to the dynamics, on one hand reflecting on the history given, but also aware of how the staff are talking about patients and their families. In their experienced approach they usually accept even the most aggressive behaviour in families as possibly defensive in nature.

Treating the patients at home during an acute psychosis involves a major shift in the provision of 'family interventions'. Family members are observed managing the crisis in a way that is not the same as any 'psychotherapy' that involves inpatient admission.

The team now call on me sometimes to intervene in difficult family dynamics, but this follows their experience of my having intervened when I detected something unusually intense, or discordant. In the following example I became aware of the change in the way the staff were talking about the patient's mother.

Camilla was a 20-year-old student who had been collected by her sister from her college in the north because of the family's awareness of something seriously wrong. On their arrival in London the police had to be called to the train station because of her bizarre behaviour. She would have been detained in hospital had our team not felt that they could work with her mother, who was prepared to take time off from her own job to stay with her constantly.

Camilla was clearly suffering from a severe psychotic illness. The junior doctor's preliminary notes on her mental state are enough to illustrate this:

> Camilla unable to give any useful history at all. She sat at dinner table eating biscuits and fruit, and barely acknowledged us. Her mother gave most of the history. Camilla's behaviour was very fluctuant. She would at one point be sitting laughing to herself, and then rapidly change to tears and intense fearfulness, with hysterical flavour. At one point she sat rocking in the armchair, with her right arm half outstretched in front of her, her hand half clasped as if holding melon-sized object, and rocking her arm from right to left, with her eyes and head following the hand. She would also repeatedly tap or rub her abdomen. She appeared to consciously withdraw her hand and arm away from me when I tried to examine it. There was no evidence of waxy flexibility.

The reference to 'waxy flexibility' was his examination for catatonia, the most severe presentation of schizophrenic illness. Camilla had to be physically fed and washed by her mother, who reported having had to stop her running out into the street wearing only a T-shirt, along with other forms of agitated activity alternating with withdrawn states. Her mother reported going to bed with her in the afternoon in some of these states.

I decided to intervene because I detected the development of an unusual antagonism to the mother by the team. Having initially been admiring of her mother for devoting her time, they had moved into criticism of her. Their complaint was that her mother was so intrusive that they could not get an interview with Camilla on her own. They expressed the belief that Camilla would not talk in her mother's presence. Her mother was praying for her, and the staff felt she might be relying on faith so much that she was not giving the medication. In the same discussion they complained that the mother was putting her tablets in her tea, and they felt this was unethical. One comment was that it seemed as if her mother was enjoying the fact of her being ill.

Camilla had told her very religious mother that she had had an abortion a few months before. Her mother accepted that this might have precipitated the illness, but at this point we were not even sure whether it was true or a delusion.

My notes on my interview

Her mother greeted us, but said that Camilla was in the shower. I noted the pictures of Camilla, surrounded by candles, like a little altar. Initially she spoke to Veronica, the key nurse with me, to describe how well Camilla had been yesterday evening. She gave details of a shopping trip, which included Camilla bringing out her savings of two £50 notes and paying for shopping, her mother thanking her. But now she seemed relapsed again this morning. There was a lot of detail about her food, her mother demonstrating Camilla cutting a pie into four. She described all this with great pleasure. I could see how her reaction could be seen as one of delighting in her daughter being ill, one of the nurses' complaints. However, I also thought of it in the context of a girl who had had to be bathed and fed by her mother, so that cutting a pie was seen as an improvement.

I let her talk to Veronica, whom she knew, but intervened with a few questions to ask mother to clarify. She gave a very full account of Camilla's personal history, but I noted to myself the defensive way she told it. For example, she gave explanations as to why, when she came to England, she left her in the care of relatives, reassuring me that this was usual in her culture. They were 'good and Christian', she said.

Throughout our conversation she seemed to need to throw in comments that suggested to me that she wondered whether Camilla might have been abused or traumatized, e.g. 'I don't think she was abused there, she was very happy'. Regarding the recent onset she said that Camilla had visited her father abroad, and she had questioned Camilla's brother as to whether anything might have happened there.

I discussed with Camilla's mother the references she had made to possible causation. My approach in such an interview is to tell, rather than ask; taking the view that if I outline a few tentative theories, the person listening can see that these are not absolute and understand that I am also willing to hear about their own theories.

I suggested that it was unlikely that Camilla's current mental state was due to a trauma such as she was looking for. Even if her mother did find that something had happened, I would doubt that it was the cause of this. She seemed relieved by my explanation. She went on to correct some of the things she had told the team. The family with whom she had left Camilla were not relatives as she had told the team; and she was actually separated from Camilla's father, something she had denied to the team, although in fact the team had already doubted her account. She gave me her theories in her description of Camilla's personality, saying that she was someone who had always been introverted.

I had to ask her a couple of times whether she would like Camilla to join us. Eventually she called Camilla, who came in and greeted Veronica with 'hello', and sat down clutching a tea towel and a bangle. Up to this point, my conversation with her mother might be seen as that of the experienced psychiatrist, but my way of interviewing has developed in the course of my analytic training.

To illustrate the difference, when I need to have an interpreter, for example, I now give careful instructions, because so many interpreters will 'helpfully' add their own bit to my words, particularly when there is a silence. I point out that I don't ask questions, and ask the interpreter not to pose my words as questions. If the person doesn't answer; 'don't say anything more,' I say, 'I will see the response.' I ask the interpreter to wait, even if there is a long silence, or if the patient or relative looks uncomfortable, tearful or angry. I explain that this is something that I need to see.

I tried to make contact with a now silent Camilla by hypothesizing on what she seemed to be communicating. She avoided eye contact, though she did look directly at me at least once. I commented on the towel she was holding and how she was doing a lot of cleaning these days and it might be that she felt she was unclean. I added that perhaps she thought she was dirty because of something she had done. (I was thinking of the termination and of sex.) There was a slight nod of agreement to both of these. I also suggested that she might think that we were unable to help her with these things because of what she had done. Again, a nod from her in response. There were other things I said that elicited no response, so I then said that obviously I was guessing and maybe I had some things wrong. She nodded yes to this.

I went on to suggest that there might be something preventing her from talking, and preventing her from telling us. (Often, the search for the phenomenology of hallucinations ignores more primitive forms of resistance.) I kept this to the idea of 'something' forbidding her. She agreed with a slight nod of her head. I then suggested that it must be very lonely for her to be trapped into not being able to talk about what was troubling her.

At this point her mother, who was clearly moved by the way I was interviewing her daughter, took the towel from Camilla as if to facilitate her paying a little more attention to me, and then, quite tearful, she left the room for me to continue the interview. Camilla did not speak to me when her mother left, confirming to the nurse present that it was not the case that she could not speak because of her mother's presence.

The effect of the interview was very powerful. Camilla's mother had had an experience of emotional contact. I could discuss with the team the relationship between mother and daughter, and outline the idea of there being a symbiotic relationship in regression. I could help them see her mother's behaviour in a more positive light as her attempt to make contact, to mother her daughter, in the face of her worry about how her previous relationship might have failed her daughter.

Camilla's mother then showed more trust in the team, for she knew that they discussed their contact with me. The team easily accepted Camilla's subsequent focus on me, with the development of a delusional transference in which she became preoccupied with the idea that I had 'stolen her eggs'. She elaborated these delusions when I saw her again, with ideas that I had been present at an operation in which her eggs were stolen against her will. Mindful as I was that I had become a persecutor, a focus for many of her delusions, I was aware that we now could contain such projections within our teamwork.

Shifting between psychoanalytic and psychiatric models in the clinical work

The concept of shifting from a psychiatric to a psychoanalytic model has been of great relevance in my work. There is an advantage in making contact with patients, but there is also a risk if one is not aware of the limitations. If, as psychiatrist, I am thinking analytically, paying attention to the meaning of communication rather than the psychiatric phenomenology, I can miss important aspects crucial to management of the illness. I became aware of this in the intensive care unit, the responsible psychiatrist with no other psychoanalysts or trained psychoanalytic psychotherapists available at all.

While working with one patient in particular, I had been listening with an analytic ear, and had not noticed the signs of relapse. During the sessions, the only change was a greater degree of freedom in his speech. I was not to know that this was more linked with the sexually disinhibited behaviour he was demonstrating elsewhere, an early sign of relapse. The nurses had not alerted me to the changes because they assumed that, given the amount of time I spent with him, I would notice. There was a degree of safety in that this took place in a secure setting, but the patient was having unescorted leave and there was a potential risk of violence. It was fortunate that there was nothing more serious before we picked this up. His arrogant attitude to the nurses, with his idealization of me, to whom he referred as 'the one who knows', had married only too well with their own enthusiasm about my new approach to the ward, so that they were too close to seeing me as 'the one who knows'.

Teaching and training

In our hospital there are limited psychotherapy resources, to such an extent that I give a weekly session to supervise junior doctors in their psychotherapy cases in the absence of available consultant psychotherapists. Thus, I had to decide whether I could give some small input into the training of students for whom I am firm head. I decided to lay a little groundwork by giving them a positive view of Freud and psychoanalysis. I use one of their tutorials to give a 'historical introduction to psychotherapy'. I find that those who have heard of Freud have only heard criticisms. In another I introduce a reflective approach, discussing the emotional impact of not just the psychiatric patients, but encouraging them to discuss many of the traumas and difficulties they face in their medical and surgical rotations.

Surely this is something that should be provided in the medical curriculum, a development from Balint's work with GPs?

In this chapter, I can only give some examples of how I bring psycho-analysis into my work. The reader may be able to discern that my training in psychoanalysis has enriched my experience as a psychiatrist to the degree where I feel I make greater contact with patients and their families. In the knowledge that this direct contact is limited, I have chosen to use this experience to teach and train. As a consultant who uses the medical model, strictly adhering to what is seen as 'evidence-based practice', I demonstrate the relevance of a psychodynamic formulation in the most acute and severe illnesses. My private work in psychoanalysis allows me the satisfaction of in-depth work with patients, along with my work with psychoanalytic colleagues which keeps me grounded so that I don't fall into the trap of seeing myself as the 'omnipotent consultant psychiatrist'. For the reader might also see in my account how powerful an attraction there is in supervising eager trainees who are keen to take on an approach that helps them with the difficulties.

References

Bion, W.R. (1957) 'Differentiation of the psychotic from the non-psychotic person-alities', *Second Thoughts*, London: Karnac.

Farde, L., Wiesel, F.A., Halldin, C. and Sedvall, G. (1988) 'Central D2-dopamine receptor occupancy in schizophrenic patients treated with antipsychotic drugs', *Archives of General Psychiatry*, 45: 71–76.

O'Connor, S. (1998) 'An analytic approach in a Psychiatric Intensive Care Unit', *Psychoanalytic Psychotherapy*, 12 (1): 3–15.

Van Putten, T., Marshall, B.D., Liberman, R., Mintz, J., Kuehnel, T.G., Bowen, L., et al. (1993) 'Systematic dosage reduction in treatment-resistant schizophrenic patients', *Psychopharmacological Bulletin*, 29: 315–320.

Chapter 13

'It was an accident waiting to happen!'

An investigation into the dynamic relationship between early-life traumas and chronic post-traumatic stress disorder in adulthood[1]

Mary Brownescombe Heller

It is difficult to think of traumatic events these days without thoughts of September 11 2001, or July 7 2005, coming to mind: 'Nine-Eleven' and 'Seven-Seven', as most people now say, in an attempt to shrink these disasters into something more manageable; yet the after-effects continue to reverberate.

My chapter is not about this kind of headline-hitting, global disaster, but it is about the way in which certain events, experienced as traumatic, can shatter the lives of individuals, leaving them changed for ever. To illustrate this I shall recount the stories of four people from the 22 participants who took part in a research project I undertook a few years ago. The aim of the research was to explore the underlying antecedents of chronic post-traumatic stress disorder (PTSD) in adults. There are parallels with July 7 and September 11, since not only does trauma rupture the containing skin of the self, which can lead to a catastrophic collapse of psychic structure, but in chronic PTSD people can feel that they are living in a terrorist state, in which action predominates and reflective thought becomes impossible.

Trauma implies a break with the continuities of life, a threat to survival, a terrifying meeting with death. This can lead to the emergence of primitive defences to ward off unbearable, unthinkable anxieties. What we shall see in these four individuals suffering from PTSD is a disintegration of ego structures, resulting in their egos becoming taken over by terrorizing objects.

Greg worked on the Teesside docks. Eight years before I saw him, he had been shifting crates when a sling-load of steel bars, being lowered by a crane, inadvertently swung around and knocked him to the ground. He lay there helpless, watching this sling-load descend ever closer. He was convinced that he was going to be crushed to death. A workmate, seeing what had happened, shouted a warning to the crane-driver who managed to stop the load inches short of where Greg lay. He was pulled free, having suffered severe bruising to his shoulder where he had been hit by the steel bars. Since then, he has experienced nightmares and almost daily 'flashbacks' of a near-delusional type. Antidepressant and anxiolytic medication has not helped, nor have several episodes of counselling and cognitive behavioural therapy

(CBT). Over the years Greg has made numerous suicide attempts and when I met him, in his early fifties, he was in a very dejected and hopeless state. He told me:

> I'll open the door to the living room . . . and it's like I'm there . . . the whole thing happening again. Steel has a taste, you know. And I can see, taste, smell, hear, feel . . . that sling-load of steel as it comes towards me. Your heart starts racing and you're physically sick. It's there . . . and you can't get away from it.

Frances was attacked by a female schizophrenic patient while on night nursing duty. This patient was one with whom Frances had a special relationship, being able to calm her down when others failed. Frances had always enjoyed her work. This unexpected attack left her with a split lip and bruising on her arms and shoulders; she was otherwise physically unhurt, but very frightened by the patient's threats to kill her. She has been unable to work since and has made at least one serious suicide attempt.

She says, some three years later:

> My whole idea of life has gone. I can't function . . . I can't work . . . I can't think . . . I see *her* all the time. She's with me wherever I go. To live every day is such an effort. All I want to do is scream. I feel terribly ashamed and guilty because my whole family is suffering.

Like Greg and Frances, it is typical for those who suffer from chronic PTSD to feel an overwhelming sense of helplessness in their attempts to defend themselves against what are experienced as mad intruders. Their traumatizing events cannot be consigned to the past so that ordinary life can continue. These events remain concretely in the here and now of the present, being endlessly repeated in their minds and bodies.

'Daphne', a professional woman in her mid-forties, was in the front passenger seat of their large car, with her husband at the wheel. They were going up a steep hill when Daphne saw a flashing light ahead coming straight towards them. She just had time to register that it was a police car being driven by a woman police officer before it hit them full on and bounced into another car, which had swerved to avoid the accident. Daphne reported how their car had 'cannoned like a snooker ball' backwards down the hill before her husband managed to stop the car by crashing it into a stone wall. Apart from seatbelt burns and whiplash, neither Daphne nor her husband was seriously injured. Nor, miraculously, were the other drivers, although all three cars were write-offs. 'What made it worse,' Daphne told me, 'was that it was a police car. The police are supposed to protect you, not crash into you!'

Since that time, four years ago, Daphne has suffered from chronic pain in her neck, back and shoulders. It is supposed that her nerve-endings have been damaged and she has had several operations to remove nerve roots – to no avail. Daphne told me that the accident had left her with 'an exaggerated startle response'. She is irritable and intolerant, breathless and jumpy. She has given up work and is constantly ruminating about death. When her husband takes her out in the car, she will scream when she sees other vehicles coming towards them. She perceives danger everywhere and now almost never leaves her home.

Peter, the last of these four participants, must be at least six feet five inches in height, and substantially built. He tells me tearfully at our first meeting, 'I've lost a lot of weight since the accident'. I understand him to be telling me that it's not just body mass that he has lost, but something much more significant.

Peter is in his early thirties and married, with two small children. Until the accident, he said he'd never had a day's illness and certainly had never been anywhere near the Mental Health Services. He was well thought of by his employers at the mining company. As part of his work, along with the other men, he would tip barrow-loads of rock through a metal grid floor down to heavy steel rollers below. From there it would be conveyed along a continuous belt to rotating teeth which broke up the larger pieces, before being carried to pulverising grinders somewhere out of sight. On this particular evening, two and a half years ago, Peter had already made a couple of trips with the heavy barrows. It was nearing the end of his shift and he was looking forward to going home and watching the match. Next week was his interview for one of the supervisor posts. He thought it was fairly certain that he would get the job. It would be good to have more money and better hours. He'd be able to go out regularly with his wife and see more of the children.

As usual, he wheeled the barrow onto the centre of the grid and began tipping the contents through the metal bars. Without warning, the metal floor gave way, catapulting him down on to the steel rollers, 15 feet below. He lay there, jack-knifed, helpless and unable to move, only the collapsed metal flooring beneath him preventing his passage along the conveyer belt and into the mouth of the rock crushers. Although he was in a great deal of pain, he was fully conscious and all he could think about was being pulled towards the metal teeth and torn to pieces.

Fortunately, one of Peter's mates had seen what had happened and ran to the main circuit switch, throwing it into reverse and stopping the conveyor belt. 'I can't have been laid there more than a couple of minutes before the power was turned off,' Peter said, 'but it felt like time had stopped for ever.'

Peter was taken by ambulance to Accident and Emergency. It was thought at first that his back was broken, but this turned out to be severe swelling and bruising. They said in the hospital that he was very lucky to have got away so lightly. Since that time Peter has been unable to work on the site. He has tried going back several times, but gets overcome with utter panic. He is often physically sick and he still has nightmares several times a week. In these, not only does he fall into the pit, but he experiences himself being crushed through the revolving teeth of the grinders. He wakes drenched in sweat, his heart pounding. He has withdrawn from his social life, he doesn't play football with the lads anymore, he can't concentrate on anything for more than a few minutes, his libido has dwindled to zero, his relationship with his wife has suffered, he is irritable with the children, he hates being in the house on his own and he is continually preoccupied with thoughts of dying. Disasters, such as the Lockerbie air crash, keep coming into his mind. He only has to look up and see a plane to think that it will come crashing to the ground, killing all the occupants. He was put on antidepressants by his GP, but they made him feel worse so he stopped taking them. Previously, Peter had looked forward to a future in which he might become a manager in the company. He is currently employed part-time on light driving duties, but he has had so much time off, he wonders how much longer the bosses will want him to continue working.

'All the men thought,' Peter told me, 'that the grid floor was properly welded in, and that it was a secure base, but it was just resting on the sides of the pit.' As he told me this, it was the only time he showed anger. Otherwise, he gave the impression of a man who'd had the stuffing completely knocked out of him. He continued, 'The company should never have allowed it to be like that. They should have made sure the base was secured. It was an accident waiting to happen!'

Given what happened to Peter, it is understandable that he should have felt severely shocked. But why should he still be suffering in such a terrible way more than two years after the event? After all, the hospital said that he had got away quite lightly, all things considered. Indeed, why should all 22 of the people involved in my research project still be so disabled?'

Those of us who have been involved in some sort of potentially life-threatening event (which would be the vast majority of us) know that for a while we tend to be hypervigilant and experience a startle reaction when something similar happens, or seems like it is about to happen. In my case, after a house fire many years ago, if I smelt smoke even several weeks later my heart would start racing. More recently, after being bumped into, on the front passenger side, by another car on a roundabout, for two or three months afterwards I would give an involuntary gasp if a car approached at speed from the left. Normally, we expect such responses to dampen down over time, so that after a few months it isn't that we've forgotten the incident, but rather there is a sense of the anxiety to do with it fading and becoming a past memory. This was certainly not the case with the four people I've just talked about. Far from fading, if anything their anxiety was becoming worse and the traumatizing incidents were still felt to be very much in the present – as Peter said, 'It felt like time had stopped for ever.'

So here are two puzzles: Why do some people recover fairly quickly from an exposure to accidents and other dangers whereas others continue to suffer from that combination of symptoms that we call PTSD; that is, of preoccupying intrusive thoughts and feelings about an event experienced as dangerous, in combination with compulsive attempts to avoid such thoughts and feelings? And why do some 10–15% (Kaplan and Sadock, 1998) of these people not recover from the acute stage of PTSD, but go on experiencing for years all the physiological and psychological consequences of a life-threatening incident as if it had happened only yesterday?

There are a number of studies which suggest that the development of PTSD and its recovery time depend on the nature, severity and perceived threat of the trauma (e.g. Weisaeth, 1984). But this can't be the whole story, since the majority of people who are exposed to potentially traumatizing incidents either don't develop PTSD or, if they do, they recover within a few months or so and are able to continue with their lives (Zohar *et al.*, 1998); so I think we would have to assume that it is not only the event in itself that determines the response. It has been proposed in the research literature that certain factors to do with the person themselves play a part in the development of PTSD. These are the ones I came across, in no particular order of significance: female gender, neuroticism, lack of social support, family history of psychiatric illness, adverse childhood experiences including violent assaults, previous exposure to traumatic events, pre-existing mental disorders, a tendency to avoid conflicts rather than confront them, inherited susceptibility, and a wish to claim compensation (Breslau *et al.*, 1999; Ehlers *et al.*, 1998; Horowitz, 1993; McFarlane, 1990; Skre *et al.*, 1993; Zohar *et al.*, 1998). While these various factors are of interest, and I will come back to some of them later in relation to my research findings, they don't in themselves take us further forward in a specific understanding of how and why, in Peter's case for example, the collapse of the metal grid base and his consequent fall into the waste pit should have produced in him such a devastating and apparently permanent *psychic* collapse and fall.

This is where I think an analytic explanation, based on early attachment experiences that have left the individual vulnerable or 'at risk', becomes so helpful. John Bowlby, a psychoanalyst and attachment theorist, pointed out that the normal function of any mother is to keep her babies safe from anxieties real or imagined, to keep them secure in the face of intrusions that might threaten their survival (Bowlby, 1988; Holmes, 1993). In the same way, it is the ordinary, instinctual expectation of the baby that there is a mother to understand and deal with his anxieties, to keep him safe from predators and other dangers. The human child, like other species that are born helpless and have a lengthy period of dependency on their parents, has both a capacity to be sensitive to danger and an expectation of maternal care (Bowlby, 1969). The internal world is developed and shaped by the actual relationship experiences of the child, but is also coloured and changed by the child's feelings and phantasies regarding these relationships. Melanie Klein pointed out that the young infant's capacity for self-preservation depends on his trust in a good mother. 'This is an essential condition for keeping alive,' she wrote; 'without at least some of this feeling, he would be exposed to an entirely hostile world which he fears would destroy him' (Klein, 1959, p. 253). Thus, the presence of the *internal* caretaking mother moderates fearful phantasies, ameliorates dangers, provides the secure base to our world, reassures us and helps put us back together when things go wrong. If the actual mother, for whatever reason, fails seriously in this containing, caretaking function, or is absent, physically or emotionally, for too long a time for the small child to hold in mind, then what is internalized is a negation where a mother should have been. The nothingness of this experience is equivalent to a disaster. The 'no mother' who is present is not just an absent mother, but an unrepresentable space, a negative presence that takes over in a frighteningly persecutory way. The situation is, of course, made so much worse when there is no father to support mother and child.

So a psychoanalytic view would argue that where there has been good enough parenting and a sufficiency of loving, consistent mothering, we internalize the capacity to care for ourselves in the bad times as well as the good. This internal presence cushions the knocks and enables us to recover our equilibrium after a potentially life-threatening event. Conversely, if there has been too much missing in terms of security, reliability, love and protection, we are likely to be left vulnerable when faced with such events. This 'vulnerability factor' can help explain why some people develop PTSD when others do not. But there is also the linked question to do with recovery – why do some people go on to develop *chronic* PTSD when others, equally affected initially by a traumatizing incident are eventually able to put the trauma into the past where it belongs? These were the questions I wanted to explore in my research, and hopefully to throw more light on them.

Psychoanalytic thinking began with Freud's 'psychical trauma' theory, which he developed in the early 1890s. In essence, Freud argued that when the young child experienced disturbing or painful events that were beyond his developmental capacity to deal with, they remained as unintegrated 'foreign bodies', lodged deep within his psyche, yet always with the potential to be reactivated. We might think of this as Peter's 'accident waiting to happen'. Since then, although the theories have become more complex and sophisticated, psychoanalytic therapists, for example Caroline Garland in her work with trauma survivors at the Tavistock Clinic (1998), have continued to argue that early disturbances in the parent–child relationship leave the individual adult vulnerable to a breakdown of adequately functioning defences, when exposed to severely stressful situations. Among others, the American psychiatrist and psychoanalyst Mardi Horowitz (1992, 1993), who was so influential in having PTSD recognized as a diagnostic entity, suggested that a predisposition to experience a particular kind of stressor as traumatic may be due to that stressor having a *meaning* that makes the nature of the event particularly shocking.

So in what way was Peter vulnerable, and what specifically did this 'accident waiting to happen' *mean* to him, that it should have left him physically recovered but mentally so dreadfully disabled? What kind of *internal* 'collapse and fall' was being repeated? For Frances too, in what way was she vulnerable and what did this attack by a female schizophrenic patient mean to her, that she now cannot escape from this mad *internal* object? And what about Daphne, who said that her *nerve endings* were damaged? Or Greg, who was constantly replaying the scene of a near-fatal accident in his living room?

Freud, from work with traumatized soldiers in the Great War of 1914–1918, described the psychologically wounding effects of trauma as a 'breaching of the protective shield' (Freud, 1920). While Freud does not specifically say this, I think it is implicit in what he writes about trauma that this protective shield represents the containing skin function of the internal mother, whose capacity to protect her offspring has been breached by the excessive force of the traumatizing stimulus. Accidents, losses and frustrations inevitably stir up intense feelings. A young child needs the understanding of a helpful adult if he or she is to be able to deal with such feelings. Otherwise, with no such 'container', these intense feelings threaten to overwhelm the child and can thus be dealt with only by such means as projection, fragmentation, somatizing or splitting (Garland, 1998). Bion describes vividly the state of an infant whose anxieties have not been contained by the maternal function of 'reverie'. Such a child is beset by what Bion calls *nameless dread* (Bion, 1962). In essence, this is to do with terrifying doubts about the possibility of survival in a world full of attacking objects. Whether we are child or adult, mother is supposed to be there watching out for us. This internal world mother functions to provide an umbrella, a safety net and a shock absorber. The negation of a mother, or 'no-mother present', generates a phantasy of malevolent objects – such as the grinding, pulverizing teeth, waiting to gobble him up, towards which Peter is inexorably drawn in his nightmares.

Peter said, 'All the men thought that the grid floor was welded in, and that it was a secure base, but it was just resting on the sides of the pit. The company should never have allowed it to be like that. They should have made sure the base was secured. It was an accident waiting to happen.'

If we substitute the parents as a couple, and mother as the primary object, for the mining company, Peter would be saying something like this: 'I expected to come into this world and have a secure base – a secure start to life. But it wasn't safe; it was dangerous ground that my parents provided me with. They should never have allowed it to be like that. My mother should have made sure the base she and my father gave me was properly secured. I was always in danger of falling into a terrible pit of despair and depression. It was *me* that was an accident waiting to happen.'

Of course, you might want to protest that what I've just said is conjecture. We need some evidence to back this up. So this brings me back to my research. Over a period of about two years, I interviewed everyone referred to the NHS Clinic where I worked in Teesside who was diagnosed as suffering from chronic PTSD (American Psychiatric Association, 1994). Twenty-three people met the criteria that there should have been a clear traumatizing incident, which did not involve a head injury, and that the condition should have been actively present for at least six months. Twenty-two agreed to take part. The traumatic events included industrial accidents, violent personal assaults, road traffic accidents, and the death or murder of a closely attached person. The 10 women and 12 men had been suffering from PTSD for between one and 20 years, averaging just over five years. They were between 31 and 66 years old, with an average age in the mid-forties. All socio-economic classes were represented, from the long-term unemployed to professions such as the police, education, the law and nursing. We can see straight away that for this group the previously found gender bias towards women did not apply, since the sexes were more or less equally represented.

Although this was not one of the criteria for selection, it was also of note that, like Frances, Greg, Daphne and Peter, all reported that they had been in good mental and physical health prior to the traumatic incident. As far as could be ascertained, all of them, too, had been in reasonably stable marital or partner relationships. So again, for this group of 22, previous findings that chronic PTSD is based on a lack of social supports, or on a psychiatric history or previous neurotic symptoms, did not apply. Indeed, of the 22 before the traumatizing incident, only one person had ever experienced a serious depressive incident – and that had been nearly 20 years before the trauma that resulted in his PTSD. This is fewer than you would expect in a normal population (Singleton *et al.*, 2002).

The main research task was to explore systematically whether some individuals might be said to have a predisposition towards the development of chronic PTSD and, if so, what was the nature of this predisposition. To do this, I used a variety of well-known psychometric tests, such as the Beck Depression Inventory, but the main research tool of the study was the 'Adult Attachment Interview' (AAI). Following the assessments, which took several visits, some participants opted to join a PTSD support group while a number of others entered psychotherapy on an individual or group basis.

The AAI is a semi-structured interview that reveals the individual's current state of mind regarding their childhood attachment relationships, along with their thinking patterns and strategies of affect-regulation in relation to these attachment experiences. It was originally devised by Mary Main and her co-workers, who based it on work by John Bowlby and Mary Ainsworth, with the intention of using it to explore the attachment histories of mothers with young children (Holmes, 1993, 2001). Mary Main wrote that the aim of the AAI was 'to surprise the unconscious into self-revelation' (1991).

The interview is audio-recorded and takes about an hour and a half to administer. The resulting narrative is coded via a content and discourse analysis. Dysfluencies in the discourse around certain events would indicate incomplete psychological processing of the event. What is important in the coding process is not so much *what* people say but *how* they say it and whether their narratives are internally consistent. Past experiences and events do not, in themselves, determine attachment status, even when these events were traumatic. What is important in determining the individual's state of mind with regard to attachment is the extent to which the parents' relation to the child, and their handling of potentially traumatizing situations, were perceived by the speaker as trustworthy, comforting and appropriately protective, whether these were neglectful or rejecting, or were overly involved, intrusive, role-reversing or excessively demanding. In other words, was there a 'good enough' loving containment and understanding of the inevitable trials, tribulations and traumas that beset childhood? If there was not, to what extent has the individual been able to work through, come to terms with and achieve a reasonably balanced view of their early relationship difficulties?

Three 'normative' attachment patterns emerged from Main's research. These were: 'secure and balanced' (approx. 55%), 'avoidant-dismissing' (approx. 24%) and 'enmeshed-preoccupied' (approx. 18%), with a small group who were 'unclassifiable'. About 20% of her whole group showed 'unresolved trauma or loss'. In essence, this was to do with issues that had not been thought about or worked through, around which a variety of defences had been constructed.

Because of the clinical nature of my research group, I employed Pat Crittenden's 'Dynamic Maturational' coding and classification system (Crittenden, 1999, 2006). This provides a set of 'clinical' categories that expand the standard AAI classifications. Crittenden's 'DM' AAI model enables a more sensitive analysis of the material, especially those patterns that were unclassifiable on Main's system, so is particularly relevant to the psychological disorders. The AAI scripts were coded 'blind' by trained AAI assessors.

Now a few words about my findings in general. No participants came in the 'normative' categories of attachment; 2 came into a 'low clinical' category and 20 in a 'high clinical' category. Whereas the 'low clinical' group achieved scores on their psychometric tests that were consistent with significant psychological distress, the 'high clinical' group all had scores indicating distress at much more extreme levels. Three groups or clusters emerged: a group of high As (compulsively avoidant-dismissing), a group of high Cs (obsessionally enmeshed-preoccupied) and a group who used a complex combination of avoidant and preoccupied attachment strategies. These very differing types of attachment behaviours would indicate that a 'one size fits all' approach to therapeutic intervention would not be helpful and could be anti-therapeutic.

Twenty out of the 22 produced evidence of serious childhood attachment traumas, with 16 of these (80%) showing up as 'unresolved losses and traumas' in the DM-AAI classifications. This included the traumatic loss of one or both attachment figures through death, divorce, serious accidents or chronic illness; the death of a sibling; serious marital violence; emotional and physical abuse (in one case sexual abuse); and/or rejection by a major caretaking figure.

What was of particular interest was the number of individuals who had experienced metaphorically or concretely equivalent traumas in childhood to the incidents in adulthood, which had resulted in their chronic PTSD. A conservative estimate (rated independently) found 16 whose current traumas bore a resemblance, at times almost uncanny, to their childhood traumatic experiences. For example, in the case of the teacher whose PTSD began after a child in his class died during a PE lesson he was taking, the AAI revealed that his father had left the country shortly after he was born and that, as a six-year-old, his much-loved granddad and father substitute had died in front of him when they were out walking together. Or the woman whose coalminer father suffered near-fatal injuries when a coal tub came loose and crashed into the back of him, fracturing his spine and leaving him severely disabled and the family destitute. She was five at the time. Her PTSD began three years before I saw her, when the car she was driving was crashed into from behind, while she was waiting for the car ahead of her to turn right. Although her car was written off, she herself suffered only minor whiplash. Nevertheless, her PTSD was so severe that she has been unable to work since. Then there was the woman who'd been mugged by a man in a stocking mask, holding a sawn-off shotgun. Her flashbacks and nightmares consisted of seeing his masked face and hearing him shouting at her, 'Give me your bag, or I'll blow your head off!' In her AAI, she told me how her mother's face and upper body had been severely mutilated by a bomb blast in the Second World War. Throughout her childhood, mother's face had often been bandaged, and she was regularly in hospital having shrapnel removed. She had always felt shame and embarrassment at having a mother so disfigured and, of course, guilty about having such feelings.

It was clear from discussions with these four people, as well as with others in the group, that these early events had never been thought about

much – nor were they consciously felt to have had any particular significance. Indeed, most of the group were initially quite resistant to making
these kinds of links. Their inability to think about these connections put me
in mind of Bion's (1962) distinction between 'alpha elements' and 'beta
elements'. Bion points out that remembering and linking, mourning and
learning from experience all derive from what he calls 'alpha function'.
Alpha function transforms raw sensory impressions, or 'beta elements', into
narrative experience that can be stored in memory in a form that makes it
accessible to reflective thinking. Beta elements can be thought of as 'psychic
noise' (Ogden, 2003). As such, they cannot be linked together into a
meaningful narrative and are fit only for evacuation.

Nevertheless, the research findings for this group of 22 indicated that the
presence of early attachment difficulties did support the dynamic hypothesis of a highly sensitized, 'at risk' vulnerability to later traumatic events
in adulthood. The research also supported those studies that found that
previous exposure to traumatic events, particularly in childhood, was
associated with the development of PTSD in adulthood. The AAI results
revealed that these traumatic events not only were based on early,
unresolved losses, but were compounded by the lack of adequately sup-
porting and containing parental attachment figures. Thus, such events
could not be integrated within the child's mind, but remained split off from
the developing ego. As Freud himself wrote in 1895, in his 'Project for a
Scientific Psychology' (p. 359), 'The very first traumas of all escape the ego
entirely'. The *chronicity* of their PTSD appeared to be linked semantically
with these early, unresolved and apparently 'forgotten' losses and traumas.
We might say that these are the 'unthought knowns' that have been so
lucidly commented on by Christopher Bollas (1987) in his book *The
Shadow of the Object*.

This led me to conclude that the main predisposing factors in my research
group's chronic PTSD were a combination of unresolved losses and other
problematic attachment features from childhood, together with an adult
life-threatening event that bore actual or metaphorical similarity to the
childhood trauma. What was past experience and what was current experience had become affectively and cognitively confused, so that the capacity
to distinguish between 'now' and 'then' had become lost, resulting in past
and present merging seamlessly into each other and forming an unassimi-
lated 'composite trauma', which endlessly repeated itself in the form of
chronic PTSD. I think this composite trauma has something in common
with what Ron Britton (2003) has described as the 'fifth dimension': that is,
a dimension of dynamic significance which is independent of time and space,
but which links events by way of the *affects* attached to them.

Before I come back to our group of four, I want to say something about
the process of symbolization, since I have found this particularly helpful in
thinking about the participants of my research study. In order to be able to

symbolize, we need to have the emotional capacity to deal with loss and change – which means to be able to mourn, to recognize the separateness and difference of other people, to reflect on ourselves in relation to others, to have some idea of how others might see us and to be able both to learn from events and to consign them to past memory systems. This involves having a reasonably clear understanding of both psychic reality and external reality – and the differences between them. Ron Britton has referred to this as the capacity to achieve a third space in the mind, while Peter Fonagy (2001) and his co-workers think of it as the capacity to mentalize.

Caroline Garland (1998), in her work on trauma, specifically states that the capacity to recollect and to remember is a symbolic level of functioning, whereas 're-experiencing', which is what happens in PTSD, indicates a failure in symbol formation. Hanna Segal (1957) points out that symbol formation is based on the individual's capacity to use substitutes for actual things and situations. These substitutes have psychic equivalence to the objects for which they stand. We use symbols to stand for things, while knowing that these symbols are not the things in themselves. The word 'spider', for example, is not the actual spider – but for some spider-phobic individuals, even the word cannot be spoken in their presence without a panic attack taking place. For such people, the word 'spider' and the feared object are equivalent. The symbol and the object have become one and the same thing. Hanna Segal has described this failure to symbolize as a *symbolic equation*. The 'composite trauma' that I have described in my chronic PTSD group, in which past and present have become indistinguishable, can be understood as just such a symbolic equation.

So now, let us go back to the four that we have been looking at in detail. Let us see how they fit with this hypothesis of 'at risk' vulnerability and 'semantic resonance' with earlier 'unthought' and unsymbolized, but unconsciously known, losses and traumas.

Frances was attacked by a schizophrenic patient. As Frances told me at our first meeting, 'The very idea of going back to nursing terrifies me. She got inside me. She wanted to kill me . . . and she would have done. She just didn't want me and no matter what, she was going to make sure I wasn't there. I feel like if I go anywhere near her, she will kill me.'

The AAI brought out a highly problematic relationship with a mother, experienced as very powerful, who had made no secret of the fact that Frances had been a mistake and unwanted. The discourse analysis revealed a split, unintegrated version of mother – on one hand idealized as very loving; on the other as harsh, cruel and frightening. This latter version of mother was denied. The schizophrenic patient's sudden and unexpected attack on Frances brought this split together with catastrophic results, leaving Frances unable to escape from a mad and murderous version of mother in her internal world, which she had never allowed conscious expression. Frances is currently in long-term group analytic psychotherapy.

As for Peter, the AAI painfully revealed his precarious, insecure child-hood, in which a drunken father consistently and violently beat up a mother whom Peter was unable to protect. These were memories he thought he had put behind him and locked away for ever. In tears, he remembered the many occasions as a small child when he had cowered helplessly in the corner while his father, in a drunken rage, attacked his mother who was screaming in terror. There was at least one occasion when she was knocked uncon-scious and Peter was sure that she had died. We can see how this past internal scenario is now reflected in his ruminations about death and in his fears of planes coming crashing from the skies. The accident waiting to happen was a violently destructive 'primal scene' leading to a catastrophic collapse of his internal world. What he had thought of as a secure base at work turned out to be every bit as precarious, insecure and dangerous as his life at home had been with his parents. He knew he was angry with his father, what he was unaware of was his sense of grievance towards his mother for allowing these things to happen. Peter declined the offer of psychotherapy, not wishing, I suspect, to open up these painful things once again. The last I heard, however, he was receiving longer-term counselling.

Daphne, whose car had cannoned down the hill like a snooker ball, and whose nerve endings were said to be damaged, experienced a series of deaths in her childhood. Her four-year-old brother died when she was six months old. Her father died when she was six, leaving her mother unable to cope with her young family. Before long, their large, comfortable house had to be sold and the family moved into a 'street house' with grandmother. When she was ten, her grandmother died and at 17, her best friend died in an accident. What the AAI revealed was a split pattern of an idealized relationship with her dead father and a preoccupied, enmeshed relationship with her alive mother. When describing her mother, Daphne commented, laughing, 'My mother's a great one for throwing herself downstairs! Not intentionally, but she's very good at cutting herself with knives and . . . she's very good at . . . she's terribly accident-prone. She was a joke as a kid. If there was any way of walking into something, rather than round it, my mother would do it.'

Her rather mocking tone changed and she added, 'I was petrified. Absolutely petrified. I can't cope with my mother's . . . I find it difficult coping with . . . er . . . if anyone's ill . . . I just can't cope . . . and that started . . . when my father died . . . and yes, I was always . . . always . . . waiting for my mother to somehow do something to herself.'

As Daphne had earlier complained, 'The police [in other words, her parents] are there to protect you, not to crash into you!'

We might say that these early losses have damaged Daphne's emotional nerve endings and cued her to respond by cannoning downhill internally, just like a snooker ball. When she was hit by the police car there was no internal mother to help her recover her equilibrium. Nor, as a young child, was there an external mother who was able to help her deal with the loss of her father. Daphne did not wish to pursue a therapy option.

As far as Greg is concerned, his AAI was one of the most brief, in that he gave monosyllabic answers to most of the questions. Greg was knocked to the ground by a sling-load of steel which, he was sure, would crush him to death. He spoke of seeing this incident as repeated flashbacks in his living room. When he was first seen for assessment he was attending a day centre for five days a week and was in a despairing state. He had experienced the loss of a number of close relatives as a child and as an adult. There was no evidence of his having come to terms with any of these losses. Greg described his childhood in idealized terms, saying 'I was always the little blue-eyed boy'. In reality, his childhood came across as emotionally deprived and bleak. There was a repeated theme of his having accidents and he also described a scene in which his father had been brought back from work having sustained a serious accident. What he remembered most vividly was the blood on his father's clothes. Perhaps most pertinent of all, because of what would have been in his mother's mind when he was a baby, was the information in the AAI that Greg had been the replacement for a boy child who had died in infancy. I take this as the psychic equivalent to the 'living room' mind of his mother that he talked of being terrified to enter, in which a deathly scene repeatedly occurred. Greg was offered a year of individual psychotherapy focusing on the expression of affect. During this time he was able to reduce his avoidant pattern, make contact with the workmates he had not seen since the accident eight years before and get on with his life – albeit in his preferred avoidant style.

So what I'm proposing, based on the evidence from this research group, is that a current, potentially life-threatening incident takes on the repetitiously traumatic form of chronic PTSD, because it resonates so closely with past, unintegrated experience that has been fuelled by emotionally charged phantasy. This idea is, of course, not new but, like so much of what we talk about today, can be traced back to Freud's early thinking (e.g. 1899).

I'll conclude briefly by coming back to my title – 'It was an accident waiting to happen'. We could also think of this as an accident *wanting* to happen. There is an earlier trauma that needs a container. The chronic PTSD seen in the 22 participants of my research study had become the vehicle through which all their earlier pain, fright, confusion, grievances, rage and distress could be expressed. For at least some of them it could then be understood, worked through and relegated to the past.

Acknowledgement

The author would like to thank all 22 participants in this research project for giving their permission for anonymized extracts from their AAI type-scripts to be quoted.

Note

1 An earlier version of this paper was given at a conference on trauma organized by the North of England Association of Psychoanalytic Psychotherapists (NEAPP) in 2003.

References

American Psychiatric Association (1994) *Diagnostic and Statistical Manual of Mental Disorders (4th edn.) (DSM-IV)*, Washington, DC: APA.

Bion, W.R. (1962) *Learning from Experience*, London: Karnac.

Bion, W.R. (1962) 'A theory of thinking', *International Journal of Psychoanalysis*, 43: 306–310.

Bollas, C. (1987) *The Shadow of the Object: Psychoanalysis of the Unthought Known*, London: Free Association Books.

Bowlby, J. (1969, 1982) *Attachment*: Vol. 1 of *Attachment and Loss*, London: Hogarth Press.

Bowlby, J. (1988) *A Secure Base: Parent–Child Attachment and Healthy Human Development*, London: Routledge.

Breslau, N., Peterson, E.L., Kessler, R.C. and Schultz, L.R. (1999) 'Short screening scale for DSM-IV post-traumatic stress disorder', *American Journal of Psychiatry*, 156: 908–911.

Britton, R. (2003) 'Discussion of Dana Birkstead-Breen's paper', *Bulletin of the British Psycho-Analytical Society*, January.

Crittenden, P., Fava Vizziello, G. and Landini, A. (1999) *A Dynamic-Maturational Approach to Mental Functioning in Adulthood: An Expanded Method for Analysing the Adult Attachment Interview*, Milan, Italy: Masson.

Crittenden, P. (2006) 'A dynamic-maturational model of attachment', *Australian and New Zealand Journal of Family Therapy*, 27: 105–115.

Ehlers, A., Mayou, R.A. and Bryant, B. (1998) 'Psychological predictors of chronic post-traumatic stress disorder after motor vehicle accidents', *Journal of Abnormal Psychology*, 107: 508–519.

Fonagy, P. (2001) *Attachment Theory and Psychoanalysis*, New York: Other Press.

Freud, S. (1895) 'Project for a Scientific Psychology', *Standard Edition*, Vol. 1, London: Hogarth Press.

Freud, S. (1899) 'Screen Memories', *Standard Edition*, Vol. 3, London: Hogarth Press.

Freud, S. (1920) 'Beyond the Pleasure Principle', *Standard Edition*, Vol. 18, London: Hogarth Press.

Garland, C. (Ed.) (1998) *Understanding Trauma: A Psycho-Analytical Approach*, London: Duckworth.

Holmes, J. (1993) *John Bowlby and Attachment Theory*, London: Routledge.

Holmes, J. (2001) *The Search for the Secure Base: Attachment Theory and Psychotherapy*, London: Karnac.

Horowitz, M.J. (1992) 'The effects of psychic trauma on mind: Structure and processing of meaning'. In J. Barron, N. Eagle and D. Wolitski (Eds.), *Interface of Psychoanalysis and Psychiatry* (pp. 489–500), Washington, DC: American Psychological Association.

Horowitz, M.J. (1993) 'Stress response syndromes: A review of post-traumatic stress and adjustment disorders'. In J.P. Wilson and B. Raphael (Eds.), *International Handbook of Traumatic Stress Syndromes*, New York: Plenum Press.

Kaplan, H. and Sadock, B. (1998) *Kaplan and Sadock's Synopsis of Psychiatry: Behavioural Sciences, Clinical Psychiatry* (8th edn.), Baltimore: Lippincott, Williams & Wilkins.

Klein, M. (1959) 'Our adult world and its roots in infancy', *Envy and Gratitude*, London: Virago Press, 1998.

Laub, D. and Auerhahn, N.C. (1993) 'Knowing and not knowing massive psychic trauma: Forms of traumatic memory', *International Journal of Psychoanalysis*, 74: 287–302.

Main, M. (1991) 'Metacognitive knowledge, metacognitive monitoring and singular (coherent) vs multiple (incoherent) models of attachment: Findings and directions for future research'. In C.M. Parkes, J. Stevenson-Hinde and P. Marris (Eds.), *Attachment across the Life Cycle*, London: Routledge.

McFarlane, A. (1990) 'Vulnerability to post traumatic stress disorder'. In M. Wolf and A. Mosnaim (Eds.), *Post-Traumatic Stress Disorder*, Washington, DC: American Psychiatric Press.

Ogden, T.H. (2003) 'On not being able to dream', *International Journal of Psychoanalysis*, 84: 17–30.

Segal, H. (1957) 'Notes on symbol formation', *International Journal of Psychoanalysis*, 38: 391–397.

Segal, H. (1993) 'The function of dreams'. In S. Flanders (Ed.), *The Dream Discourse Today*, London: Routledge.

Singleton, N., Bumpstead, R., O'Brien, M., Lee, A. and Meltzer, H. (2002) *Psychiatric Morbidity among Adults living in Private Households, 2000: Summary Report*. London: Office for National Statistics.

Skre, I., Onstad, S., Torgersen, S., Lygren, S. and Kringlen, E. (1993) 'A twin study of DSM-III-R anxiety disorders', *Acta Psychiatrica Scandinavica*, 88, 2: 85–92.

Weisaeth, L. (1984) *Stress reactions in an industrial accident*, unpublished doctoral dissertation, Oslo University, Norway.

Zohar, J., Sasson, Y., Amital, D., Iancu, I. and Zinger, Y. (1998) 'Current diagnostic issues and epidemiological insights in PTSD', *CNS Spectrums (Supplement Monograph)* 3 (7), July/August.

A brief history of mentalization-based treatment and its roots in psychoanalytic theory and practice

Peter Fonagy and Anthony Bateman

What is borderline personality disorder?

Borderline personality disorder (BPD) is a complex and serious mental disorder. It is characterized by a pervasive pattern of difficulties with emotion regulation and impulse control, and instability both in relationships and in self-image (Skodol *et al.*, 2002). The current DSM-IV definition refers to: 'a pervasive pattern of instability of mood, interpersonal relationships, self image and affects and marked impulsivity' (American Psychiatric Association, 1994). The DSM-III definition of BPD (American Psychiatric Association, 1980) was strongly influenced by a review by Gunderson and Singer (1975). The review emphasized features in areas of social maladaptation, psychotic-like cognitions, relationship difficulties, impulsive action and dysphoric affect.

The criteria for BPD have changed over the years. For example, while the DSM-III definition did not include impulsivity as an essential feature, this was introduced in DSM-IV. DSM-IV also included transient, stress-related paranoid thoughts and severe dissociative symptoms in the definition. Other criteria that have been retained from the first systematic definition in DSM-III are a pattern of unstable relationships, affective instability, intolerance of being alone, self-harm, and chronic feelings of emptiness or boredom. Because there are nine criteria for BPD, of which only five need to be present to make the diagnosis, a very large number of combinations of criteria for a BPD diagnosis are possible (Skodol *et al.*, 2002). It is possible for two individuals who receive the diagnosis to share only one of the nine criteria. Other shortcomings of the definition include the omission of the proneness to regression and the use of primitive defence mechanisms often seen in those with BPD.

BPD is a common condition that is thought to occur globally (Pinto *et al.*, 2000) with a prevalence of 0.2–1.8% of the general population (Swartz *et al.*, 1990). Most studies originate from North America and suggest a weighted prevalence of BPD of around 0.5% in the USA. The situation may be different elsewhere, but in the UK, Coid and colleagues (2006) found that the weighted prevalence of BPD in a random sample of British householders was around the same at 0.7%. The most reliable study of the prevalence of the disorder in a community sample conducted in Oslo (Torgersen *et al.*, 2001) also suggested that the prevalence of BPD was not as high as commonly assumed; only 0.7% of patients from a representative community sample were diagnosed as borderline. There therefore appears to be a remarkable agreement between studies and countries where the condition has been carefully studied. Prevalence rates increase if patients within the mental health system are sampled. Only Torgersen *et al.* studied the sociodemographic characteristics of the sample; they found significant links between BPD and younger age, living in a city centre and not living with a partner. It was not associated with gender despite the widespread belief that BPD is commoner in females. Lower rates are found in black and minority ethnic groups, although the evidence for this is limited (Singleton, 1998; Tyrer *et al.*, 1994), and it remains possible that there is a reticence to make the diagnosis in this group, although Mikton and Grounds (2007) only found a cultural bias for antisocial personality disorder.

Higher prevalence rates are found in clinical populations. Moran and colleagues (2000) found a prevalence rate of 4–6% of primary care attenders, suggesting that people with BPD are more likely to visit their GP. It is common in those with eating disorders and drug and alcohol problems and also in adolescence. Chanen and colleagues (2007) suggest a prevalence rate of 11% in adolescent outpatients and 49% in adolescent inpatients. The highest prevalence rates are found in those patients requiring the most intensive level of care – outpatient rates range from 8 to 11%, inpatient from 14 to 20%, and forensic services from 60 to 80%. In a Dutch forensic psychiatric hospital, 80% of patients fulfilled criteria for at least one personality disorder, with paranoid, antisocial, and borderline being the most common (Ruiter and Greeven, 2000). Similar rates have been found in England and Sweden (Blackburn *et al.*, 1990), with the most common being borderline and antisocial personality disorder (Dolan and Coid, 1993).

A first encounter with BPD on the couch

The first time one of us (PF) came across a borderline patient on the couch was early in his analytic career as his first membership case. The following is his account of the experience.

The patient was clearly borderline, by both psychoanalytic and psychiatric criteria. He was impulsive, at times deeply depressed to the point of suicidality, at other times desperately attempting to regulate his wildly fluctuating emotional state by excessive alcohol consumption. His life was disorganised and he had no successful relationships, yet had a deep hunger to form attachments with people he hardly knew. Early on in his analysis he told me about his father's violence and the physical abuse he routinely suffered. At the time I saw him, now well over a quarter of a century ago, I learnt to interpret the transference and try, given sufficient opportunities, to work through an idea to reconstruct childhood experiences to the best of my ability. My patient was very amenable to this approach some of the time, although completely inaccessible to communication on other days or even other times during the same session. During a session that is etched in my memory, I recall him discussing the rivalrous relationship that he had been exposed to at work. He was a professional driver and he thought that two other drivers from the same firm were trying to establish a pecking order about who was the best. I sensed that the communication also related to his uncertainty about which of us was better and I interpreted that perhaps it felt safer to discuss the competition between his colleagues than it might be to think about how the two of us might match up to each other. He accepted my comment about the rivalry and immediately went on to discuss his competitiveness, current and past, in relation to his father. When he linked this to his feeling of being excluded by his father when he came to family meals (as a child he remembered with some distress having to eat with the nanny or child carer before his father came home and when his parents would eat together) I felt I had a golden opportunity to link my patient's ambivalence about his rivalrous feelings and his sense of rejection in being excluded from the discussions that took place between his parents at dinner. He strongly agreed with my understanding of his problem and talked about his father's tendency constantly to belittle and humiliate him.

He brought a dream to the next day's session where he and his father were having a fight. In the dream he saw himself as an adult, bigger in stature than his father and able to beat him but in the end resolving the struggle by taking out a knife and smoothly, with a slicing movement, separating his father's penis from the rest of his body. He brought the dream as evidence that what we had discovered about him in the last session had been correct and of course most helpful. I had more than a slight feeling of unease while listening to this story. While theoretically I could easily link the Oedipal struggle and the intercourse from which my patient had been excluded to the castration imagery of the dream, I also sensed an absence of resistance or working through in the way the material had emerged. I began to dimly remember Rosenfeld's caution about interpreting unconscious conflict with patients with borderline personality disorder (Rosenfeld, 1965). My unease increased when he went on to remember a further segment of the dream when the image of castrating his father was quickly followed by seeing himself in the dream holding his father's severed penis up as if it were a torch. He was reminded of the Statue of Liberty and conveyed to me that illuminating the darkness represented by his unconscious mind freed him to be a person who could now genuinely engage with others.

Needless to say, neither my interpretations nor his dream the following day signalled a dramatic improvement in his condition. On the contrary, he appeared to deteriorate to become even more suicidal as I tried my best to work through the ideas of castration and bodily mutilation linked to guilt surrounding his unconscious fantasy of patricide. During my training I had of course read about concrete thinking in psychotic patients and I remembered that the work of Harold Searles and other analysts at Chestnut Lodge had impressed me in particular (Searles, 1960). This patient seemed to have a deficit in thinking capacity comparable to that which I learned characterized psychotic patients.

This early experience led to a focus on the thinking capacities of borderline patients. In an early paper effectively co-authored with George Moran, we identified the repudiation of a concern with mental states as a key aspect of borderline psychopathology (Fonagy, 1991). The first time we used the term 'mentalization' was in 1989 (Fonagy, 1989), influenced by the Ecole Psychosomatique de Paris, but we used the term as operationalized by developmental researchers investigating theory of mind (Leslie, 1987). The failure of mentalizing had of course been apparent to most psychoanalysts working with these patients, particularly Bion, Segal, Rosenfeld, Green, Kernberg and the North American object relations theorists. In an early paper reviewing ideas concerning mentalization in relation to classical psychoanalytic concepts, this intellectual indebtedness was carefully documented (Fonagy and Higgitt, 1989). The simple basic suggestion we made was that representing self and others as thinking, believing, wishing or desiring did not arrive at age four as a consequence of maturation but rather was a developmental achievement that was profoundly rooted in the quality of early object relations. Its predictable vulnerability to disappearance under stress in borderline conditions was seen as an appropriate focus for psychoanalytically oriented psychological intervention.

At around the same time the other author (AB) was treating patients with severe personality disorder in NHS clinical practice as well as seeing some patients for analysis. Clinical discussions with the team at University College centred not only on BPD but also on its overlap with narcissistic and antisocial disorders from the perspective of mentalization and technique in psychotherapy. We know that there is considerable similarity between borderline, narcissistic, and antisocial disorders and the common factor between them was thought to be a fragile, brittle self-structure either from disorganization or from excessive rigidity. Individuals with narcissistic and antisocial personality disorders tend to shelter within schematic representations of relationships to protect the self; partners have to play particular roles. Grandiose fantasies, the seeking of admiration, the control and dominance of others, and a firm belief in entitlement and compliance from others are frequent. Flexibility, doubt, uncertainty and reflection, all hallmarks of mentalization, are not apparent. Mind states become rigidified and relationships are violently forced into a specific mould, giving the erroneous impression of stability. In fact this inflexible rigid structure is brittle, much like untempered steel, and the self can shatter suddenly, with little warning, leading to violent outbursts against another person as the self is rapidly destabilized. In contrast, with BPD the self-structure is inherently unstable whenever a 'mind meets a mind' and so there is a picture of constant disorganization in relationships.

Drawing on the ideas of Rosenfeld and Racker (Racker, 1957, 1968), our theoretical and clinical discussions led to the suggestion that the role of the therapist was to interpose himself in the therapy process at the point at which mental collapse is taking place, with the primary aim of maintaining mentalizing in both himself and the patient (Bateman, 1998). Rosenfeld (1964) drew our attention to the importance of the self-structure in describing thick- and thin-skinned narcissists. The thin-skinned narcissist is vulnerable and fragile while the thick-skinned narcissist, aligned with the psychopath, is inaccessible and defensively aggressive. We suggested that both structures were flawed and inherently unstable and used the conceptualization to discuss the interrelationship between violent acts to others and the attack on one's own body in suicide attempts (Bateman, 1998). Thick-skinned narcissists are more likely to be violent to others at a point at which their dominant, grandiose self is threatened – the self-preservative violence discussed by Glasser (1998) – while the thin-skinned narcissist may be violent, usually to himself but not necessarily so, when something important to his self-regard is undermined. Patients with BPD oscillate between the two states and it is the movement between them that offers the opportunity to intervene to re-establish a process of mentalizing at the moment that it is being lost. We considered this to be the focus of therapy for these patients.

A developmental perspective on BPD

A second line of analytic inspiration came from work with children undertaken as part of a project to construct a manual for child analysis and subsequent work in developmental science between Mary Target and Peter Fonagy (Fonagy et al., 2002; Fonagy and Target, 1996, 2000, 2007; Target and Fonagy, 1996). This work helped us to think more deeply about the normal development of thinking or mentalizing capacity and the more primitive modes of thought that precede its emergence. In trying to map the emergence of mentalization on the basis of material from records of child analysis and clinical and research work with children in other contexts, we came up with a heuristic map of the emergence of mentalization that turned out to be extremely valuable in understanding some qualitative aspects of the thinking of some patients in borderline states. In particular, we noticed that the concrete thinking that many have identified as a hallmark of BPD was reminiscent of the way a two- to three-year-old normally tended to treat internal experience. The equation of internal and external, treating what is inside my head as equivalent in status to what is there in the physical world, typifies the way toddlers and preschoolers often think until they acquire full mentalizing capacity. We have called this way of thinking *psychic equivalence*. At other times they appear to be able to use the notion of mental states but paradoxically use it only when they can clearly separate it from physical reality (for example, in play). In this state of mind, which we have called *pretend mode*, thoughts and feelings can be envisioned and talked about but they correspond to nothing real. Finally, the compelling nature of physical reality is also obvious when children only impute intention from what is physically apparent. We noted that this *teleological mode* of thinking was present from a very early stage but is compelling for all of us at moments when mentalizing has ceased, when physical reassurance is demanded and required if emotion regulation is to be reinstated.

Alongside our psychoanalytic work, we also had the opportunity to develop our ideas about the capacity to mentalize in a research context. Attachment research that we were undertaking at the same time identified the parent's capacity to reflect on the mental states of their own parents, as well as their own mental states in relation to them, to be predictive of their child's security of attachment (Fonagy et al., 1991). We came upon this finding through careful analysis of narrative transcripts of attachment experiences by prospective mothers and fathers. Our operationalization of this capacity as reflective function (RF; Fonagy et al., 1998) turned out to be helpful in studying individuals with BPD. Those with a combination of childhood trauma and limited reflective function were highly likely to be diagnosed with BPD compared to psychiatric or normal controls. A further finding that linked security of attachment to a precocious capacity to engage in 'mindreading' seemed to complete the circle (Fonagy et al., 1997). A number of other studies have replicated this finding (de Rosnay and Harris, 2002; Harris, 1999; Meins et al., 1998; Ontai and Thompson, 2002; Raikes and Thompson, 2006; Steele et al., 1999; Symons, 2004; Thompson, 2000). It appeared that individuals gifted with an attuned and sensitive parent who focused on their mind would develop the capacity to understand themselves and others in mental state terms, which would equip them with a superior capacity for regulating internal states as indicated by superior affect regulative capacity and attentional control. Those whose intersubjective context was more limited, those who were neglected or overwhelmed by a misattuned caregiver, were likely to grow up to be vulnerable to temporary loss of affect regulation and to be prone to loss of voluntary control over manipulating their mental states.

Added to this conundrum was the obvious and overwhelming presence of trauma in the history of individuals with BPD. It seemed that only relatively few individuals who had experienced trauma showed the pattern of difficulties manifested by individuals with BPD, although almost all the patients with this pattern could remember a history of maltreatment or abuse. It became clear that the vulnerability originating in infancy made the experience of abuse and maltreatment less tolerable, leaving psychic devastation in its wake. The subjective experiences of our patients became understandable once we recognized that in their encounters with a torturing figure they evolved a strategy of disengaging from an interest in the internal world, both in themselves and in those around them. The loss of a sense of a psychological other was easy to understand given that many of these patients had experiences of abuse of such severity that the contemplation of the thoughts and feelings of the abuser filled with frankly malevolent ideas towards the child was simply intolerable. Their vulnerability in regulating emotional responses and generating effective strategies for controlling their thoughts and feelings challenged their capacity for thinking about their own actions in terms of subtle understandings of their thoughts and feelings. They slipped into what superficially could be described as a kind of mindless state, both in relation to others and in relation to themselves. Of course the story turned out to be more complicated than this because these incapacities, palpable at certain times, were not always evident. We noticed that at moments of emotional distress, particularly distress triggered by actual or threatened loss, the capacity for mentalization was most likely to apparently evaporate. The question quickly became how these observations could be usefully translated into a therapeutic approach that could be helpful given the prevalence and severity of this clinical problem within the public healthcare system.

Working with BPD in the NHS

One valuable insight that both of us gained from our clinical and research experience and that helped us develop a clinical programme was that, with these patients, understanding the specific unconscious links between present and past was an inappropriate focus for therapeutic work. Working with these patients actually required remarkably little 'insight' on the part of either the therapist or the patient. Our analytic trainings have taught us to make subtle links between latent and manifest content, between ideas as they are presented and underlying conflicts or concerns of varying depth and scope. The training that we undertake as analysts is essential in order to become attuned to the way the unconscious part of the mind generates conscious content and controls behaviour, either through these conscious thoughts or sometimes even totally bypassing phenomenal awareness. Our work as analysts is appropriately focused on identifying these unconscious mental structures that are in control of behaviour, thought and feeling, and bringing consciousness to bear to empower the individual to find more appropriate adaptations to internal and external experience. The difficulty of borderline patients is not simply at the level of particular troublesome unconscious ideas, but with mental regulation *per se*. The analytic approach can still be used, but with the aim of strengthening mentalization rather than generating insight. In other words, we still talk with our patients to help them to gain a better understanding of both themselves and others, but no longer with the aim of finding the hidden meaning behind the apparent superficial presentation. Rather, we aim to generate meaning from a surface that has been stripped of a psychological level of experience.

In terms of technique, then, we can forgo the interpretation of unconscious conflict, affect that is denied, thoughts that are repudiated, wishes that are repressed. What we need to focus on in every context and in relation to every interpersonal encounter is simply a re-presentation of the experience in terms of mental states, feelings, wishes, beliefs and desires. In fact the most important aspect of mentalization-based treatment is a rigorous and unwavering focus on elaborating subjective experience in relation to both self and other in as simple and as genuine a way as possible. Presenting these patients with overly complex understandings may well be a source of confusion for them, since they may not feel clear enough about how they think and feel to be able either to accept or deny them with confidence. Under these circumstances the most readily available strategy might be to disengage from the discourse altogether, as evidenced by the large proportion of patients who drop out from psychotherapy services unless special efforts are made to engage them in a manner that is consistent with the limitations in their affect regulation and attentional capacities.

A further implication that followed from our clinical formulations concerned the level of training required from those delivering this form of psychological therapy. If the aim of the treatment is not the elucidation of the dynamic unconscious but rather the enhancement of the capacity to mentalize, the training requirements for a therapist are modest relative to what is essential for those who work with neurotic patients. A further pragmatic consideration enters here concerning access to psychological therapies. If access to psychodynamically oriented psychological therapies is restricted to those who have undertaken a 4–6 year training which includes both personal therapy and supervised clinical practice on several long-term psychotherapeutic cases, we will not have the kind of access to mental healthcare that any public health service requires. Above, we have estimated the point prevalence of BPD to be around 2–3% of the population. This means between 500,000 and 800,000 individuals in the UK.

Offering psychodynamic psychotherapy to all these persons, assuming a caseload of 10 patients per therapist, would require 80,000 therapists working full-time just with these patients. We further have to bear in mind that short-term treatments are known not to be adequate for this group and all research points to a minimum duration of one to two years before the pattern of suicidal self-harming behaviour is adequately reversed (Bateman and Tyrer, 2004). It is unrealistic to hope that any country would have the resources to offer a treatment of adequate duration and intensity to more than a tiny proportion of these patients if we cannot reduce the training burden associated with delivering this type of treatment.

The development of mentalization-based treatment (MBT)

Following this line of reasoning, and given our theoretical approach, we have evolved a psychodynamic treatment that requires a relatively modest amount of additional input, given a background of work with this type of patient in a range of possible professional contexts, e.g. nurse, caseworker, psychologist, social worker, occupational therapist, art therapist. We are not claiming that the treatment can be delivered by 'anyone'. Rather, it builds on such individuals' already solid capacity to contain and hold in mind someone who is determined to disrupt exactly that type of scrutiny. For such individuals, who are able to work with this sometimes very worrying but highly deserving group of patients without responding in kind to affective dysregulation, a relatively brief three-day training can suffice to enable them to deliver a structured method of therapy that has mentalization as its focus. In part this is because MBT does not require therapists to learn and implement a wide range of techniques in highly skilled ways or to identify relational patterns in detail. Too much emphasis on schemas or behaviours might reduce the development of the patient's ability to seek his own understanding. We focus on the development of mental resources that are available to deal with recurrent patterns of behaviour and relationships rather than identification of the patterns themselves. This emphasis is non-trivial clinically. Mentalizing therapists do not get involved in discussing the structure or nature of the relationship that the patient brings, but focus more on the patient's capacity to think about the relationship. For example, the MBT therapist addresses the rigidity of schematic representations or roles rather than the roles or schemas themselves; the MBT therapist tries to enhance and facilitate flexibility and generate alternative perspectives (Bateman et al., 2007).

Mentalization-based treatment was first developed and implemented as a day hospital programme for patients with BPD. It was developed in collaboration with a team of generically trained mental health professionals with an interest in psychoanalytically oriented psychotherapy rather than by highly trained personnel within a university research department. Our research into its effectiveness took place within a normal clinical setting (St Ann's Hospital, London) and in a locality and healthcare system in which patients were unlikely to be able to obtain treatment elsewhere. This allowed effective tracing of patients within the service and accurate collection of clinical and service utilization data. Patients were treated at only two local hospitals for medical emergencies such as self-harm, enabling us to obtain highly accurate data of episodes of self-harm and suicide attempts requiring medical intervention. Although quite complex, the programme was designed so that it could be dismantled at a later date to determine the therapeutic components.

Our own evidence base remains small as far as treatment outcome is concerned, yet replication studies are under way and an increasing number of practitioners are using mentalization techniques in treatment, such that more information will become available soon. Our original randomized controlled trial (RCT) of treatment of BPD in a partial hospital programme offering individual and group psychoanalytic psychotherapy (Bateman and Fonagy, 1999, 2001) showed significant and enduring changes in mood states and interpersonal functioning associated with an 18-month programme. The benefits, relative to treatment as usual, were large (NNTs – numbers needed to treat – around two) and were observed to increase during the follow-up period of 18 months, rather than staying level as with dialectical behaviour therapy.

Forty-four patients who participated in the original study were assessed at three-monthly intervals after completion of the earlier trial. Outcome measures included frequency of suicide attempts and acts of self-harm, number and duration of inpatient admissions, service utilization, and self-report measures of depression, anxiety, general symptom distress, interpersonal function and social adjustment. Data analysis used repeated measures analysis of covariance and non-parametric tests of trend. Patients who had received partial hospitalization treatment not only maintained their substantial gains but also showed a statistically significant continued improvement on most measures, in contrast to the control group of patients who showed only limited change during the same period. This suggests that 'rehabilitative' changes had developed, enabling patients to negotiate the stresses and strains of everyday life without resorting to former ways of coping such as self-harming activity.

Health care utilization of all patients who participated in the trial was assessed using information from case notes and service providers (Bateman and Fonagy, 2003). Costs of psychiatric, pharmacological, and emergency room treatment were compared six months prior to treatment, during 18 months of treatment, and during 18 months of follow-up. There were no differences between the groups in the costs of service utilization pre-treatment or during treatment. The additional cost of day hospital treatment was offset by less psychiatric inpatient care and reduced emergency room treatment. The trend for costs to decrease in the experimental group during 18 months of follow-up was not apparent in the control group, suggesting that day hospital treatment for BPD is no more expensive than general psychiatric care and shows considerable cost savings after treatment.

Overview of the process of MBT

MBT aims to develop a therapeutic process in which the mind of the patient becomes the focus of treatment. The objective is for the patient to find out more about how he thinks and feels about himself and others, how that dictates his responses, and how 'errors' in understanding himself and others lead to actions in an attempt to retain stability and to make sense of incomprehensible feelings. It is not for the therapist to 'tell' the patient about how he feels, what he thinks, how he should behave, what the underlying reasons are, conscious or unconscious, for his difficulties. We believe that any therapy approach that moves towards 'knowing' how a patient 'is', how he should behave and think, and 'why he is like he is' is likely to be harmful. The therapist has to ensure that she retains an approach that focuses on the mind of the patient as he is experiencing himself and others at any given moment.

In an attempt to capture the therapist stance that gives the best chance of achieving mentalizing goals, we have defined a mentalizing, inquisitive, or not-knowing stance. The mentalizing or not-knowing stance is not synonymous with having no knowledge. The term is an attempt to capture a sense that mental states are opaque and that the therapist can have no more idea of what is in the patient's mind than the patient himself. When the therapist takes a different perspective to the patient this should be verbalized and explored in relation to the patient's alternative perspective, without making assumptions about whose viewpoint has greater validity. The task is to determine the mental processes that have led to alternative viewpoints and to consider each perspective in relation to the other, accepting that diverse outlooks may be acceptable. Where differences are clear and cannot initially be resolved they should be identified, stated, and accepted until resolution seems possible. The mentalizing stance requires the therapist to own up to her own anti-mentalizing errors, which are treated as opportunities to learn more about feelings and experiences – 'How was it that I did that at that time?' The therapist must articulate what has happened in order to model honesty and courage but above all to demonstrate that she is continually reflecting on what goes on in her mind and on what she does in relation to the patient, which is a central component of mentalizing itself.

We will now illustrate this mentalizing stance with a brief clinical example of the process that the therapist tries to generate in a session; involving a 'dislikable' patient.

A patient continually reported that he was aware that people did not like him and tried to avoid him. There was some validity to his concerns because he was, on occasions, threatening and also highly critical of others. The therapist questioned how the patient knew this with such certainty all of the time. Gradually taking a not-knowing stance and moving the session into current process between patient and therapist, as recommended in MBT, the therapist asked 'What makes you say that now?' The patient stated that he knew the therapist did not want to see him at the moment. The therapist responded by saying that this was news to him as it had not occurred to him that he did not want to see the patient.

This authenticity in response immediately contrasts the therapist's current 'unknowing' mental state with that of the patient. The patient said 'You need some therapy then, to help you know what is going on' and went on to describe how the therapist had said 'hello' to him in the waiting room. Rather than assuming that the patient was paranoid and being deliberately provocative, the therapist asked for clarification about how the patient had experienced his greeting of 'hello'. He also indicated that he was willing to work out what was going on in his mind as suggested by the patient. 'Maybe I do need therapy, as I am not sure exactly what was going on in my mind at the time.' Ignoring this, the patient went on to say he was clear that the therapist had no enthusiasm in his voice when he said 'hello' and so he had immediately concluded that the therapist was reluctant to see him.

Rather than doubt this interpretation, the MBT therapist initially must try to validate the patient's experience, and only if he is unable to do so should he begin to seek alternative perspectives. So the therapist asked the patient to describe a little more about what it was about his greeting that had made the patient so certain. As he did so, he stated clearly 'I was not aware of being unenthusiastic about seeing you today, but I was aware of feeling fatigued.'

The patient responded by challenging the therapist: 'You would say that, wouldn't you. It is unprofessional to want to avoid seeing a patient.'

Again the therapist responded truthfully by mentioning that he would tell the patient if he felt he did not want to see him; he would not see that as unprofessional as long as he also reflected openly on what was going on that might be making him reluctant to see the patient. He continued by saying 'On this occasion the session is making me feel a bit reluctant about continuing this dialogue, because it looks to me that whatever I say to you, you are convinced that you are right and that I am going to cover up what I am really feeling – and I am not sure what to do about that.'

As the therapist accepted his contribution to making the patient feel unwanted, the session moved on. Both therapist and patient were able to consider more carefully the sensitivities of the patient and how easily that stimulated problematic feelings for him.

The importance of this sort of dialogue for the MBT therapist is about generating a process of contrasting mental states and meaning, so that both patient and therapist continually consider alternative perspectives. It is less about determining who is correct. Both are experiencing what has happened impressionistically and both have to accept uncertainty and doubt about their experience. Rigid adherence to a specific understanding will inevitably initiate prototypical – almost choreographed – interactions, with patient and therapist holding fixed opinions on which they later base unwarranted decisions. For example, the patient may well decide that it is not worth coming to see a therapist who does not want to see him, and a therapist may decide that the therapy is not working and should end.

There are three main phases to the trajectory of MBT. Each phase has a distinct aim and harnesses specific processes. The overall aim of the initial phase is assessment of mentalizing capacities and personality function and engaging the patient in treatment. Specific processes include giving a diagnosis, providing psycho-education, establishing a hierarchy of therapeutic aims, stabilizing social and behavioural problems, reviewing medication, and defining a crisis pathway. During the middle phase the aim of all the active therapeutic work is to stimulate an ever-increasing mentalizing ability. In the final phase preparation is made for ending intensive treatment. This requires the therapist to focus on the feelings of loss associated with ending treatment and how to maintain gains that have been made as well as working with the patient to develop an appropriate follow-up programme tailored to his particular needs.

At St Ann's there are two variants of MBT. The first is a day hospital programme in which patients attend initially on a five-day-per-week basis. This programme is a combination of individual and group psychotherapy focusing on implicit mentalizing processes and expressive therapies promoting skills in explicit mentalizing. The exact structure and content of each group is less important than the interrelationship of the different aspects of the programme, the working relationship between the different therapists, the continuity of themes between the groups, and the consistency with which the treatment is applied over a period of time. Such non-specific aspects probably form the key to effective treatment, and the specificity of the therapeutic activities remains to be determined. Integration within the programme is achieved through our focus on mentalizing. All groups have an overall aim of increasing mentalizing and within a framework that encourages exploration of minds by minds, even if the route to this goal is via explicit techniques such as artwork and writing. The maximum length of time in this programme is 18–24 months.

Entrance to the day hospital programme requires the patient to show at least some of a number of features that include high risk to self or others, inadequate social support, repeated hospital admissions interfering with adaptations to everyday living, unstable housing, substance misuse, and fragmented mentalizing. Patients who show some capacity for everyday living and have stable social support and accommodation are more likely to be treated within the second adaptation of MBT, the intensive outpatient programme, particularly if their mentalizing processes are characterized only by vulnerability in close emotional relationships. At present there is no agreed measure of severity of personality disorder and so it remains impossible to assign individuals to one programme or the other according to a score on a recognized instrument. The primary considerations are risk and instability of social circumstances.

A patient's journey through MBT

A 24-year-old female patient was referred from forensic services following her arrest for setting fire to her university dormitories. She had a history of recent suicide attempts and regularly burned herself with cigarettes and a hot iron. Feelings of rejection in her current relationship with her partner could trigger serious self-harm. She was admitted to the day hospital programme and offered individual (one session per week) and group (three sessions per week) psychotherapy; with the addition of art therapy (two sessions per week) within the expressive therapy programme. The programme was organized over five days and amounted to nine hours of therapy per week, with three-monthly reviews of her antipsychotic and antidepressant medication. In individual sessions the initial focus of treatment was clarification of her own feelings and of others' experiences of her. The eventual focus was on how her experiences of self-doubt and emotional turbulence led to a sense of fragmentation which was controlled only by experiences of intense physical pain. The individual therapist identified these processes, while focusing on the way she represented her own mental states and those of others with whom she interacted. Gradually this was explored within the relationship with her therapist – 'It never occurred to me that what I did had an effect on anyone else'. In groups, the patient was frequently challenged about the effect of her behaviour on other group members, resulting from her frequent threats to leave the group. The individual and group therapists collaborated in helping to maintain her attendance in treatment. In art therapy she was encouraged to express her inner states in her paintings, to explain her pictures to others and to consider the ways in which other people reacted to, and understood, her paintings.

During the period of treatment she terminated her relationship with her abusive partner and stopped her medication. She re-entered university and continued with MBT as an outpatient. At the end of 36 months she was discharged and a year later she joined training courses for professionals wishing to learn more about MBT.

The second programme is an 18-month intensive outpatient (IOP) treatment consisting of an individual session of 50 minutes, once per week, and a group session of 90 minutes, once per week. As in the day hospital programme, the group therapist is different from the individual therapist. The requirements placed on patients are more onerous than those placed on day hospital patients because participants are less chaotic and have better mentalizing abilities and some capacity for attentional and affective control.

All patients now enter an introductory mentalizing group before admission to the day hospital or IOP programme. This 12 week introduction to MBT consists of weekly modules focusing on problems related to personality disorder. The initial session on how to use mentalizing for everyday living is followed by sessions emphasizing how mentalizing can help to manage affective dysregulation, interpersonal interactions, cognitive distortions, and self-destructive behaviour. The significant feature of this programme is not so much its content but rather the development of a process that stimulates the patients to consider the mind as an important focus for managing problems associated with personality disorder, particularly those that are triggered by relational problems.

Day hospital and IOP programme – some common factors

After the first few sessions and after discussion with the treatment team the individual therapist makes an initial formulation which is given in written form to the patient. The purpose of the formulation of the patient's problems is to place feelings and behaviour within an individual context and to commence the development of a coherent interpersonal and developmental narrative. Frequently borderline patients have an incoherent narrative that makes little sense to them, leaving them unable to explain their personality development with any lucidity. They become schematic and categorical, linking specific events with explicit problems. The development of the formulation is the beginning of helping the patient to understand himself by exploring his personal story. Any formulation must be jointly developed and be understandable to patient, therapist and team. It is written down as a working hypothesis rather than a veridical truth established by a therapist and is reviewed throughout the treatment programme. In the formulation the initial goals should be clearly stated and linked to those aspects of treatment that will enable the patient to attain them. There should be a brief summary of the joint understanding that has developed with a focus on the underlying causes of the patient's problems in terms of mentalizing, their development and their current function. The formulation should also include longer-term goals in terms of the patient's social and interpersonal adjustment which are likely to be important indicators of improved mentalizing.

All patients both in the partial hospital programme and in IOP have a review with the whole treatment team every three months. The group therapist, the individual therapist, the psychiatrist and other relevant mental health professionals meet with the patient to discuss progress, problems, and other aspects of treatment. Practitioners meeting together jointly with the patient ensures not only that the views of everyone are taken into account and integrated into a coherent set of ideas but also that mentalizing as manifested through the discussion of the different viewpoints is modelled as a constructive activity that furthers understanding. These regular reviews lead to a reformulation which can then form the basis of ongoing treatment.

The hardest work for the patient takes place in the middle phase. For the therapist this phase may appear easier because by the time the initial phase has been negotiated many of the crises will have subsided, the level of engagement in treatment will be clear, the patient's motivation may have increased, and the capacity to work within individual and group therapy may be more pronounced. In addition the therapist may have a better understanding of the patient's overall difficulties and so have a more robust image of him in mind, while the patient has also become aware of the therapist's foibles and way of working. For other patients and therapists the treatment trajectory may continue to be disrupted, and a primary task of the therapists is to repair ruptures in the therapeutic alliance and to sustain their own and the patient's motivation while maintaining a focus on mentalizing.

Recent research has shown that, contrary to the long-prevailing misconception that personality disorder is intractable and untreatable, borderline patients naturally improve over time. Two carefully designed fully powered prospective studies have shown that the majority of BPD patients experience a substantial reduction in their symptoms far sooner than previously assumed. After six years, 75% of patients diagnosed with BPD severe enough to require hospitalization achieve remission by standardized diagnostic criteria (Shea et al., 2004; Zanarini et al., 2003). However, the improvement is primarily in impulsive behaviour and symptoms of affective instability. Complex interpersonal interaction, intricate negotiation of difficult social situations and interaction with systems may be less responsive to treatment. The borderline patient who no longer self-harms may still lead a life severely curtailed by his inability to form constructive relationships with others. Patients remain incapacitated in how they live their lives unless they develop constructive ways of interacting with others. The focus of the final phase is on the interpersonal and social aspects of functioning, provided that the symptomatic and behavioural problems are well controlled, along with integrating and consolidating earlier work.

The final phase starts at the 12-month point when the patient has a further six months' treatment. In keeping with the principles of dynamic therapy, we consider the ending of treatment and associated separation responses to be highly significant in consolidation of gains made during therapy. Inadequate negotiation by the patient of the experience of leaving (and incidentally inadequate processing of the ending on the part of the therapist) may provoke in the patient a re-emergence of earlier ways of managing feelings and a concomitant decrease in mentalizing capacities. The consequence is a reduction in social and interpersonal function.

Responsibility for developing a coherent follow-up programme and for negotiating further treatment is given to the patient and individual therapist. No specific follow-up programme is now routinely offered. Most patients ask for further follow-up. Some patients may have had a 'career' over many years interacting with mental health services; to leave this behind requires a massive change in lifestyle that may not be fully embedded by the end of 18 months. For the severe personality disordered patient who has had many years of failed treatments, multiple hospital admissions, and inadequate social stability, it is unlikely that they will be able to walk away from services never to return after 18 months, irrespective of success of the treatment. Most patients require further support as they adapt to a new life. Many patients choose intermittent follow-up appointments rather than further formal psychotherapy. This is organized within the treatment team. Senior practitioners who have known the patient and who are known to the patient offer individual appointments on a four to six weekly basis for 30 minutes. During follow-up appointments the therapist continues to use mentalizing techniques exploring the underlying mental states of the patient and discussing how understanding themselves and others is leading to resolution of problems, enabling them to reconcile difference, and helping them to manage problematic interpersonal areas and intimate relationships. The follow-up contract is flexible and the patient can request an additional appointment if there is an emotional problem that cannot easily be managed. But in general, the trajectory over follow-up is to increase the time between appointments over a six-month period to encourage greater patient responsibility. How long a patient is seen in this manner is dependent on the therapist and patient and should be agreed between them. Some patients elect to be discharged relatively early during follow-up on the basis that they may call and request an appointment at any time in the future. Other patients prefer an appointment many months ahead and this provides adequate assurance within their own mind that we continue to have them in mind, giving them greater confidence and self-reliance to negotiate the stresses and strains of everyday life.

In MBT the principal aims are always the same – to reinstate mentalizing at the point at which it is lost, to stabilize mentalizing in the context of an attachment relationship, to minimize the likelihood of adverse effects, and to allow the patient to discover himself and others through the experience of a mind considering a mind. Careful focus on the patient's current state of mind will achieve these aims. As one patient said – 'Before I did all this it never even occurred to me that what I did or thought had any effect on anyone else. Sometimes I still think that life was better because sometimes I don't like what other people think. But it does make life more interesting.'

Conclusion

Psychoanalysis was and remains the most comprehensive psychology. The clinical setting of psychoanalysis is a laboratory where those eager to learn about 'how the mind works' can invariably find inspiration and occasionally answers to important questions about some of the most perplexing aspects of human experience. Borderline phenomena, originally described by Knight (1953) and elaborated upon by some of the greatest minds in psychoanalysis – Kernberg, Bion, Rosenfeld, Winnicott, Mahler and many others – has provided a key testing ground for psychoanalytic theories of personality, particularly during the second half of the last century. Our modern psychoanalytic ideas are still informed and enriched by these classical observations, although our inspiration now derives from neuroscience and molecular genetics as well as the consulting room. Our clinical responsibilities have similarly expanded from the relatively intimate setting of the psychoanalytic practitioner devoting years to a single private patient to an opening-up of psychotherapeutic services to allow and encourage access for the massive numbers whose lives could be changed by appropriate psychological intervention. The scaling-up of psychological therapies to meet population demands has thus far privileged short-term interventions such as CBT, but not all disorders respond to psychotherapy when delivered within a brief, time-limited framework. Nevertheless, the onus is on the psychoanalytic clinician privileged by his expertise in understanding mind to be creative in developing an effective but potentially comprehensively available method that succeeds in preserving the key subtleties and respect for complexity of mind that psychoanalysis offers in its unparalleled richness, while at the same time enabling more than the few to have the benefit of its long-term value. This is the goal which we set ourselves on this journey that began 20 years ago, and we sincerely hope that we have advanced some of the way towards achieving it.

References

American Psychiatric Association (1980) *Diagnostic and Statistical Manual of Mental Disorders (3rd edn., DSM-III)*, Washington, DC: American Psychiatric Press.

American Psychiatric Association (1994) *Diagnostic and Statistical Manual of Mental Disorders (4th edn., DSM-IV)*, Washington, DC: American Psychiatric Association.

Bateman, A.W. (1998) Thick- and thin-skinned organisations and enactment in borderline and narcissistic disorders', *International Journal of Psychoanalysis*, 79 (Pt 1): 13–25.

Bateman, A.W. and Fonagy, P. (1999) 'The effectiveness of partial hospitalization in the treatment of borderline personality disorder – A randomised controlled trial', *American Journal of Psychiatry*, 156: 1563–1569.

Bateman, A.W. and Fonagy, P. (2001) 'Treatment of borderline personality disorder with psychoanalytically oriented partial hospitalization: An 18-month follow-up', *American Journal of Psychiatry*, 158 (1): 36–42.

Bateman, A.W. and Fonagy, P. (2003) 'Health service utilization costs for borderline personality disorder patients treated with psychoanalytically oriented partial hospitalization versus general psychiatric care', *American Journal of Psychiatry*, 160 (1): 169–171.

Bateman, A.W., Ryle, A., Fonagy, P. and Kerr, I.B. (2007) 'Psychotherapy for borderline personality disorder: Mentalization based therapy and cognitive analytic therapy compared', *International Review of Psychiatry*, 19 (1): 51–62.

Bateman, A.W. and Tyrer, P. (2004) 'Psychological treatment for personality disorders', *Advances in Psychiatric Treatment*, 10: 378–388.

Blackburn, R., Crellin, M., Morgan, E. and Tulloch, R. (1990) 'Prevalence of personality disorders in a special hospital population', *Journal of Forensic Psychiatry*, 1: 43–52.

Chanen, A.M., Jovev, M. and Jackson, H.J. (2007) 'Adaptive functioning and psychiatric symptoms in adolescents with borderline personality disorder', *Journal of Clinical Psychiatry*, 68: 297–306.

Coid, J., Yang, M., Tyrer, P., Roberts, A. and Ullrich, S. (2006) 'Prevalence and correlates of personality disorder in Great Britain', *British Journal of Psychiatry*, 188: 423–431.

de Rosnay, M. and Harris, P.L. (2002) 'Individual differences in children's understanding of emotion: The roles of attachment and language', *Attachment & Human Development*, 4 (1): 39–54.

Dolan, B.M. and Coid, J. (1993) *Psychopathic and Antisocial Personality Disorders: Treatment and Research Issues*, London: Gaskell.

Fonagy, P. (1989) 'On tolerating mental states: Theory of mind in borderline patients', *Bulletin of the Anna Freud Centre*, 12: 91–115.

Fonagy, P. (1991) 'Thinking about thinking: Some clinical and theoretical considerations in the treatment of a borderline patient', *International Journal of Psycho-Analysis*, 72: 1–18.

Fonagy, P., Gergely, G., Jurist, E. and Target, M. (2002) *Affect Regulation, Mentalization and the Development of the Self*, New York: Other Press.

Fonagy, P. and Higgitt, A. (1989) A developmental perspective on borderline personality disorder, *Revue Internationale de Psychopathologie*, 1: 125–159.

Fonagy, P., Steele, H., Moran, G., Steele, M. and Higgitt, A. (1991) 'The capacity for understanding mental states: The reflective self in parent and child and its significance for security of attachment', *Infant Mental Health Journal*, 13: 200–217.

Fonagy, P., Steele, H., Steele, M. and Holder, J. (1997) 'Attachment and theory of mind: Overlapping constructs?' *Association for Child Psychology and Psychiatry Occasional Papers*, 14: 31–40.

Fonagy, P. and Target, M. (1996) 'Playing with reality: I. Theory of mind and the normal development of psychic reality', *International Journal of Psycho-Analysis*, 77: 217–233.

Fonagy, P. and Target, M. (2000) 'Playing with reality: III. The persistence of dual psychic reality in borderline patients', *International Journal of Psychoanalysis*, 81 (5): 853–874.

Fonagy, P. and Target, M. (2007) 'Playing with reality: IV. A theory of external reality rooted in intersubjectivity', *International Journal of Psychoanalysis*, 88 (Pt 4): 917–937.

Fonagy, P., Target, M., Steele, H. and Steele, M. (1998) *Reflective-Functioning Manual, version 5.0, for Application to Adult Attachment Interviews*, London: University College London.

Glasser, M. (1998) 'On violence: A preliminary communication', *International Journal of Psychoanalysis*, 79: 887–902.

Gunderson, J.G. and Singer, M.T. (1975) 'Defining borderline patients: An overview', *American Journal of Psychiatry*, 132: 1–10.

Harris, P.L. (1999) 'Individual differences in understanding emotions: The role of attachment status and emotional discourse', *Attachment and Human Development*, 1 (3): 307–324.

Knight, R. (1953) 'Borderline states', *Bulletin of the Menninger Clinic*, 17: 1–12.

Leslie, A.M. (1987) 'Pretense and representation: The origins of "Theory of Mind"', *Psychological Review*, 94: 412–426.

Meins, E., Fernyhough, C., Russel, J. and Clark-Carter, D. (1998) Security of attachment as a predictor of symbolic and mentalising abilities: A longitudinal study, *Social Development*, 7: 1–24.

Mikton, C. and Grounds, A. (2007) 'Cross-cultural clinical judgment bias in personality disorder diagnosis by forensic psychiatrists in the UK: A case-vignette study', *Journal of Personality Disorders*, 21: 400–427.

Moran, P., Jenkins, R. and Tylee, A. (2000) 'The prevalence of personality disorder among UK primary care attenders', *Acta Psychiatrica Scandinavica*, 102: 52–57.

Ontai, L.L. and Thompson, R.A. (2002) 'Patterns of attachment and maternal discourse effects on children's emotion understanding from 3 to 5 years of age', *Social Development*, 11 (4): 433–450.

Pinto, C., Dhavale, H.S. and Nair, S. (2000) 'Borderline personality disorder exists in India', *Journal of Nervous and Mental Disease*, 188: 386–388.

Racker, H. (1957) 'The meanings and uses of countertransference', *Psychoanalytic Quarterly*, 26: 303–357.

Racker, H. (1968) *Transference and Countertransference*, London: Hogarth Press.

Raikes, H.A. and Thompson, R.A. (2006) 'Family emotional climate, attachment security, and young children's emotion knowledge in a high-risk sample', *British Journal of Developmental Psychology*, 24 (1): 89–104.

Rosenfeld, H. (1964) 'On the psychopathology of narcissism: A clinical approach', *International Journal of Psycho-Analysis*, 45: 332–337.

Rosenfeld, H. (1965) *Psychotic States: A Psychoanalytic Approach*, New York: International Universities Press.

Ruiter, C. and Greeven, P. (2000) 'Personality disorders in a Dutch forensic psychiatric sample: Convergence of interview and self-report measures', *Journal of Personality Diorder*, 14: 162–170.

Searles, H. (1960) *The Nonhuman Environment*, New York: International Universities Press.

Shea, M.T., Stout, R.L., Yen, S., Pagano, M.E., Skodol, A.E., Morey, L.C., *et al.* (2004) 'Associations in the course of personality disorders and Axis I disorders over time', *Journal of Abnormal Psychology*, 113 (4): 499–508.

Singleton, N. (1998) *Psychiatric Morbidity among Prisoners in England and Wales*, London: Office of National Statistics.

Skodol, A.E., Gunderson, J.G., Pfohl, B., Widiger, T.A., Livesley, W.J. and Siever, L.J. (2002) 'The borderline diagnosis I: Psychopathology, comorbidity and personality and personality structure', *Biological Psychiatry*, 51 (12): 936–950.

Steele, M., Steele, H., Croft, C. and Fonagy, P. (1999) 'Infant mother attachment at one year predicts children's understanding of mixed emotions at 6 years', *Social Development*, 8: 161–178.

Swartz, M., Blazer, D.G., George, L. and Winfield, I. (1990) 'Estimating the prevalence of borderline personality disorder in the community', *Journal of Personality Disorder*, 4: 257–272.

Symons, D.K. (2004) 'Mental state discourse, theory of mind, and the internalization of self–other understanding', *Developmental Review*, 24: 159–188.

Target, M. and Fonagy, P. (1996) 'Playing with reality II: The development of psychic reality from a theoretical perspective', *International Journal of Psycho-Analysis*, 77: 459–479.

Thompson, R.A. (2000) 'The legacy of early attachments', *Child Development*, 71: 145–152.

Torgersen, S., Kringlen, E. and Cramer, V. (2001) 'The prevalence of personality disorders in a community sample', *Archives of General Psychiatry*, 58: 590–596.

Tyrer, P., Merson, S., Onyett, S. and Johnson, T. (1994) 'The effect of personality disorder on clinical outcome, social networks and adjustment: A controlled clinical trial of psychiatric emergencies', *Psychological-Medicine*, 24 (3): 731–740.

Zanarini, M.C., Frankenburg, F.R., Hennen, J. and Silk, K.R. (2003) 'The longitudinal course of borderline psychopathology: 6-year prospective follow-up of the phenomenology of borderline personality disorder', *American Journal of Psychiatry*, 160 (2): 274–283.

Part 4

Analytic support to health service staff

Chapter 15

Relating psychoanalysis to general psychiatry

The role of the psychosis workshop

Richard Lucas

In this chapter, I shall be considering the role that a weekly psychosis workshop can play in helping junior doctors to relate meaningfully to patients in psychotic states (Garelick and Lucas, 1996). Following a description of the context behind the workshop, some differing analytic attitudes to psychosis will be briefly considered from a historical perspective. It is my premise that a differing analytic framework is necessary when approaching disorders that are psychotic compared to those that are neurotic. This framework is described and a clinical example given, to show the application of the framework in practice in a psychosis workshop.

The background context

In all training guidelines for junior doctors starting in psychiatry, a basic requirement is that they learn how to develop a therapeutic alliance with their patients. These skills are best developed through working with less disturbed patients under psychotherapy supervision. However, before the junior doctor has the chance to develop confidence in these skills, on their very first day in psychiatry they are plunged into the world of psychosis. These doctors have no previous in-depth knowledge of psychiatry, nor an analytic or dynamic framework to help them with their bewildering first encounters with psychotic states of mind. Within a very short time of starting their psychiatric training they find themselves on emergency duty where, metaphorically speaking, they are thrown in at the deep end in the paradoxical world of psychosis, with no one having taught them how to keep afloat in such dangerous waters.

During the day, the psychiatric junior doctor is not allowed to send a patient on leave without the consultant's written endorsement, yet that same evening he or she may be alone in the emergency clinic trying to make sense of psychotic states of mind, while faced with the decision as to whether or not the patient should be admitted. Patients in psychotic states tend to disown and project their troublesome feelings into others, thus creating an even more confused and disturbing state in the minds of these newly started junior doctors.

The situation is not helped by background psychiatric teaching that emphasizes the biological roots of psychosis. Although medication may clearly be both indicated and needed, a pharmacological model will not help the junior doctors to make sense of, and put to clinical use, these troublesome feelings that are engendered in them by the patient. The challenge also remains as to how to contemplate in one's own mind how a therapeutic alliance may be developed with the patient, such that the psychotic monologue may be converted into a dialogue between patient and doctor. This is a very different proposition from that involved in relating to a less disturbed patient.

The following vignette illustrates the problem.

At a weekly seminar I held with junior doctors who were new to psychiatry, a senior house officer (SHO) on night duty in the emergency clinic encountered a patient in a psychotic state who accused the junior doctor of being an impostor. The doctor prescribed medication and arranged to see the patient again. The seminar's response to the junior doctor was to tell him that next time he saw the patient he should wear a white coat! This response can be seen as a concrete attempt by the SHOs to protect their colleague's identity from attack. The directive to wear a white coat was all the armoury that they had at their disposal at the time, being unable to process the experience any further.

This vignette reminded me of a patient who, having smashed up his flat in a psychotic furore, was admitted under section to hospital. When I saw him on the locked ward the next day, he was in a calm state with no evidence of psychosis apart from the fact that he asked how he should know that I was a doctor rather than an impostor. He suggested that he should phone the police to check my credentials. The use of analytic concepts can help us appreciate the dynamics underlying this behaviour. Through projection and reversal into the opposite, I had become the impostor. In reality, it was the patient, now acting in a calm manner, who was the impostor in the sense that it was he, only the day before, who had smashed up his home. By sharing this experience with the SHOs, it became possible to stimulate their interest in the complexity of interactions with patients with psychotic states of mind.

The challenge for myself, working with a background in general psychiatry, has been to develop an analytic framework of direct relevance to those working in the NHS and to put it to use in weekly seminars with junior doctors.

Analytic attitudes to general psychiatry and psychosis

General psychiatry and psychosis have often been regarded as an arid area for analytic exploration: interestingly, Freud did not share this view. In 1916, writing on the subject of 'Psychoanalysis and Psychiatry' as part of his 'Introductory Lectures on Psychoanalysis' (1916–1917a), Freud had this to say: 'there is nothing in the nature of psychiatric work which could be opposed to psycho-analytic research. What is opposed to psycho-analysis is not psychiatry but psychiatrists.' This quotation would make for a lively debate at the AGM of the Royal College of Psychiatrists!

In a later paper in the Introductory Lectures series (1916–1917b) on 'The Libido Theory and Narcissism', Freud goes further in his support for the need for an analytic presence in general psychiatry.

> There are difficulties that hold up our advance. The narcissistic dis-orders and the psychoses related to them can only be deciphered by observers who have been trained in the analytic study of the trans-ference neuroses. But our psychiatrists are not students of psycho-analysis and we psycho-analysts see too few psychiatric cases. A race of psychiatrists must first grow who have passed through the school of psycho-analysis as a preparatory science.

At the time, Freud's hope was that this should occur in America.

Ernest Jones, the founder of the British Psychoanalytical Society, added his view in a paper entitled 'Psycho-analysis and Psychiatry' (1930).

> The normal, the neurotic, and the psychotic have reacted differently to the same fundamental difficulties of human development. Parentheti-cally, I wish to express here my conviction that the strategic point in the relationship between the three fields is occupied by the psychoneuroses. So-called normality represents a much more devious and obscure way of dealing with the fundamentals of life than the neuroses do, and it is correspondingly a much more difficult route to trace. The psychoses, on the other hand, present solutions so recondite and remote that it is very hard for the observer to develop a truly empathic attitude towards them, and unless this can be done, any knowledge remains intellec-tualistic, external and unfruitful.

In order to develop a 'truly empathic attitude', we need to tune in to the psychotic wavelength; ordinary empathy, applied to psychotic disorders, is not enough (Lucas, 1993).

Over the years analysts have, at times, tried to impose their own views to explain behaviour in psychosis. Reacting to the inhumanity of the early physical interventions such as leucotomy and insulin coma, Laing and the anti-psychiatry movement blamed schizophrenia on society's intolerance of eccentricity (Lucas, 1998), later becoming disenchanted when the psychosis did not remit with their *laissez-faire* attitude. In the United States, at Chestnut Lodge, the roots of psychosis were attributed to infantile trauma, following Fromm-Reichmann's concept of the 'schizophrenogenic' mother. Outcome studies, however, failed to produce a positive response when compared to borderline states (Fromm-Reichmann, 1957). In the United Kingdom during the 1960s, emerging Kleinian theory was applied to the mind in psychosis and led to an enthusiasm to treat individual cases of schizophrenia through analysis, with many important seminal insights gained from this work (Rosenfeld, 1965; Segal, 1957; Sohn, 1985). The prevailing optimistic climate also led to the creation of specialist analytic units in the NHS at Shenley and The Maudsley Hospitals (Jackson, 2001). However, following this initial enthusiasm the specialist centres closed, perhaps with the realisation of the intransigent nature of the chronic psychoses.

Following on from the work of Klein, and based on his individual analytic case studies, Bion introduced a completely new perspective to psychosis with his consideration of a psychotic part of the personality that develops and functions completely differently from the non-psychotic part (Bion, 1957). As junior doctors, we were invited by Bion to keep these two separate parts in mind and, in all major psychotic disorders, always to address the needs of the psychotic part first and foremost. It has been left to those few analysts still working in the field to add Bion's insights to preceding theories, in order to assemble a framework that is of relevance both to the task of relating to patients with psychosis and in aiding junior doctors in their work.

In modern day psychiatry, with its emphasis on evidence-based approaches, everything that is undertaken is expected to be open to objective measurement. At present, this does not include evidence arising from a consideration of the individual countertransference experience. Such evidence would be regarded as too subjective and unscientific, yet this is of crucial importance in the deciphering of experiences with psychotic states. I have found it essential to provide the space in a psychotic workshop to support the SHOs in the exploration and valuing of their individual emotional experiences, rather than these being ignored as idiosyncratic.

In the introduction to his book *Sex, Death, and the Superego* (2003), Ronald Britton compares this current emphasis on an 'evidence-based' approach in medical research with what he terms an 'experience-based' one. He points out that, in contrast to learning new medical skills, it takes decades to gain experience in psychoanalysis. In the meanwhile the young doctor has to rely on information gleaned from papers and from the supervision of others who have already gained such experience. He warns, however, that we all carry 'overvalued ideas' that can become treated as 'selected facts' (Britton, 2003). This means that we must always retain our own critical faculties when listening to others, no matter how experienced they may be in the field. This idea is highly relevant for SHOs starting out in psychiatry who, when presenting at workshops, need to be encouraged to retain their own critical faculties and individual sensitivities. Using Winnicott's terminology, we need to foster a 'facilitating environment' for the development of the next generation of psychoanalytically oriented psychiatrists (Winnicott, 1965).

For myself, despite an analytic training and seven years at the Maudsley Hospital, which included the privilege of working under Henri Rey in the psychotherapy department where we saw borderline patients, as well as time spent on the specialist psychosis inpatient unit, run initially by John Steiner and then by Murray Jackson, nothing prepared me for arriving at Claybury Hospital in 1978. The setting was a busy asylum, with responsibility for 28 acute beds, 125 long-stay beds, a day hospital, outpatient clinics and forensic visits. This was very different from the small caseload and academic atmosphere I had encountered at the Maudsley. I found that I had to act as a scavenger, gleaning any useful analytic contributions on psychosis from wherever I could find them, while at the same time being wary of overvalued ideas in myself or others. In this way I began building up a framework with which to relate to patients and their psychopathology. It has been a hard and demanding experience, but in the end a gratifying one in which I have been able to offer help to new psychiatrists starting out on their own voyages of discovery.

Developing a model of the mind applicable to psychosis

As a psychoanalyst who works in general psychiatry and carries clinical responsibility for patients during protracted admissions in very ill states of mind, my perspective is very different from that taken by the analytic psychotherapist in other areas of clinical work. The theory I work with is one that must take account of the following issues.

1. The usefulness as well as the limitations of the medical model; that is, the phenomenological and diagnostic classifications employed in psychiatry

The medical model, as applied within psychiatry, is very limited in flexibility. While it helps to clarify that we are dealing with a major psychotic disorder, it provides only a snapshot and cannot take account of dynamic movement, since this requires the introduction of an analytic model. Without a psychoanalytically based teaching, SHOs will not be introduced to this perspective.

2. The role of medication

Antipsychotic medication may help to act as a container and ease the psychoanalyst's pathway in relating to the patient. Antidepressant medication can sometimes be a helpful adjunct in facilitating the continuation of analysis in severe cases of depression where, for example, the patient is finding it difficult to get up for morning sessions. The fundamental point is that when we are dealing with psychosis we have to relinquish the omnipotent view (whether analytic or organic) that only one pathway should prevail. In other words, we need to be prepared to introduce flexibility into our thinking.

3. The notion of cure

The history of schizophrenia, from both organic and analytic perspectives, is redolent with optimistic attempts to cure the condition, since such an illness does not fit into our familiar preconceptions. When the asylums closed a decade ago, it was felt that chronic schizophrenia was the result of institutionalization. It followed from this idea that effective community care would obviate the need for inpatient beds, thus leading to an acute shortage of beds in the district hospitals. During the alarming early years of the illness, with its potential for suicidal acts, the danger is that we may focus too much on an attitude of achieving therapeutic success. This focus on therapeutic zeal may result in losing sight of the importance of providing support for the patient to come to terms with the condition, through helping to assemble a containing environment.

4. Theories of infantile trauma

Most analytic models of the mind place a central emphasis on infantile trauma in order to explain the development of psychopathology. However, we need to consider the limitations of over-relying on this approach when relating to patients with schizophrenia (Lucas, 2003). What is needed is an open mind in each individual case.

5. The need to differentiate psychotic processes from major psychiatric disorders

There is a need to differentiate severe borderline states from schizophrenia, since each has differing implications in terms of its modes of management and prognosis. Borderline patients teach us a lot about psychotic processes (Rey, 1994), and their management is enabled through an analytic approach. The transference directed towards the therapist has a particular intensity and the patient may well be very committed to the therapy.

For example:

A reclusive and eccentric character was referred to our hospital psychotherapy department, as he was very insistent on having individual therapy. No sooner was he in treatment with his very experienced psychotherapist than he threatened to complain to the hospital management that his therapist was incompetent. Such a patient, presenting as he did, is far more likely to have a severe borderline state than schizophrenia: the latter's management would involve the full community mental health team and the relatives, rather than remain focused on the individual therapy, as in this case.

6. A view of the 'death instinct'

Nothing in Freud's theorizing has generated more controversy among his followers than his introduction of an inherent destructive force, the death instinct or death drive. Freud introduced the concept belatedly to his metapsychology in order to complement his notion of the life instinct. As Laplanche and Pontalis (1973) pointed out in a detailed review of the death instinct, a dualistic tendency is fundamental to Freudian thought. At first Freud was tentative about the notion, but he ended up strongly endorsing it. He wrote, 'To begin with, it was only tentatively that I put forward the views that I have developed here, but in the course of time they have gained such a hold on me that I can no longer think in any other way' (Freud, 1930). Taken purely at a theoretical level, academic minded analysts have argued strongly against the validity of such a concept. In reviewing the concept, Black concluded, 'the death drive, as such, probably merits no future in psychoanalytic thinking' (Black, 2001). Schwartz went even further, saying, 'we should stop thinking of a death drive but directly in terms of destructiveness'. He added forcibly that, 'we should stop teaching the death drive in our training'. However, what is missing in their discussions is any clinical material to support this thesis.

When practising in general psychiatry and relating to patients with major psychotic disorders, I find I cannot think in any other way than that described above by Freud.

> A patient I once saw summarized the conflict of the contradictory nature of the life and death forces in his opening remark to analysis, when he said, 'Dr Lucas, I'm in a terrible state and really need analysis, but man to man as adults, I'm perfectly alright!' Later in the analysis, he graphically conveyed what is meant by death instinct material, when he related a dream where a nuclear explosion had occurred. There was devastation everywhere except for some vegetation remaining on an outer planet. His response to my observation on this sign of life was a mocking one. 'So you think that there is still some hope, do you?' He had said previously, in relation to his father's wish for him to have analysis, 'I am going to grind you and my father into nothing'. It is hard to keep going against such forces, whether seeing a patient individually or, more pertinently, for junior staff in everyday psychiatry.
>
> (Lucas, 1992)

Classical rehabilitation studies have echoed the same tune of Bion's description of the never-decided conflict between the life and death instincts in chronic schizophrenia. They found that people with learning difficulties, or following a stroke, could learn and retain new skills taught to them. This contrasts with the patient with chronic schizophrenia who will rust over as soon as the occupational therapist's back is turned and require constant stimulation. These negative symptoms of schizophrenia could be thought of as manifestations of the death instinct (Wing and Brown, 1961).

The question often arises, why not just view aggressiveness as a positive reaction to frustration, without the need to invoke such a draconian idea as the death instinct? When this point arose some time ago in a discussion at a British Psychoanalytic Society meeting, I recall Hanna Segal, a leading exponent on the death instinct, saying that the best way she could describe its manifestation in everyday life was 'human bloody-mindedness' – something we can all recognise. This certainly resonates with my own clinical experience when relating to patients with major psychotic disorders.

7. Tuning into the 'psychotic wavelength'

Identifying the dominating psychopathology, while retaining an overall empathy for the patient in his struggle to cope with crises within his own limited mental capacities, is a central issue in teaching SHOs to regard their patients as human beings rather than objectifying them as 'the psychotic'.

> A patient came into hospital having changed his name by deed poll to Jesus Christ, but complaining that he had no money and he was angry with God. He was unable to cope in his present state, so in his psychotic way he had hoped that, by his changing his name, God would help him out. Unfortunately for him, changing his name had not resolved his financial troubles. We can feel sympathy for him trying to cope with his predicament within his limited mental resources, rather than just considering the presenting material in phenomenological terms.

8. The importance of the countertransference experience

Since patients in psychotic states project, our countertransference experiences are of crucial importance when striving towards an overall understanding. For example, since there are two separate parts operating simultaneously in psychosis, we are frequently left questioning ourselves as to whether we are being fair when doubting the veracity of the patient's account. Is what the patient telling us evidence of psychosis, or is it the truth? If we experience this doubting countertransference, it usually indicates that we are in the realm of psychosis.

For the leader and participants of a psychosis workshop, it is a frequent experience to feel that we have nothing to contribute when we hear about florid psychotic material that makes no sense. It is only with time that we come to recognise that we have been on the receiving end of powerful projections from the psychotic part of the patient. This part is engaged in negating and evacuating thoughts that have been arrived at through the thinking work of the non-psychotic part. It is as if the psychotic part has a contemptuous murderous reaction, a 'so what!' response to any thinking that might take place. As the workshop proceeds, so it begins to come to life as we hear everyone's associations to the projected material. This enables the initial aridity to turn into a workshop that becomes creative and fruitful.

9. The deciphering of ideographs, and the relationship between hallucinations and delusions

Bion described how the psychotic part of the mind is incapable of thinking; it can only act as a muscular organ. It stores memories, termed ideographs, in which it projects feelings, for the purpose of evacuation or communication. Our task in everyday psychiatry is to decipher the meaning of these ideographs. This is comparable to solving crossword puzzle clues, and is helped by the simultaneous use of our countertransference experiences (Bion, 1958). Such work, importantly, introduces humour and interest into the team's involvement in work that might otherwise threaten to become arid, demanding and soul-destroying.

> A patient in a manic state complained of having contracted avian flu. If we think of the delusion as an attempt by the psychotic part to evacuate his sanity, the symptom becomes alive and interesting, rather than just a dry phenomenological description of a delusion requiring medication. I described the avian flu that the patient had caught from chickens as his attempt to fly away from his need to co-operate with our treatment for him. I said that he was chickening out of attending the day hospital and receiving full community support, rather than facing up, with us, to his problems. Interpreting in this way led to a smile from the patient and helped the care team feel less disabled by the patient's mania.

10. The psychotic and non-psychotic parts

Most importantly of all, I have learned to think always in terms of two separately functioning parts of the mind, rather than one person, when relating to such major psychotic disorders as schizophrenia, bipolar affective disorders and major depressive episodes. I would also include anorexia nervosa, as becomes evident in the clinical illustration that follows later.

In his seminal paper 'On Narcissism', Freud (1914) described two completely separate modes of functioning of the mind. These were the anaclitic and the narcissistic, with the narcissistic mode predominating in schizophrenia and depression. We might consider the narcissistic mode as fuelled by the death instinct, with envy as its external manifestation (Freud, 1914). Bion (1957) expanded on Freud's theme of duality in his paper that differentiated the psychotic from the non-psychotic parts of the personality, with narcissism the dominant mode in the psychotic part (Segal and Bell, 1991).

As a general psychiatrist, whenever I am asked to consider sectioning a patient under the Mental Health Act, I have to determine whether I am relating to a sane part of the patient or to a mad part that is masquerading as normal. Denial and rationalisation, rather than hallucinations and delusions, are the commonest presenting symptoms in psychosis. We can frequently be fooled by the patient's denials and rationalisations into underestimating the severity of the disturbance in their underlying state of mind. A common occurrence of this dynamic in everyday analytic practice is in severe depression, where we might think we are relating to a non-psychotic part that is seeking insight, whereas the dominating psychotic part is not in the least interested in understanding, since all it wants is fusion with an idealised object (Lucas, 2003).

I think that most analysts who are not familiar with working in general psychiatry may still feel uncomfortable with the notion of two separate parts, rather than thinking in terms of split-off parts of the personality requiring reintegration. Such splitting, though a fundamental concept, properly belongs to the workings of the non-psychotic part. For myself, I find this concept of two separate parts of the personality to be of enormous help when I am trying to orient myself to the presenting psychosis. For example, if a patient says that he is feeling fine, yet the nearest relative has alerted the professionals to an alarming relapse, who are we to believe? It is crucial, in my view, that approved social workers carry this model of the two parts in mind when they are conducting an assessment under the Mental Health Act, otherwise they can be left with the view that asserts that the patient is fine and the problem lies solely with the relative (Lucas, 2003).

With this background framework in mind, I will now turn to material presented at a psychosis workshop by an SHO to his colleagues, who were all relatively new to psychiatry. I hope that the example will illustrate why analytic concepts need to be pitched to the psychotic wavelength if they are to impact on, and be of use to, the SHOs.

Clinical example

The background history

At a weekly psychosis workshop, held in an informal setting, an SHO who was working on the eating disorder unit presented the problem of a 19-year-old girl with a history of severe anorexia, since the age of 15. She had spent 18 months in a non-specialised hospital and had then been transferred for a year to an inpatient adolescent unit. After discharge, she started primary school teacher training, but within a year required readmission. She had been on the eating disorder unit for two months at the time of the presentation.

We were told that although she was prepared to walk, she would neither eat nor drink. Under the Mental Health Act she was having to be forcibly fed twice a day through a naso-gastric tube. She kept pulling out the tube and it took six nurses to hold her down, while she screamed and resisted the tube being reinserted.

This young woman came from a Catholic background. She was the fifth of seven children and there was no family history of mental illness. She had always been shy, which was regarded as indicative of her being very determined or very stubborn, depending on how it was looked at. She had been diagnosed as having a psychotic depression as well as anorexia nervosa, because she experienced visual hallucinations and kept saying that she wanted to die. The visual hallucinations involved seeing people who were dead. In the past, these visions of dead people had frightened her, but now she was saying that she did not mind if she joined them. Other people could stab her or give her an overdose, she said, but she would not do this; she could only try to die through starving herself. As part of her treatment on the eating disorder unit she was seeing a psychotherapist for individual sessions, but this person was not present at the workshop.

The discussion

In the ensuing discussion, the following issues emerged.

1   In his countertransference experience, the presenting SHO felt that her illness was like a bulldozer. He also complained of a monologue, mainly in the form of a controlling silence by the patient. There was no dialogue and only on rare occasions did the patient appear as if near to tears.

2   The SHO also wondered if her religious background played a part, as she had initially asked to see the visiting Catholic priest, who was described as a warm and homely person. However, she now no longer wished to see him.

3   Another SHO at the workshop recalled that when on duty and having to be involved in her naso-gastric feeding, he at first felt sad for her, then frustrated and angry with her resistance to intubation, it being so very difficult for him to do. Finally, when at last he succeeded with the intubation, he felt like he was raping her.

4   Another doctor felt that we were stuck at a level of intubating her in response to her actions and that we were also stuck at that physical level when relating to this patient.

5   Apart from my SHO, all the other SHOs thought of the hallucinations solely in phenomenological terms, as part of the picture of a psychotic depression. My SHO had been with me for several months and, unlike the other SHOs, was a GP in training rather than a psychiatrist in training. This meant that he was not weighed down by phenomenology training for exam purposes. He expressed a different view, saying that the hallucinations told him of a worrying change of forces inside her; where first she had been frightened of an identification with dead people, now she was not.

Teaching points

The psychotic wavelength

If anorexia nervosa and depression are psychotic disorders, it means that we cannot rely solely on our ordinary sensitivities to make sense of what is happening. We need to tune into, and relate to, the specific psychopathology.

1   *The psychotic and non-psychotic parts.* In psychotic disorders, as Bion (1957) pointed out, we will not make progress unless we think of two separate parts rather than one person, and it is the psychotic part that we have to deal with first. In anorexia nervosa, the psychotic anorexic part has a fundamental hatred of appetite and is murderous towards any sign of its presence in the non-anorexic part (Sohn, 1985). This way of thinking can help the SHOs to understand why the patient would not stab herself or take an overdose. In her madness, this behaviour would imply an appetite for something and thus represent a need, however destructive this was. Thus others would have to do these things to her; she could only kill herself passively through starvation.

2   *The limitations of the phenomenological approach.* While the phenomenological approach is important for diagnostic purposes, in a dynamic clinical situation where a different approach is needed, the eyes of the SHOs can be opened to its limitations. The differing ways of approaching the visual hallucinations are a telling example.

3   *From monologue to dialogue.* The psychotic part evacuates the insight arrived at by the thinking work of the non-psychotic part, in the never-

ending conflict between the life and death instincts. Hence the non-psychotic part has a need for a warm priest as a supportive figure. The psychotic part has disowned these feelings, via projection, into the priest and now does not want to see him anymore. If we had thought of her behaviour in a more conventional way, we might simply have concluded that she was just showing ambivalent feelings towards Catholicism. A problem had arisen in this young woman in which a very powerful anorexic part became dominant. This part hated the sane, non-anorexic part that had an appetite for living. We can see that the presenting situation is not an ordinary separation anxiety, nor is it a fear of living – as suggested by the SHO – or, indeed, a fear of growing up, as some have suggested is the cause of anorexia.

The SHOs' basic problem, and this applies to all cases presented at the psychosis workshop, is how do we find a way of talking meaningfully to the patient? In other words, how is it possible to imagine a way of converting a psychotic monologue into a two-person dialogue? In this anorexic patient, the mental conflict has been reduced through projection solely into a physical battle around feeding. The conflict needs to be reinstated as a mental problem. At the physical level the anorexic part has to be helped to realise that the non-anorexic part is being given equally powerful support in its need to survive during a dominating anorexic episode. While over the course of many years, with the help of psychotherapy, the non-anorexic part may be helped to grow in reflective strength, the SHO, in this moment of time, needs a meaningful framework to grasp hold of – which can then be spelled out to the patient. That is, that the battle between the two parts can be described, while the staff continue to support a dominated, tearful sane part that currently remains in a suppressed state, but which wants to live and to train as a teacher. Only when this is being spelled out to the patient can periods of non-naso-gastric feeding be tried out within the context of an attempted mental dialogue. Nevertheless, we would have to expect that there might be long spells when all sanity remained projected into the staff while the anorexic behaviour remained predominant.

In psychotic disorders, staff may have to endure stages of seemingly never-ending intransigence, such as those that occur with protracted episodes of depression in hospitalised cases. While waiting for these episodes to relent, it is essential to keep a live dialogue going, even if it seems confined solely to the staff and carers. It is at such difficult times that these analytic concepts can really resonate for SHOs and care staff alike. If the SHOs can become freed from the dogma of purely phenomenological thinking, they can then be free to be their individual selves and thus take an interest in their own responsiveness to the material. Through the analytic framework, they are introduced to the means of developing a confidence in speaking in a more real way to their patients, and thus moving the relationship from a monologue to a dialogue – even if this is taking place only in their own minds.

In conclusion, it has been my hope that in conducting these weekly psychosis workshops, those SHOs most receptive to these analytic ideas and concepts will form the basis for the next generation of medically trained psychoanalysts; indeed, I have already found this to be the case in practice. In this way, we are fulfilling Freud's wish that a psychoanalytic presence remains in the field of general psychiatry.

References

Bion, W.R. (1957) 'Differentiating of the psychotic from the non-psychotic personalities'. In *Second Thoughts* (pp. 43–64), New York: Jason Aronson (1967).

Bion, W.R. (1958) 'On hallucination'. In *Second Thoughts* (pp. 65–85), New York: Jason Aronson (1967).

Black, D.M. (2001) 'Mapping a detour: Why did Freud speak of a death drive?', *British Journal of Psychotherapy*, 18: 185–197.

Britton, R. (1998) *Belief and Imagination*, London: Routledge.

Britton, R. (2003) *Sex, Death and the Superego: Experiences in Psychoanalysis*, London: Karnac.

Freud, S. (1914) 'On narcissism: An introduction', *Standard Edition*, Vol. 14, London: Hogarth Press.

Freud, S. (1916–1917a) 'Psycho-analysis and psychiatry: Introductory lectures on psycho-analysis', *Standard Edition*, Vol. 16, pp. 254–255, London: Hogarth Press.

Freud, S. (1916–1917b) 'The libido theory and narcissism', *Standard Edition*, Vol. 16, London: Hogarth Press.

Freud, S. (1930) 'Civilization and its discontents', *Standard Edition*, Vol. 21, London: Hogarth Press.

Fromm-Reichmann, F. (1957) *Principles of Intensive Psychotherapy*, Chicago: University of Chicago Press.

Garelick, A. and Lucas, R. (1996) 'The role of a psychosis workshop in general psychiatric training', *Psychiatric Bulletin*, Royal College of Psychiatrists, 20: 425–429.

Jackson, M. (2001) *Weathering Storms: Psychotherapy for Psychosis*, London: Karnac.

Jones, E. (1930) 'Psycho-analysis and psychiatry'. *Papers on Psychoanalysis* (p. 336), London: Maresfield Reprints.

Laplanche, J. and Pontalis, J.B. (1973) *The Language of Psychoanalysis*, London: Hogarth Press.

Lucas, R. (1992) 'The psychotic personality: A psychoanalytic theory and its application in clinical practice', *Psychoanalytic Psychotherapy*, 7: 3–17.

Lucas, R. (1993) 'The psychotic wavelength', *Psychoanalytic Psychotherapy*, 7: 89–101.

Lucas, R. (1998) 'R.D. Laing – His life and legacy', *International Journal of Psychoanalysis*, 79: 1229–1239.

Lucas, R. (2003) 'Psychoanalytic controversies: The relationship between psychoanalysis and schizophrenia', *International Journal of Psychoanalysis*, 84: 3–15.

Rey, J.H. (1994) *Universals of Psychoanalysis in the Treatment of Psychotic and Borderline States*, London: Free Association Books.

Rosenfeld, H. (1965) *Psychotic States: A Psychoanalytic Approach*, London: Hogarth Press.

Segal, H. (1957) 'Notes on symbol formation'. *The Work of Hanna Segal* (pp. 49–65), New York: Jason Aronson.

Segal, H. and Bell, D. (1991) 'The theory of narcissism in the work of Freud and Klein', In J. Sandler, E.S. Person and P. Fonagy (Eds.), *Freud's On Narcissism: An Introduction. Contemporary Freud, Turning Points and Critical Issues* (pp. 149–174), New Haven, CT: Yale University Press.

Sohn, L. (1985) 'Narcissistic organisation, projective identification and the formation of the identificate', *International Journal of Psychoanalysis*, 66: 201–214.

Wing, J.K. and Brown, G.W. (1961) 'Social treatment of chronic schizophrenia: A comparative survey of three mental hospitals', *Journal of Mental Science*, 107: 338–340.

Winnicott, D.W. (1965) *The Maturational Process and the Facilitating Environment.* London: Hogarth Press.

Chapter 16

Doctors in trouble[1]

Rob Hale and Liam Hudson

This chapter describes a service for 'doctors in need of psychological help'. It is run by a psychoanalyst, and while offering a broad range of services the fundamental understanding is psychoanalytic. The service is funded by the postgraduate medical dean and is available to all those qualified doctors in the area who are in a training role, whether as trainers or trainees. Individuals come because they recognize that they are in trouble, or because others find their professional behaviour unacceptable and are worried about their mental health – or, of course, a combination of the two. Doctors coming to the service are offered up to six assessment sessions. Should this be required, they are then referred to another agency for further treatment. In the first 22 months since the regional dean took over the funding of the service, 64 doctors were seen. While this chapter concentrates on the treatment of doctors, many of the principles enunciated are applicable to health workers in general.

The overriding principle governing any such service is that of confidentiality. While the postgraduate dean funds the service, neither she nor her staff has access, direct or indirect, to the information it yields about identifiable individuals. There are a few exceptions. These arise when the therapist believes that doctors in treatment may be a danger to their patients. In these cases, and following discussion with the doctors themselves, disclosure may from time to time be necessary. Further, the treatment is offered in an institution both geographically and organizationally separate from the one in which the doctor works, and doctors can use it without fear of being noticed. Shift systems within medicine are a reality too, and these must be accommodated. To do this runs counter to different defensive structures. We, as doctors, develop our own pattern of defences, their shape determined by the interaction of the personality we bring to medicine with the distinctive anxieties of the branch of medicine in which we specialize. Psychodynamic theory conceives of the individual as an equilibrium-seeking system, within which anxiety causes us to partition experience between the acknowledged and the ignored or denied (Hudson, 1998). From a more specifically psychoanalytic perspective, it is the relationships and experiences of childhood that are seen as the key determinants of such adult adaptations. Not only do these focus the expression of genetic and intrauterine influences, translating them into culturally recognizable forms, but they contribute causally in their own right by establishing – or failing to establish – those primitive bonds of trust between child and parent on which, later in life, resilience to stress is going to depend. There is a further argument, itself psychoanalytic in inspiration (Jaques, 1955; Menzies, 1961), which conceives of institutions – firms, hospitals – as themselves taking on the form they do as a defence against the anxiety and depression of those who work inside them.

In this chapter, two cases are presented. The doctors in question are alike in that the sources of their distress are predominantly internal; the psychological concomitants of developmental crises left unresolved. They differ in that the first doctor is seriously ill whereas the second is not. They also differ culturally, in that the first springs from a background of pronounced cultural fissure and personal dislocation; the second from a background that is altogether more coherent. A plausible reading of the evidence about them is that the fissured background of the first has contributed materially to the severity of her illness, and that the coherence of the second's background has served as a source of psychological strength.

Dr Y

Reluctant to seek help, Dr Y first made contact with the service at the suggestion of a doctor already in treatment. She is aged 40, and works in a relatively small general practice with two other partners and a list of some 7,000 patients. Depressed, she says that her partners are to some extent aware of the depths of her difficulties and are 'very supportive'. Her difficulties seemed to start three years ago, when she realized a relationship was going to fail. In fact, it ran on for two more years before it eventually broke up. The break-up coincided with the onset of her mother's fatal illness from chronic heart failure. Dr Y now lives with her ageing father. She feels, irrationally, that she precipitated her mother's illness, and experiences an overwhelming sense of pointlessness and failure.

She is the youngest of six children, and the only one now unmarried. Her parents came to the UK in 1972, at least in part so that she, the youngest, could have a proper education. Her father and oldest brother urgently wanted her to study medicine, and in doing so she became the family's success story – in her own phrase, its 'status symbol'. Her mother on the other hand remained sceptical, hoping that she would become a wife and mother. Dr Y herself, she now claims, entertained doubts. Often she would say to her mother, 'I wish I was like you. Uneducated. A mum.' In her early twenties, Dr Y entered a marriage that had her family's approval, and went abroad with her new husband. After two years, it was clear that the marriage was not going to succeed, and she decided to end it. Pregnant at the time, and feeling the need to choose between her husband and her unborn child, she had a termination: 'I feel now that I'm being punished for what I did then. I feel so guilty about what I did.'

Although Dr Y's troubles surfaced in her late thirties, their sources lay in a familiar but, in her case, unresolved conflict between career and motherhood. Her father had taken one view; her mother another. Where her father wanted her to embrace the values of Western society, her mother remained rooted in those of her more traditional culture – the one within which Dr Y had grown up until she was a teenager, and which embodied strong expectations about the destiny of women as mothers and home-makers. It is one thing for an able teenaged girl to be uprooted from one culture and transplanted to another if both parents adopt similar attitudes towards the move. It is quite another if her mother pulls in one direction and her father in another. In as much as Dr Y could commit herself wholeheartedly to the values and mores of modern Britain, she was severing herself from the assumptive world within which she had grown up and in which her mother remained firmly lodged. Worse, the removal from a traditional culture to a modern culture was one that was to be justified in her father's eyes, in part at least, by her professional success, her future as the family's 'status symbol'.

The literature on outsiders and emigrés suggests that the removal from one culture to another is often accompanied by a release of imaginative energy and entrepreneurial vigour (Hudson and Jacot, 1986). In Dr Y's case, no such release occurred – presumably because, at some primitive level, her identifications and loyalties were divided. Her career as a doctor was the expression not so much of her own longings, but of her father's and eldest brother's longings for her. Not only has she reached the age of 40 as the only member of her family unmarried and childless, but there is a sense, it follows, in which she sacrificed her career as a mother to her medical career – a career about which she was bound to be equivocal, and about which she became increasingly uncertain as the pressure exerted on her by her patients mounted. She is aware now that she is not investing herself in the practice as she should, and often finds herself resenting the demands her patients make. These she finds trivial. 'I feel I'm constantly having to give.'

Dr Y's efforts to help herself are interspersed with episodes that are openly self-destructive. She has taken three overdoses; tried to strangle herself; and on her fortieth birthday drove up and down the motorway at high speed hoping that someone would cause her to crash. 'When you are suicidal, you think of nothing else. Afterwards, it's frightening to realize how crazy you've been.'

At the end of the first meeting with her therapist (RH), it was clear that Dr Y needed both immediate support and long-term psychotherapy. With her permission, her GP was contacted – he was the family's doctor but was unaware of her difficulties and had not previously been consulted by her about them. He was asked to prescribe paroxetine, an antidepressant drug, and agreed. Dr Y and her therapist arranged to meet again in three days' time.

Subsequently, Dr Y was to spend a substantial period off work. In a session four months after the first contact, she spoke of the anxieties she had experienced in her first return to general practice. She found herself doubting her own judgement. She said that she had been looking through the notes of cases that she had been dealing with before she had gone sick. There was a woman who had presented with a cough. In the intervening two months the cough had persisted. Dr Y's partner had referred the patient and a carcinoma had been found. Dr Y felt at once that the fault was hers. The therapist pointed out to Dr Y that she was her own harshest critic. Most doctors would have acted as she acted, but would not now feel guilty. Normally, she would have been able to cope. She agreed: 'Yes, I would've laughed it off.' She went on to describe how her patients were demanding so much of her and how hard she found it. They were waiting for her to come back. Her therapist replied that perhaps they were also telling her that they were angry with her for having gone away in the first place. She said that she couldn't stand up to her patients as she once could. She told of a woman who – yet again – had come in demanding medication that she, Dr Y, knew was unnecessary. In the past Dr Y had stood up to her. Recently the patient had been to see a consultant who had confirmed in a letter that the patient did not need the medication. The patient told Dr Y, nevertheless, that the consultant had said that she should have a small amount of the medication just in case there was a crisis. Dr Y said that she had given in to the patient because she couldn't face an argument. The therapist suggested that she was upset because neither she nor the patient could face the anxiety underlying the patient's insistent request. She knew that the patient's demand expressed her terror of being left without a safety line. In her still fragile state Dr Y realizes that her own anxieties are mirrored in those of her patients. As she recovers, she recognizes that she must keep separate her patients' unacknowledged terrors from her own.

Dr C

Tall, elegant and trendily dressed, Dr C is for all the world the epitome of the successful young doctor. She comes from a medical family, her cultural background as coherent as Dr Y's is fissured. Despite a rebellious adolescence in which she became a punk, she managed by the time she was 17 to have a choice between art school, music school and medical school. By the time she was 26, she had a first in her BSc. Honours in one part of her finals, and had passed both parts of her Membership at her first attempt. Now, two years later, she is established in a registrar's post in a top London postgraduate hospital. Unlike Dr Y, she is in no obvious sense ill.

Something was nonetheless sufficiently amiss with her life, both professional and private, to bring her into therapy.

The account given here is drawn from a single session, as usual on a Saturday morning. It pays attention to the detail of her exchanges with her therapist.

> Dr C: After I saw you a fortnight ago I felt really pissed off. You made me recognize how hard a time I was giving my boyfriend. I apologized and all he could do was chuck it back in my face. He said he couldn't cope with my moods. He couldn't understand that I was telling him that I recognized how much I loaded onto him. He said he just couldn't cope with me.

I said that she must feel angry with me for making her vulnerable. She seemed to be telling me that therapy was removing her defences – an inevitable consequence of therapy in its early stages.

> Dr C: Well, it's been a pretty lousy fortnight anyway. My boss has been away, and there has been this terribly sick woman; we thought she was going to die. The awful thing was that we couldn't find out why. She had septicaemia and we couldn't find the cause. We just had to watch her going downhill. The other consultants came and gave their opinions but they didn't seemed concerned in the way he is. It was all very well for those consultants. She wasn't their patient. They could just walk away from her. On my nights off, I just couldn't sleep.

Her last session had evidently shaken her, and I asked why.

> Dr C: It was realizing that I was still the Princess who gets what she wants, and people do what she wants.

I noticed then that she was crying. On the last occasion but one, I reminded her, she had turned up at the clinic, although I had told her well in advance I would be away. Again, I pointed out to her the omnipotent nature of her thought: the assumption that I would be waiting for her, when she knew, consciously, that I was not going to be there. At the time, she had jumped back into her car with a mixture of anger and disappointment and real relief; relief that there were things inside her that she wouldn't have to face.

> Dr C: You are just not expected to be weak when you are a doctor. The day before yesterday, I was caught in the corridor by the wife of a man who has leukaemia. The consultant was going to tell him at lunchtime, but his wife had already guessed. She was furious with me. Why couldn't I tell her? I had been up all the night before and really couldn't

cope with her shouting at me. I didn't handle it at all well. I went to the sluice and locked the door and cried for a bit. Then I realized I had to tell the patient straightaway. As I was going to tell him, his wife came in. I had to tell her to go away. I hated myself for what I was doing because I knew she was so frightened.

I replied that she was telling me about life-shattering events for which she felt responsible and with which she was expected to cope. At the back of her mind, she was uneasy about where her boss had been – and, more importantly, where I had been. I pointed out that she had rung me the previous week to say that she could not make the session because she was still coping with the patients she had admitted the night before. She must feel, somewhere, that I should make time for her in the way that she made time for her patients.

> Dr C: Yes, but look what it does to you when you really care about your patients. My boss, Brian – he has been a consultant for only two years. He's 39, but he looks 20 years older. He's balding and going grey.

I made no comment.

> Dr C: He's the one that everyone wants to refer patients to because he cares. He works morning, noon and night.

I said that she was worried about who looked after Brian, and that she felt responsible for him as well as for her patients.

> Dr C: Well, I don't want to look after him, and I'm not sure now that I want to be him. The other day, I found myself sitting in the middle of the ward saying out loud 'Where am I going?', and people said 'Now Sarah is really losing her marbles'.

I asked how people cope without losing their marbles.

> Dr C: Well, most medics do. They can just shut off. They can look at it as an intellectual exercise. Even Brian does that at times. We had a postmortem over the woman who had just died. We all sat round and talked about the pathology findings. Nobody really talked about what they felt inside.

I said that I thought she was struggling to find a place where she could talk about these feelings, and that in a way she was bringing the need of her whole unit with her to our sessions.

Dr C: Yes, but that's not much use, because how can I feed it back into them when they can't hear it?

I said that she was telling me today about the dilemma of being the omnipotent medical Princess yet of having to face the reality that people die and that you can do nothing. Part of her was telling me too that therapy didn't help either. It was the end of the session. She got out her diary, and we made the next appointment, fitting it in with her time off-duty.

The course of psychotherapy is hard to foresee. In the cases of Dr Y and Dr C, the hope is that they will learn to recognize as dysfunctional their own preoccupations and traits: Dr Y's guilt and Dr C's omnipotence. It is also hoped they will learn, in their therapy, to distinguish more clearly between their patients' unacknowledged anxieties and their own. Both may well move within the profession towards niches in which the demands made on them are more congruous with their own capacities to cope. It could be, for example, that Dr Y will move from general practice, and the incessant emotional demands its patients make, into work where contact with patients is more carefully regulated – or even into laboratory research. Dr C could move too. In her case, the prestige of her present position is bound to make a sideways move seem like a defeat; but she could nonetheless switch from physical medicine to a specialty where her psychological sensitivity would become an advantage. She might move, for example, in the direction of psychiatry or pediatrics – or fill Dr Y's place in the ranks of the GPs.

Patients who are referred

With both Dr Y and Dr C, who had come to the service voluntarily, the enterprise of therapy was collaborative. Unsurprisingly, when approached for permission to publish the clinical material, albeit appropriately disguised, each gave her permission. Unlike them, approximately one-third of the doctors seen in the service were referred by their consultant or clinical tutor. Working with doctors who have been referred in this way, the therapist becomes forcefully aware that different anxieties are in play; the doctors' preoccupations are often paranoid in character, and the fantasies are those of persecution. Questions of allegiance and absolute confidentiality here become crucial issues and, for this reason, it was felt inappropriate to present clinical material in this chapter from a doctor who had been referred.

It should be said, nevertheless, that the position of the referred doctor is rarely simple. One doctor may become the focus and scapegoat for a troubled unit or hospital. In effect, doctors may come for therapy on their firm's behalf. Often it takes a crisis, sometimes a crisis with legal implications, for the need – whether individual or collective – to be recognized.

For the doctors on whom such pressures play, there is the reasonable fear of being labelled sick, mad, or inadequate – the weak link in a macho team. Small wonder that many doctors, junior or senior, can regard seeking psychological help as tantamount to professional suicide. This is particularly so for those working in the specialties with the highest prestige, and in teams where excellence is sustained on the strength of the prime movers' latent psychopathology.

The position of the referred doctor has a further complication. Often a clash of cultures plays its part in the story, as it did for Dr Y, and with such clashes come the possibility of ethnic or racial prejudice. A feature of the present service bears on this possibility. Nearly three-quarters of the doctors using the service were trained in the UK. Of these, just over half were self-referred, the others being referred either by their consultants or by their clinical tutors. The remaining quarter of the doctors using the service were foreign-trained; of these, all but three came because they were referred by their consultants or clinical tutors. Many of the home-trained experience themselves as troubled and come for help of their own accord; in other words, this pattern is unusual among the foreign-trained (Hale and Hudson, 1992). The consequence is that many of those foreign-trained doctors who use the service do so seized with thoughts of rejection and persecution that obstruct the development of a collaborative atmosphere. Regrettably, then, the experience of collaborative therapy within the service is at present very largely restricted to work with doctors trained in the UK.

A final thought

Our hospitals grew out of institutions that were religious in nature, informed by religious values. Altruism remains central to the practice of medicine in the British Isles to this day. Recently, however, new and more commercial values have been introduced. A small but significant proportion of the doctors who refer themselves to the service as patients do so as a result of these changes. Typically, their firms are experiencing difficulty in meeting financial targets, a constraint that not only is unfamiliar but seems to violate the doctors' ethic of care. Usually it is the consultant who comes on these grounds, but more than once it has been a junior doctor who comes, as it were, as emissary.

The new ways of the Health Service undermine the existing defences of many doctors, both at a personal level and at the level of the institution. Many of the pressures exerted are indiscriminate, causing anxiety in the minds of the more and less dedicated alike. They may also be gratuitous in that, with appropriate care, their effect could be mitigated or avoided altogether. It may not be unduly difficult to design forms of medical training that preserve the doctor's traditional altruism, but at the same time acknowledge the severity of the psychological demands that the practice of medicine in a cost-conscious Health Service can make.

Note

1 This chapter was originally published in J. Firth-Cozens and R.L. Payne (Eds.) (1999), *Stress in Health Professionals*, Chichester, UK: Wiley.

References

Brown, R. (1986) *Social Psychology* (2nd edn., pp. 635–685), London: Collier Macmillan.

Firth-Cozens, J. (1992) 'The role of early family experiences in the perception of organizational stress', *Journal of Occupational and Organizational Psychology*, 65: 61–75.

Friedman, E.S., Clark, D.B. and Gershon, S. (1992) 'Stress, anxiety and depression', *Journal of Anxiety Disorders*, 6: 337–363.

Hale, R. and Hudson, L. (1992) 'The Tavistock study of young doctors', *British Journal of Hospital Medicine*, 47: 452–464.

Holmes, T.H. and Rahe, R.H. (1967) 'The social readjustment rating scale', *Journal of Psychosomatic Research*, 11: 213–218.

Hudson, L. (1998) *Strangely Familiar: The Psychological Significance of Boundaries and of What Lies Beyond Them*. Tanner Lecture on Human Values, Yale University, 14 April 1997, Salt Lake City, UT: University of Utah Press.

Hudson, L. and Jacot, B. (1986) 'The outsider in science'. In C. Bagley and G.K. Verma (Eds.), *Personality, Cognition and Values*, London: Macmillan.

Jaques, E. (1955) 'Social systems as a defence against persecutory and depressive anxiety'. In M. Klein, P. Helmann and R.E. Money-Kyrle (Eds.), *New Directions in Psychoanalysis*, London: Tavistock.

Menzies, I.E.P. (1961) *The Functioning of Social Systems as a Defence against Anxiety*, Tavistock Pamphlet No. 3, London: Tavistock.

Morgan, D.R. (Ed.) (1992) *Stress and the Medical Profession*, London: British Medical Association.

O'Leary, A. (1990) 'Stress, emotion, and human immune function', *Psychological Bulletin*, 108: 363–382.

Rycroft, C. (1968) *Anxiety and Neurosis*, Harmondsworth: Penguin.

Richings, J.C., Khara, G.S. and McDowell, M. (1986) 'Suicide in young doctors', *British Journal of Psychiatry*, 149: 475–478.

Taylor, G.J. (1987) *Psychosomatic Medicine and Contemporary Psychoanalysis*, Madison, CT: International Universities Press.

Chapter 17

Teaching a psychoanalytic approach to public sector mental health workers

Graham Ingham and Vic Sedlak

In this chapter we describe our efforts to offer a relatively short, psycho-analytically oriented programme of reading seminars and work discussion groups to a wide range of mental health professionals. Our aim was to give participants a sense of a psychoanalytic approach to their work and as a means of understanding their patients/clients. Our experience of working in the National Health Service (NHS) over many years had been that young and inexperienced colleagues had increasingly been asked to take on and treat more and more disturbed patients. We had noted that this could have a number of different effects, such as a wish to find quick, simplistic interventions. We had observed that when these failed, therapists could become quite demoralized and then they sometimes sought more sophisticated and psychoanalytical frames of reference in which to understand their patients and the destructive and repetitive patterns of their pathology. With this in mind we wanted to offer something that would be of help to members of NHS staff who wished to learn of ways of understanding and intervening in the lives of such patients.

Both of us were essentially in private practice; although we were involved with providing supervision and personal analysis to a number of NHS staff, this was on a private basis. We were fortunate therefore that two local psychotherapy departments were sufficiently aware of the need for the sort of programme we wanted to offer to create a setting in which it could take place. They collaborated to provide us with a paid session each in which to prepare and carry out the programme, as well as accommodation and administrative help. Without such support it would have been very difficult to set up and carry out our intervention. For example, these NHS departments already knew potential applicants who had expressed previous interest in a psychoanalytic way of thinking, and they were able to advertise our proposal and to field enquiries. We produced a leaflet to advertise the programme; it is worth quoting from it as a means of describing the kind of problems we wanted to address.

Working with difficult patients will put various strains on mental health professionals. They can be of two sorts: the difficult patient will by definition be difficult to treat and will tax the clinician's capacity to formulate the patient's problem in a manner that can lead to appropriate and effective intervention. Secondly, the difficult patient will stir up in the clinician uncomfortable emotions that will challenge his or her ability to function in a helpful and professional manner.

The seminars offered will address both of these areas by offering a reading seminar in which core psychoanalytic concepts of theory and technique will be taught and discussed. Secondly, a work discussion group will focus on an understanding of the emotional dynamics of the patient's presentation and the therapist's reaction, in order to apply this to a deeper understanding of the presenting problems.

We had over 60 participants in the five years that we offered the seminars. The basic structure of the course, a one-year programme of reading seminars and work discussion group, is one that was established at the Tavistock Clinic over 20 years ago and adapted by us to our limited local resources. Within each year there were two groups, each conducted by one of us, and, halfway through the year's programme the conductors would swap groups. Hence the groups stayed the same to facilitate cohesion and trust, and each group had experience of both conductors.

Over the five years we evolved a series of seminar topics as we learnt from our experience of what students found useful and as we gained in understanding of what they needed from us. Later in this chapter we will describe the rudiments of our reading list as a means of communicating our understanding of what that we feel is useful and pertinent to the types of patients that our colleagues deal with in the NHS. It should be borne in mind that our intention was to employ selected psychoanalytic papers as a means of introducing certain basic concepts that we regarded as pertinent to the struggle faced by our course members to make sense of the often very disordered material and behaviour presented by patients; it was not to present a balanced introduction to psychoanalytic thought, even less a comprehensive overview.

The structure of our programme remained unchanged: we offered a one-year course with weekly seminars over three terms. Each meeting consisted of a reading seminar (participants were expected to have done the reading prior to the meeting and to come prepared to discuss it) and then a work discussion group in which participants took it in turns to bring their work with a patient for discussion. We will briefly describe the work discussion group before presenting a more detailed account of the reading seminars.

In the work discussion groups we tried to insist that participants brought a good description of the presenting problems, some historical background, a resumé of the main themes of the treatment to date and then process notes on at least one session. We found a wide divergence in participants' ability/willingness to provide such material; some could see very quickly that the best way of psychoanalytically understanding clinical problems was through a microscopic view of the transference/countertransference as it manifested itself in the session; others were extremely resistant to this. We continued to insist on this since we felt that it was an essential part of what we wanted to get across to our students: that patients should be listened to very carefully and each of their communications should be considered as meaningful. Similarly, in the work discussion groups we laid great stress on the parameters of the therapy that was being described and we tried to convey the importance of the setting, the contract with the patient, the importance of distinguishing between an assessment and a treatment and the importance of any changes in these parameters. Some students really valued this emphasis and were able to understand it while others remained resistant.

As we have indicated, one of the main aspects of a psychoanalytic approach that we wished to convey and teach was that patients should be listened to carefully and that their individuality as it emerged in their material should be taken seriously. Furthermore, we tried to emphasize that the treatment offered to them should have an appropriate setting that was adhered to as much as possible and that the effects of any variation in the setting should be investigated. While such premises might appear to be self-evident, we wish to emphasize them in this report since it was very striking how often they were neglected and how resistant were some participants to actually adhering to them in their practice.

The first term of the reading programme reflected our concern to stress the importance of a psychoanalytical attitude to the setting and to the ways that the therapist listens to the patient. We began by reading the two opening chapters from Roy Schafer's book *The Analytic Attitude*. We found this author particularly jargon-free and our students valued the humane and careful attention that he advocates. We found that these chapters were successful in communicating the ways that analytic attention rested not only on the same ordinary values that pertain to decent ordinary relationships but also on extra-ordinary psychoanalytical values, particularly those of acceptance and neutrality. In the following three seminars we went back to Freud and looked at three of his technical papers: 'Recommendations to physicians practising psychoanalysis'; 'On beginning the treatment' and 'Observations on transference love'. Schafer's chapters are, in effect, a distillation of these three papers and discussing the Freud papers in detail gave the students something of a historical sense and perspective on the discipline of clinical psychoanalysis, as well as an opportunity to reinforce and elaborate on the principles described by Schafer.

The papers of course describe the invention of the psychoanalytical situation and hence provided us with our first opportunities to discuss with our students the differences between the situation in which psychoanalysts work and those that our students were working in. Throughout the course we would return to this many times and we constantly discussed with our students the ways that the knowledge gained from the practice of psychoanalysis could be applied to their work situation. This involved discussion of the difficulties and the occasional impossibility of this application. It would often lead to an acknowledgement of the impossibility of being able to help in a fundamental manner many of the cases brought for discussion, as well as the additional acknowledgement that a full psychoanalytic treatment would also come up against the same obstacles. (We found that one of the most important parts of our course was an open acknowledgement of the grave problems that many of our students' patients had and the very limited impact that any intervention could have.)

To return to the reading: our next seminar looked at a much more modern paper, Betty Joseph's 'On transference love: Some current observations'. We followed this up with 'Transference: The total situation', by the same author. These two papers illustrate that modern psychoanalysis rests firmly on Freud's great discoveries; they put great emphasis on the here and now of the current clinical situation and on the way that this immediate situation is where one can observe and comment upon the transference as it is happening. They also served us well in introducing, via detailed clinical example, the kind of clinical intervention that we wanted our students to understand as quintessentially analytical: the putting into words in as neutral a way as possible the clinician's understanding of the patient's current state of mind.

We next went back to Freud and read 'Remembering, repeating and working-through'. We found that this placed Joseph's papers in a theoretical context that explained the potential usefulness of the type of interventions she advocates. Freud's paper also allowed us to introduce a subject that we would return to many times in our subsequent reading: the enormity of the psychic forces that are involved in many pathological presentations. We used the paper to discuss Freud's discovery of the 'repetition compulsion' and we would go on in the second term of the reading to look more closely at some of the factors involved in many persistent pathological organizations.

In the following seminar we looked at Peter Fonagy's paper on 'Memory and therapeutic action'. This reinforced many of the points we had already tried to bring out in the previous papers. It also addressed directly one of the most common misconceptions that we found among our students, namely that they could treat their patients principally by discussing their history with them and produce thereby some kind of therapeutic catharsis. We found it useful to be able to stress that what patients need is to realize that they repeat their history and do so in the clinical situation, and it is this realization that can be therapeutic.

An essential part of our aim was to help our students engage in an alive and emotionally challenging relationship with their patients. It was possible to bring particular attention to this in the discussions of these opening papers, but it was a theme that remained a central concern throughout the seminars. In order to promote this we always tried to choose papers that contained clinical material.

We tried to convey to our students some of the principal ways that psychoanalysts understood emotional development and its vicissitudes and pathologies. Hence we next moved on to look at a Hanna Segal paper and a number of chapters from her *Introduction to the Work of Melanie Klein* since we found these to have the virtues, for our purposes, of clarity and of both being summaries of bodies of work and containing vivid clinical illustrations. They were: 'The Oedipus Complex Today'; 'The Paranoid Schizoid Position'; 'The Psycho-pathology of the Paranoid Schizoid Position'; 'Manic Defences'; 'The Depressive Position'. In total we spent four weeks looking at these papers. We used them also to convey the fact that psychoanalysis had developed theories about healthy and pathological maturation and that these were grounded in the developmental tasks of infancy and childhood and their various manifestations in adult life. These papers completed the first term.

In the second term we focused primarily on those factors of the personality that make for the kinds of difficult and sometimes intractable clinical presentations that our students were bringing to the work discussion seminars. They were: Klein on 'Mourning and Its Relation to Manic Depressive States'; Brenman on 'Separation: A Clinical Problem'; Winnicott on 'The Capacity to Be Alone'; Segal's 'On the Clinical Usefulness of the Concept of the Death Instinct'; Joseph on 'Envy in Everyday Life'; Spillius on 'Varieties of Envious Experience'; Rosenfeld on 'A Clinical Approach to the Psychoanalytic Theory of the Life and Death Instincts'; Riviere on 'A Contribution to the Analysis of the Negative Therapeutic Reaction' and Steiner on 'The Interplay between Pathological Organizations and the Paranoid-Schizoid and Depressive Positions'. Study of these papers allowed us to discuss some of the factors that can make for enormous difficulties with patients. The choice of papers is largely determined by what we ourselves had found helpful and influential, and a bias towards Kleinian thinking is clear. We were aware of this but chose these papers because of their clinical clarity. We always tried to bear in mind that modern Kleinian theory puts great stress on the capacities of the caretaker to be able to contain and modify destructive instincts, and we tried to help the students think about the implications of this on their clinical attitude and practice. (It should be borne in mind that we continually modified our reading list and it is likely that a subsequent one would be slightly different; for instance, three papers on envy, in hindsight, was excessive.)

The next raft of papers we looked at took us from the second to the third and final term of the programme. We wanted to help the students think about the difficulties they experienced in addressing much of their patients' pathology in a clinically useful way. Our understanding was that it was not only a lack of knowledge that contributed to this but also, of course, the emotional effect the patients were having on them. Hence we next studied a number of papers that specifically addressed the countertransference. We began with Caper's paper 'On the Difficulty of Making a Mutative Interpretation' and then looked at Birksted-Breen's 'Working with an Anorexic Patient' and Symington on 'The Analyst's Act of Freedom as an Agent of Therapeutic Change'. This was followed by Sandler's paper on 'Countertransference and Role Responsiveness'; Brenman Pick on 'Working through in the Countertransference' and Carpy on 'Tolerating the Countertransference: A Mutative Process'.

The above reading led us naturally to looking at the concept of 'projective identification' and we discussed two papers: Spillius's 'Clinical Experiences of Projective Identification' and Feldman's 'Projective Identification: The Analyst's Involvement'.

The last batch of papers was a somewhat eclectic collection and addressed specific questions that we had found to be of interest to the students. These papers tended to vary a little from year to year but in the last year were: two papers by Martindale and Lucas on 'Psychosis'; Milton on 'Why Assess?'; Main's 'The Ailment' (nearly all our students worked in institutions and were hence interested in the dynamics stirred up in the organization by difficult patients). We also, in the last year, looked at four papers that addressed specific issues that the students had asked about: Milton's 'Abuser and Abused'; Garland on 'Thinking about Trauma'; Phillips on 'Homosexuality' and Birksted-Breen's paper 'Working with an Anorexic Patient'. The last reading seminar looked at 'Termination reconsidered' by Pedder.

Discussion

In terms of what we considered to be important to convey to the students, we would argue that the papers looked at in the first half of the first term were essential.

In discussion of the setting, the desirability of a regular and reliably quiet, uninterrupted place and time was noted, but we were always at pains to stress the crucial importance of an internal setting that reflected analytic attitudes. These, following Schafer, consisted of neutrality (emphasizing the patient's need to impact on this); a non-judgemental attitude (the subordination of one's own personality, values, needs – including the need to be helpful); the avoidance of black-and-white, either/or thinking; respect for complexity; empathic listening (tolerance, patience, undemandingness, etc.); the patient's need to take responsibility for his/her difficulties and for efforts to resolve them (conveyed in the session by the understanding that the patient will bring their thoughts and feelings to the session); recognizing the universality of psychic inertia (the work, pain and sheer difficulty in effecting personal change).

Our focus in much of the reading but also in the work discussion groups was on the way in which, whatever the setting, the patient/client brings their mode of relating to the encounter with the therapist/worker. We always tried to show our students that the patient will attempt to recreate characteristic (object) relationships within this setting and will do so via words and actions unconsciously aimed at eliciting and provoking particular feelings and behaviours in the therapist. As Joseph puts it, 'It is after all the patient's prerogative to misuse the situation, according to her personality and pathology'. Tolerance and disciplined examination of these emotional impacts is, of course, of the essence of psychoanalytic clinical work and remains a demanding and at best partially achieved aim after many years of analytic training and experience. Nonetheless our experience was that these principles chimed with and made sense of the clinical difficulties faced by a significant number of course members and, from the evidence of work presentations, continued as an internal reference point throughout the course.

For others a psychoanalytic approach clearly felt incompatible with their existing ways of understanding and working with their patients. Given a fairly inclusive selection policy for the course and our presentation of an undiluted psychoanalytic model, it might be anticipated that some students would 'drop out'. The proportion varied from year to year but averaged around 20 per cent. On the other hand, about six or seven of our students found psychoanalysis to be hugely interesting, to the point of this affecting their future career plans.

The limitations of such a course can be seen as: its having a 'take it or leave it' attitude (it was not easy for the student to select particular elements and dispense with others); it offered little in the way of a 'skills package'; it could conflict with aspects of the prevailing ethos in course members' work settings; its emphasis on the intractability of much mental disturbance could be experienced as pessimistic and as providing scant encouragement or consolation for the hard-pressed worker.

In our view, however, these limitations are indistinguishable from the strengths of the course. Our unapologetic psychoanalytic subscription was evident and straightforward, and this commitment supports clarity and depth in the teaching, consistently returning to the understanding that working with very troubled patients is inevitably troubling, but can provide considerable relief. So can knowing that the patient's defences and difficulties constitute, in Freud's words, *an enemy worthy of his mettle* and usually possess substantial arguments in their favour as a means of managing distress. Unsurprisingly, the basic principles outlined also underpin our approach to individual supervision of NHS staff.

What we hope this short description has established is that in our experience these principles and elements can be translated into a relatively formal teaching situation, without requiring that the students have prior knowledge of psychoanalysis.

Reading programme

Term 1

- *Seminar 1*: Schafer, R. (1983) 'The analytic attitude: an introduction' and 'The atmosphere of safety: Freud's papers on techniquie (1911–1915)'. In *The Analytic Attitude*, London: Hogarth Press.
- *Seminar 2*: Freud, S. (1912) 'Recommendations to physicians practising psychoanalysis', *Standard Edition*, Vol. 12: 111, London: Hogarth Press.
- *Seminar 3*: Freud, S. (1913) 'On beginning the treatment', *Standard Edition*, Vol. 12: 123, London: Hogarth Press.
- *Seminar 4*: Freud, S. (1915) 'Observations on transference love', *Standard Edition*, Vol. 12: 157, London: Hogarth Press.
- *Seminar 5*: Joseph, B. (1993) 'On transference love: Some current observations'. In *On Freud's 'Observations on Transference Love'* (p. 102), New Haven, CT: Yale University Press.
- *Seminar 6*: Joseph, B. (1985) 'Transference: The total situation', *International Journal of Psychoanalysis*, 66: 447.
- *Seminar 7*: Freud, S. (1914) 'Remembering, repeating and working-through', *Standard Edition*, Vol. 12: 145, London: Hogarth Press.
- *Seminar 8*: Fonagy, P. (1999) 'Memory and therapeutic action', *International Journal of Psychoanalysis*, 80: 215.
- *Seminar 9*: Segal, H. (1997) 'The Oedipus complex today'. In *Psychoanalysis, Literature and War* (p. 86), London: New Library of Psychoanalysis.
- *Seminar 10*: Segal, H. (1982) The psychopathology of the paranoid schizoid position. In *Introduction to the Work of Melanie Klein* (Ch. 5, p. 54), London: Hogarth Press.
- *Seminar 11*: Segal, H. (1982) 'Manic defences'. In *Introduction to the Work of Melanie Klein* (p. 82), London: Hogarth Press.
- *Seminar 12*: Segal, H. (1982) 'The depressive position'. In *Introduction to the work of Melanie Klein* (p. 67), London: Hogarth Press.

Term 2

- *Seminar 1*: Klein, M. (1940) 'Mourning and its relation to manic depressive states'. In *Love, Guilt and Reparation* (p. 344), London: Hogarth Press (1981).
- *Seminar 2*: Brenman, E. (1982) 'Separation: A clinical problem'. *International Journal of Psychoanalysis*, 63: 303.

- *Seminar 3*: Winnicott, D.W. (1958) 'The capacity to be alone'. *International Journal of Psychoanalysis*, 39: 416.
- *Seminar 4*: Segal, H. (1993) 'On the clinical usefulness of the concept of the death instinct'. *International Journal of Psychoanalysis*, 74: 55.
- *Seminar 5*: Joseph, B. (1989) 'Envy in everyday life'. In E. Bott Spillius and M. Feldman (Eds.), *Psychic Equilibrium and Psychic Change*, London: New Library of Psychoanalysis.
- *Seminar 6*: Spillius, E. (1993) 'Varieties of envious experience', *International Journal of Psychoanalysis*, 74: 1199.
- *Seminar 7*: Rosenfeld, H. (1974) 'A clinical approach to the psychoanalytical theory of the life and death instincts: An investigation into the aggressive aspects of narcissism', *International Journal of Psychoanalysis*, 52: 169.
- *Seminar 8*: Riviere, J. (1936) 'A contribution to the analysis of the negative therapeutic reaction', *International Journal of Psychoanalysis*, 17: 304–320.
- *Seminar 9*: Steiner, J. (1987) 'The interplay between pathological organisations and the paranoid-schizoid and depressive positions', *International Journal of Psychoanalysis*, 68: 69.
- *Seminar 10*: Caper, R. (1995) 'On the difficulty of making a mutative interpretation', *International Journal of Psychoanalysis*, 76: 91.
- *Seminar 11*: Birksted-Breen, D. (1989) 'Working with an anorexic patient', *International Journal of Psychoanalysis*, 70: 29.
- *Seminar 12*: Symington, N. (1983) 'The analyst's act of freedom as an agent of therapeutic change', *International Review of Psycho-Analysis*, 10: 283.

Term 3

- *Seminar 1*: Sandler, J. (1976) 'Countertransference and role-responsiveness', *International Review of Psycho-Analysis*, 3: 43.
- *Seminar 2*: Brenman Pick, I. (1985) 'Working through in the Countertransference', *International Journal of Psychoanalysis*, 66: 157.
- *Seminar 3*: Carpy, D.V. (1989) 'Tolerating the countertransference: A mutative process', *International Journal of Psychoanalysis*, 70: 287.
- *Seminar 4*: Spillius, E. (1992) 'Clinical experiences of projective identification'. In R. Anderson (Ed.), *Clinical Lectures on Klein and Bion* (pp. 59–74), London: Tavistock/Routledge.
- *Seminar 5*: Feldman, M. (1997) 'Projective identification: The analyst's involvement', *International Journal of Psychoanalysis*, 78: 227.
- *Seminar 6*: Lucas, R. (2003) 'The relationship between psychoanalysis and schizophrenia', *International Journal of Psychoanalysis*, 84: 3. Also work on psychosis by Martindale (see Chapter 7 of the present volume).

- *Seminar 7*: Milton, J. (1997) 'Why assess? Psychoanalytic assessment in the NHS', *Psychoanalytic Psychotherapy*, 11 (1): 47–58.
- *Seminar 8*: Main, T. (1989) 'The ailment'. In J. Johns (Ed.), *The Ailment and Other Psychoanalytic Essays*, London: Free Association Books.
- *Seminar 9*: Milton, J. (1994) 'Abuser and abused: Perverse solutions following childhood abuse', *Psychoanalytic Psychotherapy*, 8 (3): 243–255.
- *Seminar 10*: Garland, C. (1998) 'Thinking about trauma'. In *Understanding Trauma: A Psychoanalytic Approach* (Ch. 1), London: Duckworth.
- *Seminar 11*: Phillips, S. (2003) 'Homosexuality: Coming out of the confusion', *International Journal of Psychoanalysis*, 84: 1431.
- *Seminar 12*: Pedder, J. (1988) 'Termination re-considered', *International Journal of Psychoanalysis*, 69: 495.

Index